666 SONGS

to Make You Bang Your Head Until You Die

A guide to the monsters of **ROCK** and **METAL**

BRUNO MACDONALD

Bruno MacDonald gratefully thanks Robert Dimery,
Jo Lightfoot, Charlotte Selby and Jane Laing for their
support, Herita MacDonald for her designing and
patience, and Sonia MacDonald for letting me go to
gigs, accompanying me on expeditions to Shades,
and never telling me to turn it down.

LAURENCE KING

Published by
Laurence King Publishing Ltd
361-373 City Road
London EC1V 1LR
United Kingdom
Tel: +44 20 7841 6900
E-mail: enquiries@laurenceking.com
www.laurenceking.com

A catalogue record for this book is available
from the British Library

ISBN: 978-1-78627-652-0

Commissioning Editor: Jo Lightfoot
Editor: Charlotte Selby
Design: Herita MacDonald
Production: Davina Cheung
Picture research: Tom Broadbent

Printed in China

Laurence King Publishing is committed to
ethical and sustainable production. We are
proud participants in The Book Chain Project ®
bookchainproject.com

WELCOME TO HELL
Bruno MacDonald

'I sure as hell don't think Metallica's metal, or Guns N' Roses is metal, or Kiss is metal,' Gene Simmons declared to *Kerrang!* 'It just doesn't deal with the ground opening up and little dwarves coming out riding dragons!'

Dwarves and dragons aside, Kiss inspired and embodied much that we love about metal: anthemic choruses, pyrotechnic showmanship and brain-melting volume. Simmons even claimed to have pioneered the use of devil horns in rock 'n' roll – although, in the words of Ronnie James Dio (who actually *did* pioneer the use of devil horns in rock 'n' roll), 'Gene Simmons will tell you that he invented it but, then again, Gene invented breathing, and shoes, and everything...'

The biggest challenge in compiling a list of 666 metal songs is deciding what metal is. If we limit it to acts who actually admit to being metal, there would be a lot of Judas Priest, Manowar and Saxon in this book, and not much else.

Certainly not Nirvana – even though they created *the* anthem of their generation, covered a Kiss song, called one of their own 'Aero Zeppelin', featured a drummer who idolises Metallica and were led by a man whose first concert was Iron Maiden and whose intention for his own band was to blend The Beatles and Black Sabbath.

Certainly not Led Zeppelin, whose frontman professed to be embarrassed that they had inspired so many of the genre's clichés and whose bassist snottily declared that, after *Led Zeppelin IV*, no one would ever again compare them to Black Sabbath.

Certainly not AC/DC or Aerosmith or Van Halen or Motörhead, all of whom would probably claim to be rock 'n' roll or, if pushed, quaint old 'hard rock' (or, and let's all stifle our screams, 'heavy blues').

And certainly not the Prodigy, even though – for two decades after *Kerrang!* readers voted 'Breathe' the best song of 1996 – they played metal festivals without anyone reaching for holy water or smelling salts.

Things get sticky from the start, in fact. Metal scholar Joel McIver will beat to a bloody pulp anyone who dares suggest The Kinks invented it (Joel, skip the first pages of this book, mmm-kay?), when everyone knows Black Sabbath did.

And he's right, of course – but that doesn't mean The Kinks, Jimi Hendrix, Blue Cheer and Iron Butterfly didn't lay bloody big building blocks. Even hoary old Steppenwolf were singing about 'heavy metal thunder' when Sabbath were still calling themselves Polka Tulk and murdering 'Blue Suede Shoes'.

So we applied a more liberal definition: does it, or does it not, rock?

Does it compel you to drum on the nearest surface? Does it make you grab a tennis racquet, broom or docile cat to use as an air guitar? Does it whisk you to a muddy field of likeminded fans, having your retinas scorched by pyro and kissing your hearing goodbye?

If it does, it doesn't matter whether it's Burzum or Bon Jovi, Pantera or Paramore, Rammstein or Rush, Jeff Beck or Jay-Z, Deicide or Def Leppard.

In other words: if it looks like a duck, sounds like a duck, and walks like a duck... it's probably Angus Young.

HOW THE SONGS WERE CHOSEN
This is a personal selection and so is based on my tastes. These songs give a good sense of metal's evolution, but 666 different ones would tell the same story in an equally valid way.

I've tried to represent the subgenres and ensure that international acts get a fair crack of the whip. My apologies to fans of AFI, Death Angel, the Misfits and Riot. And I feel a bit guilty that there's only one by Whitesnake.

I hope you find at least one old or new favourite on every spread. If you don't, let's not share a tent at Download.

Cheers!

The author with Dio on the *Sacred Heart* tour in 1986. Photograph from *Kerrang!*, by Pete Cronin (petecronin.com)

RUMBLE
Link Wray & His Ray Men

BY Milt Grant, Link Wray | PRODUCED BY Milt Grant FROM 'Rumble' (Cadence, 1958)

'Link Wray invented heavy metal,' declared Bob Dylan, 'but who knows it?' Jimmy Page, for one: his delight on hearing this power-chord-pioneering instrumental is evident in the film *It Might Get Loud*. 'So much profound attitude,' Page marvels. Guitarist Wray, however, demurred at the 'father of heavy metal' tag: 'I don't think I sound at all like Metallica! I think the guitar player in Metallica has got his own sound. And I'm positive that guy does not listen to Link Wray... I don't think Link Wray is heavy metal at all. But thanks, Bob, for saying it.'

YOU REALLY GOT ME
The Kinks

BY Ray Davies | PRODUCED BY Shel Talmy | FROM *Kinks* (Pye, 1964)

'An interviewer once asked Dave [Davies, guitarist] if he thought The Kinks had gone heavy metal in the eighties,' Peter Buck of R.E.M. told *Rolling Stone*. 'He said, "It wasn't called heavy metal when I invented it."' 'That one song, "You Really Got Me", it *was* the Bible!' gasped Steven Tyler. 'Oh my god, it was the shit!' The song's prophetic rifferama was resurrected by Van Halen. 'I bought a double album from K-Tel or something that had thirty Kinks tunes,' recalled David Lee Roth. 'We learned all of one side and played them into the dirt during the club gigs.'

THE TRAIN KEPT A-ROLLIN'
The Yardbirds

BY Tiny Bradshaw, Syd Nathan, Howie Kay | PRODUCED BY Giorgio Gomelsky | FROM *Having a Rave Up with The Yardbirds* (Epic, 1965)

'The best riff...' Joe Perry declared. 'It sounds good on electric or acoustic guitar, banjo, sitar, whatever!' The Yardbirds cut it again as 1966's 'Stroll On', with Jeff Beck *and* Jimmy Page – the latter doling out a sound he would revisit on Zep's 'Wearing and Tearing' (*see* 1982). Meanwhile, Aerosmith made it a live staple. 'I know how great The Yardbirds were,' Steven Tyler told *Rolling Stone*. 'But I don't think everyone else knows it. [Their] music is a goldmine waiting to be stumbled upon.' Check out Metallica's version, featuring Beck, Page *and* Perry.

WILD THING
The Troggs

BY Chip Taylor | PRODUCED BY Larry Page | FROM *From Nowhere* (Fontana, 1966)

An unheralded blues rocker by The Wild Ones became an anthem for the ages in the hands of The Troggs. Why? Over to Professor Joe Elliott: 'Strip it down to three [chords], because they're the root chords and you don't really need the others. That's why "Wild Thing" is the most well-known song in the world... Cut off the fat and just get down to basics.' There's no shortage of great covers – from Hendrix to Aerosmith, via The Runaways and Sam Kinison – but hunt down Jeff Beck's deconstruction (on a 1986 Epic single) for the heaviest of all.

PURPLE HAZE
The Jimi Hendrix Experience

🇺🇸 🇬🇧
BY Jimi Hendrix |
PRODUCED BY Chas
Chandler | FROM *Are
You Experienced*
(Reprise, 1967)

Jimi Hendrix, Joe Perry told *Blender*, 'was walking on Jupiter while the rest of us just dreamed it.' The inspiration for generations of guitar heroes staked his claim in the intro of 'Purple Haze': 'A heavily overdriven and dissonant riff,' wrote Joel McIver, 'based on a tritone (the diminished fifth or *diabolus in musica*, an interval actually regarded as evil in medieval times).' 'Such a well-structured, almost perfect riff,' Slash observed to pastemagazine.com. 'It's very unique, just in terms of structure and technique. Very original for a rock 'n' roll riff.'

SUNSHINE OF YOUR LOVE
Cream

🇬🇧
BY Eric Clapton,
Jack Bruce, Pete
Brown | PRODUCED
BY Felix Pappalardi |
FROM *Disraeli Gears*
(Reaction, 1967)

Jimmy Page, Roger Waters declared to *Rolling Stone*, 'must have looked at Cream and thought, "Fuck me, I think I'll do that," and then put together Led Zeppelin.' Cream's influence can be distilled to this one gem. 'Such a cool-sounding song...' noted Alex Lifeson. 'They were a trio and there was a lot of activity in their playing, so that was an inspiration for Rush.' 'A desert island classic,' enthused Sammy Hagar. 'I go back to that song again and again.' And a last word from Slash: 'When I heard that, I was like, "That's what I wanna do!"'

YOU KEEP ME HANGIN' ON
Vanilla Fudge

🇺🇸
BY Brian Holland,
Lamont Dozier, Eddie
Holland | PRODUCED
BY Shadow Morton |
FROM *Vanilla Fudge*
(Atco, 1967)

'They were our heroes,' Ritchie Blackmore told *Guitar World* of the Fudge. 'They used to play London's Speakeasy and all the hippies used to go there to hang out – Clapton, The Beatles... According to legend, the talk of the town during that period was Jimi Hendrix, but that's not true. It was Vanilla Fudge. They played eight-minute songs, with dynamics. People said, "What the hell's going on here?"' And so it is with this cover, which adds four minutes of trippy sludge to The Supremes' original but still made the US top ten.

BECK'S BOLERO
Jeff Beck

🇬🇧
BY Jimmy Page |
PRODUCED BY Mickie
Most | FROM *Truth*
(Columbia, 1968)

Conceived as a sideline for then-Yardbird Beck – and credited to him when it debuted as the b-side of the 1967 hit 'Hi Ho Silver Lining' – 'Bolero' became a dry run for Led Zeppelin. Inspired by composer Ravel's *Boléro*, it stars Beck, Jimmy Page, John Paul Jones, Keith Moon and pianist Nicky Hopkins. 'I said, "Jim [Page], you've got to break away from the bolero beat – you can't go on like that!"' Beck told Douglas J Noble. 'So we stopped it dead... then we stuck that riff in... You can hear Moon screaming in the middle of the record over the drum break.'

HELTER SKELTER
The Beatles

BY Paul McCartney, John Lennon | PRODUCED BY George Martin | FROM *The Beatles* (Apple, 1968)

'"Helter Skelter" was a key track in the birth of hard rock,' Nikki Sixx noted to *Classic Rock*. 'It spoke to us in its guitars and in its lyrics. It also spoke to us because of the Manson murders… it became a real symbol of darkness and evil.' Inspired by Paul McCartney's desire to outdo what he had read about The Who's 'I Can See for Miles', the song became a theme for cult leader Charles Manson. 'It was mentioned as if we were sending him messages…' said George Harrison ruefully. 'But it's such a lot of bullshit. The Beatles never told anyone to do anything.'

SUMMERTIME BLUES
Blue Cheer

BY Jerry Capehart, Eddie Cochran | PRODUCED BY Abe 'Voco' Kesh | FROM *Vincebus Eruptum* (Philips, 1968)

Blue Cheer, observed *Kerrang!*, 'can justifiably lay claim to have invented heavy metal.' 'We're pretty flattered…' remarked singer/bassist Dickie Peterson to Nightwatcher's House of Rock, 'although we really don't consider ourselves heavy metal *per se*. We're a power trio. We're all low end. Heavy metal is high end; we're not.' To Robert Plant, however, 'Blue Cheer was as heavy metal as Iron Maiden.' Their reworking of Eddie Cochran's rock 'n' roll gem was followed by The Who's in 1970. Both influenced Rush's version, on 2004's *Feedback*.

HUSH
Deep Purple

BY Joe South | PRODUCED BY Derek Lawrence | FROM *Shades of Deep Purple* (Parlophone, 1968)

'Somebody once said to me, "Your band are the fathers of heavy metal,"' recalled Jon Lord. 'I said, *The child is not mine!*' Purple's triumphantly funky version of Joe South's song, however, laid the foundations of their place alongside Sabbath and Zeppelin as the holy trinity of hard rock. 'It was four-and-a-half minutes long and it ended with a one-and-a-half-minute organ solo,' Lord noted to DJ Tommy Vance, 'and it sold over a million in the States!' 'We were superstars…' Ritchie Blackmore said drily. 'We had a record in the top one hundred!'

IN-A-GADDA-DA-VIDA
Iron Butterfly

BY Doug Ingle | PRODUCED BY Jim Hilton | FROM *In-A-Gadda-Da-Vida* (Atco, 1968)

'One of the first heavy metal songs,' observed Alice Cooper. 'If that came out and Metallica did it, everyone would go, "Oh yeah, that's heavy metal."' (Slayer trimmed the seventeen-minute epic to a still-epic-for-Slayer three-minutes-nineteen-seconds on 1987's *Less Than Zero* soundtrack.) Of the original – also celebrated in *The Simpsons* – Dave Grohl told *Q*: 'The riff and the groove are dirgy and sinister. The whole track is so spooky and haunting. I heard it as a young kid and it freaked me out. It reminded me of bad things and still does.'

VOODOO CHILD (SLIGHT RETURN)
The Jimi Hendrix Experience

BY Jimi Hendrix | PRODUCED BY Jimi Hendrix | FROM *Electric Ladyland* (Track, 1968)

'I heard "Voodoo Chile" on the radio,' recalled Iron Maiden's Dave Murray, 'and I thought, 'Fucking hell! What is *that*?"' *That* was the Experience's all-killer-no-filler take on a fifteen-minute jam cut the day before by Hendrix, with Traffic's Steve Winwood and Jefferson Airplane's Jack Casady. Both versions appear on *Electric Ladyland*, Hendrix's only US No.1. The shorter 'Voodoo Child' – aka 'Voodoo Chile' – was his only British chart-topper. 'It was the first time I'd heard an electric guitar made to sound like that,' Bruce Dickinson recalled to *Classic Rock*.

BORN TO BE WILD
Steppenwolf

BY Mars Bonfire | PRODUCED BY Gabriel Mekler | FROM *Steppenwolf* (ABC/Dunhill, 1968)

Yes, literature fans, William Burroughs used the phrase 'heavy metal' in his *Nova* books in the mid-sixties. But he was talking about drugs. To be fair, Steppenwolf were probably talking about motorbikes – but, as DevilDriver's Dez Fafara told noisecreep.com, 'The phrase "heavy metal thunder" said it all to me when I was young.' Immortality beckoned when 'Born to Be Wild' and 'The Pusher' were featured in the 1969 film *Easy Rider*. 'And once that all took place,' recalled chief 'wolf John Kay, '"Born to Be Wild" reached its global anthem status.'

21ST CENTURY SCHIZOID MAN
King Crimson

BY Robert Fripp, Ian McDonald, Greg Lake, Michael Giles, Peter Sinfield | PRODUCED BY King Crimson | FROM *In the Court of the Crimson King* (Island, 1969)

'Distorted vocals that unsettle you right from the first syllable,' Gene Simmons noted to musicradar.com of prog's heaviest pre-Tool cut. 'This song has no chorus, but the whole thing is held together by that monster riff. You can imagine Sabbath doing a version of this. Or late-period Beatles, with Lennon screaming his lungs out.' King Crimson, Ozzy Osbourne observed to *Classic Rock*, 'had all this great musicianship, but there was a fuckin' nasty edge. I covered "21st Century Schizoid Man". That's me in a fuckin' nutshell.'

CALEDONIA
Cromagnon

BY Austin Grasmere, Brian Elliot | PRODUCED BY Austin Grasmere, Brian Elliot | FROM *Cromagnon* (ESP Disk, 1969)

As mad as Ministry, as sinister as Sabbath, this might have been influential if anyone had heard it. Few did, because the LP wasn't widely issued until the nineties (as *Orgasm*) and noughties (as *Cave Rock*). Cromagnon's mission, said drummer Sal Salgado, 'was to progress from different decades of music. Like, in '59 Elvis was shaking his pelvis... Ten years later Hendrix was pouring lighter fluid on his guitar... We were trying to carry it on to the next decade.' 'Super-strange,' marvelled Opeth's Mikael Åkerfeldt to *Classic Rock*. 'Super fucked-up and evil.'

OH WELL
Fleetwood Mac

🇬🇧

BY Peter Green | PRODUCED BY Fleetwood Mac | FROM *Then Play On* (Reprise, 1969)

'This,' warned Joe Perry, 'is not your mother's Fleetwood Mac.' Instead, as Mark Blake wrote in *Classic Rock*, it's 'a masterclass in dynamics: a jabbing riff segued into a mini-symphony filled with Spaghetti Western guitars, orchestral drums and [Peter] Green's new discovery, the cello'. The result? 'A seminal live tune,' raved Scott Holiday of Rival Sons. 'A hot riff and so full of style.' Green, said Glenn Tipton, 'took that style of music somewhere else.' Need more metal? It was engineered by Martin Birch. And just listen to 'Beating Around the Bush' by AC/DC...

AMERICAN WOMAN
The Guess Who

🇨🇦

BY Randy Bachman, Burton Cummings, Garry Peterson, Jim Kale | PRODUCED BY Jack Richardson | FROM *American Woman* (RCA Victor, 1970)

'A lot of people called it anti-American,' sighed bassist Jim Kale, 'but it wasn't really. We weren't anti-anything. John Lennon once said that the meanings of all songs come after they are recorded.' US record-buyers evidently weren't offended by suggestions that The Guess Who's native Canada might have the edge over the States: 'American Woman' spent three weeks atop *Billboard*'s Hot 100, selling half a million copies. Most likely they were seduced by Randy Bachman's riff, on a '59 Les Paul that now resides in the Rock and Roll Hall of Fame.

KICK OUT THE JAMS
MC5

🇺🇸

BY Rob Tyner, Wayne Kramer, Fred 'Sonic' Smith, Michael Davis, Dennis Thompson | PRODUCED BY Jac Holzman, Bruce Botnick | FROM *Kick Out the Jams* (Elektra, 1969)

Tearing heads off with riffs is a fine way to start a song – listen to 'Whole Lotta Love', 'Phantom of the Opera' (*see* 1980) or 'Welcome to the Jungle' (*see* 1987). But even those pale beside Rob Tyner gleefully announcing, 'Right now, it's time to... kick out the jams, motherfuckers!' This proto-grunge-punk-metal monster – which, wrote Dave Marsh, 'just about defines exciting' – has been covered by Rage Against the Machine, Blue Öyster Cult, Monster Magnet and Entombed. 'I wanted to be the MC5,' Lemmy told *Spin*, 'playing fast, loud rock 'n' roll.'

THE NILE SONG
Pink Floyd

🇬🇧

BY Roger Waters | PRODUCED BY Pink Floyd | FROM *More* (Columbia, 1969)

Pink Floyd dabbled in rifferama from day one. 'Things like "Interstellar Overdrive" or "Astronomy Domine",' noted drummer Nick Mason, '...were quite heavyweight: sort of heavy-metal thrash with a little bit of avant-garde.' But pity the poor hippies who – lulled by *More*'s opening 'Cirrus Minor' – had their karma crushed by track two: a piledriver unrivalled in the Floyd lexicon until *The Wall*'s 'In the Flesh?' (*see* 1979) and 'Young Lust'. (*More*'s own 'Ibiza Bar' is just a weedier reworking of 'The Nile Song'.) Voivod tackled it on 1993's *The Outer Limits*.

DAZED AND CONFUSED
Led Zeppelin

🇬🇧 **BY** Jimmy Page | **PRODUCED BY** Jimmy Page | **FROM** *Led Zeppelin* (Atlantic, 1969)

'My world stood still the first time I heard this,' Ozzy told *Rolling Stone*. There had been acid rock, garage, hard rock and proto-metal – not least by The Yardbirds, with whom Jimmy Page trialled his version of Jake Holmes' 'Dazed and Confused'. But this was a cut above. 'Holy shit,' deadpanned Joe Perry, 'these guys really *are* better than Iron Butterfly and Grand Funk Railroad!' To David Lee Roth, 'It was classic, quintessential blues.' But, as Steven Tyler told *Q*, 'Real heavy metal to me was Led Zeppelin playing "Dazed and Confused".'

HEARTBREAKER
Led Zeppelin

🇬🇧 **BY** Jimmy Page, John Bonham, Robert Plant, John Paul Jones | **PRODUCED BY** Jimmy Page | **FROM** *Led Zeppelin II* (Atlantic, 1969)

'What did Led Zeppelin bring to the table?' mused Gene Simmons. 'Fucking great big, huge balls!' *Led Zeppelin II* makes that clear, courtesy of side openers 'Whole Lotta Love' and this slice of swagger, topped by a scorching solo. 'It was recorded after we had finished "Heartbreaker",' Jimmy Page told *Guitar World*. 'It was an afterthought... If you notice, the whole sound of the guitar is different... It was made up on the spot.' And its legacy? 'It all changed when my sister came home with *Led Zeppelin II*,' said Steve Vai, 'and I heard "Heartbreaker".'

BLACK SABBATH
Black Sabbath

🇬🇧 **BY** Tony Iommi, Ozzy Osbourne, Geezer Butler, Bill Ward | **PRODUCED BY** Rodger Bain | **FROM** *Black Sabbath* (Vertigo, 1970)

'When we first played it,' Tony Iommi told BBC DJ Tommy Vance, 'the reaction of the kids at that time was amazement: "What's this sort of stuff?" Even *we* wondered what this sort of stuff was.' The song that bore Black Sabbath's name was, of course, the true genesis of heavy metal. 'I can't even begin to imagine what people were thinking back then when they first heard that song,' marvelled Derek Felix of Void King.

To mimic the cathartic thrill of horror films – including the 1963 one after whom they were named – the quartet

'THIS SONG SCARED THE SHIT OUT OF ME. IT'S BEYOND HEAVY'
JAMES HETFIELD

packed 'the most evil song ever' (Rob Halford) with rain, thunder and marrow-freezing music.

Ozzy Osbourne's lyrics were intended, Geezer Butler recalled, 'as a warning to people that were getting heavily involved in black magic... If you listen, they're saying, "If you're going to get into it, be serious about it. Otherwise, don't dabble in it." But everybody thinks it's about worshipping Satan.'

'You get old business tycoons wanting to go with young chicks, so they go along to black magic rituals and get themselves involved...' Ozzy explained to *NME*. 'They're sick. I believe in black magic but I've not tried it and I won't.' (A third verse, cut from the original, appears on bootleg versions and the one on Ozzy's 1997 collection, *The Ozzman Cometh*. In it, a mother stands in the fires of hell and a child cries. It doesn't end well.)

'There is no more ominous rock 'n' roll record...' Slash observed. 'On every level, it's the sound of pure evil.'

WAR PIGS
Black Sabbath

'WAR IS THE REAL SATANISM. POLITICIANS ARE THE REAL SATANISTS'

GEEZER BUTLER

🇬🇧 BY Tony Iommi, Ozzy Osbourne, Geezer Butler, Bill Ward | PRODUCED BY Rodger Bain | FROM *Paranoid* (Vertigo, 1970)

Black Sabbath blueprinted metal's future with their debut in February 1970. Seven months later, the bastards did it again. This time, they added jazzy intricacy and air-raid sirens, and dripped contempt on the elite. 'We wrote "War Pigs" because American bands were frightened to mention anything about the [Vietnam] war,' Geezer Butler told *Guitar World*. 'So we thought we'd tell it like it is.'

'It's about VIP people who are sitting there saying, "Go out and fight," and all the everyday people are forced to, but the VIPs never do,' Ozzy Osbourne explained to *NME*.

'We're not a political group. It's just that most of our songs have messages.'

Intended as their second album's title track (hence *Paranoid*'s baffling artwork), 'War Pigs' was demoed as 'Walpurgis', in which form it appears on Ozzy's 1997 collection, *The Ozzman Cometh*. The song's theme remained relevant in ensuing decades. 'All my brothers were in the army...' lyricist Butler told the *Telegraph*. 'We all thought we were gonna get called up as well, to go and fight.' 'My philosophy,' chipped in Ozzy, 'was always that I'd rather be a live coward than a dead hero.'

Faith No More covered it, said bassist Bill Gould, 'to piss off the punk bands we played with'. They placed a version on 1989's *The Real Thing* because, said Gould, 'We played that song over 150 times live, so it seemed a shame to waste it.' A live take graced their *You Fat Bastards* album and 1994's Sabbath tribute *Nativity in Black*.

CHILD IN TIME
Deep Purple

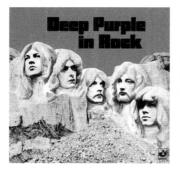

🇬🇧 BY Ritchie Blackmore, Ian Gillan, Roger Glover, Jon Lord, Ian Paice | PRODUCED BY Deep Purple | FROM *Deep Purple In Rock* (Harvest, 1970)

Written in ten minutes after Jon Lord began, said Ian Gillan, 'noodling away' at 'Bombay Calling' by psychedelicists It's A Beautiful Day, this proved Purple were a force to be reckoned with. Looted roots aside, the mini-epic showcases the band's virtuosity, particularly that of Ritchie Blackmore and Gillan. The latter, said Manowar's Eric Adams, 'was the only singer that inspired me in the early days... He just blew me away when they did "Child in Time".' 'I had never heard a bloke sing that high before,' said Michael Schenker. 'But it's great – I love it!'

MISSISSIPPI QUEEN
Mountain

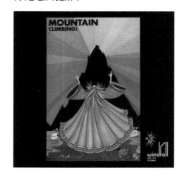

 BY Leslie West, Corky Laing, Felix Pappalardi, David Rea | PRODUCED BY Felix Pappalardi | FROM *Climbing!* (Windfall, 1970)

'Leslie West's voice and guitar are undeniable,' enthused Black Stone Cherry's Ben Wells. 'The cowbell, the riff... It's the whole package.' That introductory cowbell, explained riffmeister West to songfacts.com, 'was just in there because Felix [Pappalardi, producer and bassist] wanted Corky [Laing, drummer] to count the song off... And it became the quintessential cowbell song.' 'This one brings back memories of my very first US tour with Black Sabbath,' said Ozzy, who covered it – with West – for 2005's box set, *Prince of Darkness*.

IMMIGRANT SONG
Led Zeppelin

🇬🇧 BY Jimmy Page, Robert Plant | PRODUCED BY Jimmy Page | FROM *Led Zeppelin III* (Atlantic, 1970)

'With that hypnotic riff and Robert's bloodcurdling scream,' Jimmy Page told the *Guardian*, 'I thought, "That's the way to open an album."' Indeed, after 'Good Times Bad Times' and 'Whole Lotta Love', this completed a hat-trick of stone-cold classic openers, but with an eerie international flavour. 'What they showed to all their peer group, as musicians, was that there was, first of all, a very powerful and dramatic way to perform simple, direct rock music and also to introduce elements of more eclectic music...' observed Jethro Tull's Ian Anderson.

'IN '69 AND '70, THERE WAS SOME FREAKY SHIT GOING ON, BUT ZEPPELIN WERE THE FREAKIEST'
DAVE GROHL

'"Immigrant Song" was written after we had been to Iceland,' Robert Plant explained. 'It was a cultural exchange – although who they sent over here, I can't imagine... Of course, it ended up spawning generations of guys with crossed axes tattooed on their arms.'

'Robert's input [was] magical,' Page enthused to *Guitar World*. 'His sort of "Bali Ha" [a song from *South Pacific*] melody line was really inspired.' ('To this day, [Eddie Van Halen's ex-wife Valerie Bertinelli] thinks Led Zeppelin wrote *South Pacific*,' sniped David Lee Roth.)

The song, Plant protested, 'was supposed to be powerful and funny. [Iceland] was light all day and it was a hoot. People go, "Led Zeppelin had a sense of humour?" But I guess with a riff as relentless as that...'

Kept alive by Trent Reznor and Karen O's cover and a *Thor* soundtrack, the cut remains bewitching. 'I still get goosebumps when I hear "Immigrant Song",' said Joe Perry. 'Utterly fantastic,' agreed Michael Schenker. 'One of the most powerful rock tracks I've ever heard.'

UNDER MY WHEELS
Alice Cooper

🇺🇸 BY Michael Bruce, Dennis Dunaway, Bob Ezrin | PRODUCED BY Bob Ezrin, Jack Richardson | FROM *Killer* (Warner Bros., 1971)

Love It to Death, in 1971, birthed the Alice band as we know them, its gems including 'Ballad of Dwight Fry'. But it was on the same year's *Killer* that the group and their producer cruised into top gear. Bob Ezrin, recalled the Coop, 'said... "For all anyone knows, you could be The Electric Prunes. What we're going to do is work on your vocals, so that when people hear this music, they know it's Alice Cooper."' Seek out Alice, Axl, Slash 'n' Izzy Stradlin's gleeful cover of 'Under My Wheels' on 1988's *The Decline of Western Civilization Part II* soundtrack.

SWEET LEAF
Black Sabbath

🇬🇧 BY Tony Iommi, Bill Ward, Ozzy Osbourne, Geezer Butler | PRODUCED BY Rodger Bain | FROM *Master of Reality* (Vertigo, 1971)

Sampled by the Beastie Boys ('Rhymin' and Stealin'') and resurrected by the Red Hot Chili Peppers (check out the close of 'Give It Away'), 'Sweet Leaf' is primeval Sabbath at their most gleeful. 'I'd come back from Dublin, and they had these cigarettes called Sweet Afton...' Tony Iommi recalled to *Guitar World*. 'I took out a cigarette packet and, as it's got on the lid, "The sweetest leaf you can buy!" I was like, "Ah, Sweet Leaf!"' And the opening cough? 'Ozzy rolled this big joint and brought it out. I had a couple of puffs and nearly choked myself.'

WHEN THE LEVEE BREAKS
Led Zeppelin

🇬🇧
BY Memphis Minnie, Jimmy Page, Robert Plant, John Paul Jones, John Bonham | PRODUCED BY Jimmy Page | FROM *Led Zeppelin IV* (Atlantic, 1971)

'It's incredible to have a rock drummer that powerful, that crazy, that bad-ass, but with a groove so smooth...' Dave Grohl marvelled to *Mojo*. 'It's pure chocolate fuckin' sex. I could loop that track in my iPod for hours. This is the best groove of all time – better than any James Brown track.' The Bonzo-dominated 'When the Levee Breaks' is as eerie as it is relentless. '*Led Zeppelin IV* in particular put me on my path as a musician...' said Slipknot's Joey Jordison. 'Nobody will ever be able to match John Bonham's wide-open drum sound.'

CROSS-EYED MARY
Jethro Tull

🇬🇧
BY Ian Anderson | PRODUCED BY Ian Anderson, Terry Ellis | FROM *Aqualung* (Chrysalis, 1971)

Infamous for beating Metallica at the 1989 Grammys, Tull are a skeleton in several closets. Joe Elliott praised *Aqualung*'s 'title track and its brilliant riff, all the way through to... "Locomotive Breath", and there's so much great stuff in-between... "Mother Goose", "Cross-Eyed Mary"'. The latter is the concept album's most sinister track; 'Aqualung's got a thing about little girls,' admitted singer Ian Anderson. The song became an Iron Maiden b-side that, noted manager Rod Smallwood, 'was one of the only things we ever had played on American radio.'

I DON'T NEED NO DOCTOR
Humble Pie

🇬🇧
BY Jo Armstead, Nick Ashford, Valerie Simpson | PRODUCED BY Humble Pie | FROM *Performance Rockin' the Fillmore* (A&M, 1971)

'Kiss was originally heavily influenced by Humble Pie,' confessed Paul Stanley. Before Kiss's *Alive!* came the Pie's *Performance*, whose soul cover became their anthem. ('I just can't keep singing "I Don't Need No Doctor" forever...' Steve Marriott grumbled in 1976, 'even though it's a great song.') Their influence stretched from David Lee Roth ('My first concert was late high school, Humble Pie at the Long Beach Arena') to W.A.S.P. (who unleashed a sterling cover of 'I Don't Need No Doctor' in 1986) and Pantera (the Pie, said Rex Brown, 'could do anything').

HIGHWAY STAR
Deep Purple

🇬🇧
BY Ritchie Blackmore, Ian Gillan, Roger Glover, Jon Lord, Ian Paice | PRODUCED BY Deep Purple | FROM *Machine Head* (Purple, 1972)

'Highway Star,' said Kerry King, suggested 'Ritchie [Blackmore] was more interested in playing faster rhythms than Sabbath.' Slayer covered the song, as did Type O Negative, Metal Church, Dream Theater, Faith No More and Buckcherry. 'Highway Star' was born on a tour bus driving to Portsmouth – and, said Ian Gillan, 'We played it on stage that night.' 'In '72 alone we did six separate tours of America, one of Japan, and made *Machine Head*...' recalled Roger Glover. 'I was looking down a list of every gig we've ever played, and it is exhausting.'

SCHOOL'S OUT
Alice Cooper

BY Alice Cooper, Michael Bruce, Glen Buxton, Dennis Dunaway, Neal Smith | PRODUCED BY Bob Ezrin FROM *School's Out* (Warner Bros., 1972)

Guitarist Glen Buxton, recalled producer Bob Ezrin, 'came up with this amazing riff. Shep [Gordon, manager] called me in Toronto and said, "I think the boys just wrote a hit."' 'It was a very bratty riff, almost like him going "nah-nah-nah-nah" on the guitar,' said Alice. 'It was the only time I told Bob Ezrin, "If this isn't a hit, I might as well start selling shoes." Every part of that song was on the money.' As guitarist Michael Bruce mused to *Rolling Stone,* 'What moment of the school year does every kid look forward to? Summer – when school's out.'

SILVER MACHINE
Hawkwind

BY Bob Calvert, Dave 'Sylvia MacManus' Brock | PRODUCED BY Hawkwind, Dave 'Dr Technical' Brock | FROM *Glastonbury Fayre* (Revelation, 1972)

'They only let me sing vocals on "Silver Machine" because none of the others could hit the right notes,' Lemmy told *Uncut.* 'It's a great riff... Dave [Brock, frontman] called it a Chuck Berry riff played backwards.' It even hit the UK chart. 'One of the songs that kept us off the top was "School's Out",' Brock noted. 'I met Alice Cooper later and he said he was a fan, which made me feel a bit better.' Its legacy lives on: at festivals, Brock said, 'A black metal band on the bill will come over to shake my hand and say, "Without Hawkwind, we wouldn't be here."'

FRANKENSTEIN
The Edgar Winter Group

BY Edgar Winter | PRODUCED BY Rick Derringer | FROM *They Only Come Out at Night* (Epic, 1972)

'I thought, "Wow, everything about this song stands out,"' Dave Grohl told *Mojo.* '"The riffs, the keyboards and particularly the drums."' It arose from jams by Edgar and his brother Johnny. 'I played Hammond B3, alto sax and we had two sets of drums onstage,' Edgar explained. 'I'd play a duel drum solo with Johnny's drummer... It was fifteen minutes long. The only way we could think to put that song on the album was to edit it down into something usable... Chuck Ruff, the drummer, mumbled the immortal words, "Wow, man, this is like Frankenstein."'

SUPERNAUT
Black Sabbath

BY Tony Iommi, Ozzy Osbourne, Geezer Butler, Bill Ward | PRODUCED BY Patrick Meehan, Black Sabbath | FROM *Vol 4* (Vertigo, 1972)

Fiendishly funky even before Al Jourgensen and Trent Reznor, as 1000 Homo DJs, remade it in 1990, 'Supernaut' twinned grinding guitar with samba-style percussion. A favourite of John Bonham, it featured in an unrecorded Sabbath-Zeppelin studio jam. It also found favour with another star: 'We were in Chicago...' recalled Ozzy. 'There was a note waiting for us, inviting us to a party being held by Frank Zappa... We get there and we sit by him, and he's playing Black Sabbath... He goes, "I really like that song 'Supernaut'. Would you like some cake?"'

MAMA WEER ALL CRAZEE NOW
Slade

🇬🇧 BY Jim Lea, Noddy Holder | PRODUCED BY Chas Chandler | FROM *Slayed?* (Polydor, 1972)

'Rock and Roll All Nite,' Gene Simmons admitted, 'is a direct bastard child of Slade's "Mama Weer All Crazee Now".' 'I loved Slade,' said Paul Stanley, 'because of the singalong directness of their songs... There would probably never be us without them.' But Kiss weren't the band's only admirers. 'When Slade broke in 1972, I began to get really nervous,' said Ritchie Blackmore. 'Here I am killing myself to write the next incredible riff [and here are] four blokes pounding out four chords over and over and loving every minute of it.'

JUST GOT PAID
ZZ Top

🇺🇸 BY Billy Gibbons, Frank Beard, Bill Ham | PRODUCED BY Bill Ham | FROM *Rio Grande Mud* (London, 1972)

'A very danceable song,' David Lee Roth wrote. 'It's rock; you can dance to it. That was a kind of music you could dance to and not spill your beer.' The minor hit 'Francine' took ZZ's second album within a whisker of the Top 100, but the biting 'Just Got Paid' was *Rio Grande Mud*'s hidden gem. It was inspired, said Billy Gibbons, 'by Peter Green's opening figure in [Fleetwood Mac's] "Oh Well" [*see* 1969]. I was living in Los Angeles... It was raining and I couldn't go anywhere, so I was trying to learn this figure. It got all tangled up. And it stayed tangled.'

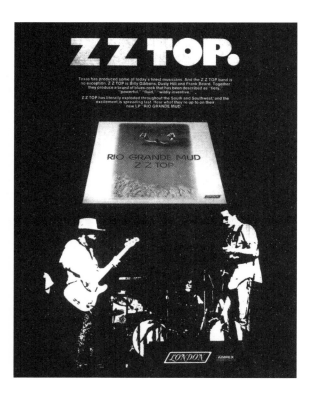

CRAZY HORSES
The Osmonds

BY Alan Osmond, Merrill Osmond, Wayne Osmond | PRODUCED BY Alan Osmond, Michael Lloyd | FROM *Crazy Horses* (MGM, 1972)

Behold the dawn of Mormon metal. 'They have an effect, which will produce another effect,' David Bowie postulated to *NME*. 'Whether it will be obvious when it does happen, or whether it will be a subliminal kind of effect that nobody will notice... it gets very much into a Buddhist kind of thing.' The Osmonds mingled with Zeppelin, and later earned tributes from Ozzy ('I just want you to know that "Crazy Horses" is one of my favourite rock 'n' roll songs of all time') and Zakk Wylde (Black Label Society's 'Crazy Horse').

EASY LIVIN'
Uriah Heep

BY Ken Hensley | PRODUCED BY Gerry Bron | FROM *Demons and Wizards* (Bronze, 1972)

On their fourth album in under two years, guitarist Mick Box remembered to m-magazine.co.uk, Uriah Heep 'found a very magical and mystical way of writing lyrics that captured everyone's imagination. There were some great songs on there, too – "Easy Livin'" really took us to the world stage'. The pumping classic, by organist Ken Hensley, became Heep's only US top forty hit, and earned *Demons and Wizards* their first of four gold awards (to be followed by the same year's *The Magician's Birthday* and 1973's *Sweet Freedom* and *Uriah Heep Live*).

I'M GOING MAD
Scorpions

BY Michael Schenker, Rudolf Schenker, Klaus Meine, Lothar Heimberg, Wolfgang Dziony | PRODUCED BY Conny Plank | FROM *Lonesome Crow* (Brain, 1972)

'We were just a young band trying to find our way,' Klaus Meine told metalexiles.com, 'trying to shape an artistic style to find the Scorpions' DNA.' Their debut album opened with this swirling slice of spacey samba – or, as Meine put it, 'a great rocker with Michael Schenker playing great solos.' Schenker – who later claimed to have written most of *Lonesome Crow*'s group-credited songs – was just sixteen when it was recorded in 1971. He promptly quit his brother Rudolf's band for opening act UFO, only to return for songs on 1979's *Lovedrive*.

PAPER PLANE
Status Quo

🇬🇧

BY Francis Rossi, Bob Young | PRODUCED BY Status Quo | FROM *Piledriver* (Vertigo, 1972)

As 1973 dawned, it had been nearly five years since Quo's last hit singles, and all four of their albums had bombed. But by the end of January, 'Paper Plane' and *Piledriver* were in the UK top ten, the latter destined for a thirty-seven-week stay. (Ultimately, no band would place more hits on the UK chart than them.) 'We didn't go out and consciously write the song as a single,' Rossi explained to *Disc*. 'It was just the right length and had plenty of balls.' (Notoriously critical of Quo's work, he later complained, 'It sounds horrendously out of tune.')

MOVIN' OUT
Aerosmith

🇺🇸

BY Steven Tyler, Joe Perry | PRODUCED BY Adrian Barber | FROM *Aerosmith* (Columbia, 1973)

'Right from their first album,' observed Izzy Stradlin, 'there is great guitar stuff.' Move past 'Mama Kin' (pretty weedy in its original incarnation) and ditch 'Dream On' (more a head-nodder than a banger); the real killer on *Aerosmith* is this hammer-heavy deep cut. '"Movin' Out" was the first song I wrote with Joe [Perry]...' noted Steven Tyler. 'It sealed the bond between me and Joe, and we didn't waste a lot of time with the rhymes. Joe quotes Jimi Hendrix's "Voodoo Chile" [*see* 1968] the way he quotes the Beatles and Stones elsewhere on the record.'

SABBATH BLOODY SABBATH
Black Sabbath

🇬🇧

BY Tony Iommi, Ozzy Osbourne, Geezer Butler, Bill Ward | PRODUCED BY Black Sabbath | FROM *Sabbath Bloody Sabbath* (WWA, 1973)

'All the compelling themes are on Black Sabbath's records: beauty, atrocity, the seven deadly sins...' Dave Navarro told *Rolling Stone*. 'The title song of *Sabbath Bloody Sabbath* has all of the stuff I'm talking about.' To Lars Ulrich, it was simply, 'Scary, crazy shit.'

The band's fifth album was initially threatened by Tony Iommi's writer's block. 'We had a good time in LA and we moved back there for *Sabbath Bloody Sabbath*, hoping to recreate the sound of *Vol 4*...' he recalled to *Guitar World*. '[We] rented the same house, the same studio, the same

'SABBATH BLOODY SABBATH WAS A GREAT ALBUM... NOBODY WOULD DARE DO WHAT WE WERE DOING, AND GET AWAY WITH IT'
OZZY OSBOURNE

drugs, everything. But we weren't able to create anything there, so we returned to England... We rented an old castle in Wales and rehearsed in its spooky old dungeon. After we wrote "Sabbath Bloody Sabbath", things just started coming fast and furious.'

'It was the end of our musical drought,' said Geezer Butler. 'It meant the band had a present, and a future.'

'The drum tracks might have been more technically precise if I hadn't been using drugs,' noted Bill Ward, 'but... I think I did okay. The title track is great to play live. There's a bit at the end with a nice percussion thing going on.'

Fans had no reservations about the album. 'The greatest heavy metal band's greatest songs...' wrote Tom Morello. 'It's just unbeatable for its power and heaviness. I dare anyone to try to come close to replicating it.' 'Creepy, spooky, and heavier than God...' suggested Billy Corgan. 'This album always makes me think of the soundtrack Sabbath would make to a final day on Earth.'

NO MORE MR. NICE GUY
Alice Cooper

BY Michael Bruce, Alice Cooper | PRODUCED BY Bob Ezrin FROM *Billion Dollar Babies* (Warner Bros., 1973)

Billion Dollar Babies, Alice's only US chart-topper, was stuffed with self-mythology: 'I Love the Dead', 'Sick Things', the title track and this witty hit, later covered by Megadeth. 'A plain great [guitarist] Michael Bruce song, as many of them were,' enthused bassist Dennis Dunaway to *Classic Rock*. 'All we did was learn it.' 'A real basic pop song with a funny lyric…' Alice told *Billboard*'s Craig Rosen. 'We figured everyone hated us so much, we would take it to the extreme: "You think we are bad now – wait until you see what's coming."'

BREADFAN
Budgie

BY Tony Bourge, Burke Shelley, Ray Phillips | PRODUCED BY Budgie | FROM *Never Turn Your Back on a Friend* (MCA, 1973)

'Hugely underrated, very sadly missed,' declared *Kerrang!* of this Welsh trio. Happily, the patronage of Metallica (who covered 'Breadfan' and 'Crash Course in Brain Surgery'), Soundgarden ('Homicidal Suicidal') and Iron Maiden ('I Can't See My Feelings') ensured they would not be forgotten. Metallica's devotion, however, didn't extend to duplicating 'Breadfan' in its entirety. 'They went into some hippy-trippy mellow bit in the middle…' James Hetfield cackled to *Guitar World*. 'We said, "Well, either we have to make fun of it or just fucking forget that part."'

WOMAN FROM TOKYO
Deep Purple

BY Ritchie Blackmore, Ian Gillan, Roger Glover, Jon Lord, Ian Paice | PRODUCED BY Deep Purple | FROM *Who Do We Think We Are* (Purple, 1973)

Frazzled from touring, the Mark II Purple were pushed into making a fourth album in under three years. The strain proved too much: within months of its release, singer Ian Gillan and bassist Roger Glover were out. But in the meantime, there was 'Woman from Tokyo' – which, after previous album openers 'Speed King,' 'Fireball' and 'Highway Star', was positively languid. But its laidback charm – built on a riff inspired by Cream's 'Cat's Squirrel' – signalled the band's funkier future, even as the lyric tipped a hat to an earlier hit, 'Black Night'.

SEARCH AND DESTROY
Iggy and the Stooges

 BY Iggy Pop, James Williamson | PRODUCED BY Iggy Pop | FROM *Raw Power* (Columbia, 1973)

Raw Power was wrecked by David Bowie's mixing, but its songs were unstoppable. The opener's lyrics, Iggy told *Clash*, 'I just sorta took out of *Time* magazine; the concept of "search and destroy". I used to read *Time* obsessively, because they were the representatives of the ultimate establishment… I kinda liked to look in there and see what they were talking about, and then I'd use that inventory in other ways.' 'If you put "Search and Destroy" on, man, I pop to attention every time!' Nikki Sixx declared to *Kerrang!* 'Oh my god, one of the greatest songs ever.'

THE OCEAN
Led Zeppelin

BY John Bonham, John Paul Jones, Jimmy Page, Robert Plant | PRODUCED BY Jimmy Page | FROM *Houses of the Holy* (Atlantic, 1973)

'It's not only that we think we're the best group in the world,' boasted Robert Plant. 'It's just that, in our minds, we're so much better than whoever is number two.' This confidence fed into Zep's fifth album, which soared on 'The Song Remains the Same' and swaggered on 'The Ocean'. The latter was introduced by John Bonham – 'He would just get drunk and start singing things,' reported Jimmy Page – and addressed the 'oceans' of fans over whom Plant presided on stage. Its irresistible riff later anchored the Beastie Boys' 'Rhymin' and Stealin''.

RAZAMANAZ
Nazareth

BY Pete Agnew, Manny Charlton, Darrell Sweet, Dan McCafferty | PRODUCED BY Roger Glover | FROM *Razamanaz* (Mooncrest, 1973)

Nazareth, Brian Johnson recalled to *Mojo*, 'were a great band… what I would call the first modern hard rock band.' The Scottish band's third album, named after its explosive opener, was their breakthrough. 'Roger [Glover, producer and Deep Purple bassist] said, "I'd really love to do this. This material could make a really great album,"' bassist Pete Agnew told *Classic Rock*. 'It made complete sense, because we were a poppier version of Deep Purple… We actually stole the riff to the song "Razamanaz" from [*Deep Purple In Rock's*] "Speed King".'

GIMME THREE STEPS
Lynyrd Skynyrd

BY Allen Collins, Ronnie Van Zant | PRODUCED BY Al Kooper FROM (*Pronounced 'Lĕh-'nérd 'Skin-'nérd*) (MCA, 1973)

More fun than 'Freebird', 'Gimme Three Steps' introduced the riffing wit that would fuel the likes of 'Sweet Home Alabama'. It was a true story, too. 'This guy was gonna whip Ronnie [Van Zant, frontman] for dancin' with his girlfriend...' recalled guitarist Gary Rossington. 'I don't know if you've got a gun pulled on you,' Van Zant remarked to *Melody Maker*, 'but, Jesus, I'm sure you've had someone say, "Stay away from that woman. She's mine." Well, this guy wanted to do me in, and there I was, saying, "Gimme three steps towards the door."'

ROCK THE NATION
Montrose

BY Ronnie Montrose | PRODUCED BY Montrose, Ted Templeman | FROM *Montrose* (Warner Bros., 1973)

'Negativity around the band was probably the only thing that stopped them...' Joe Elliott said of Sammy Hagar's alma mater. 'People thought they were the poor man's Zeppelin. The album *was* very reminiscent of Zeppelin, but its production was bigger.' 'It was just better than the other American bands of the time...' Gene Simmons told thequietus.com. 'The songs were undeniable.' Hagar himself told *Classic Rock*: 'If Ronnie [Montrose, guitarist] had been easy to work with, I would have done Montrose reunions all the time. I loved that band.'

WE'RE AN AMERICAN BAND
Grand Funk Railroad

BY Don Brewer | PRODUCED BY Todd Rundgren | FROM *We're an American Band* (Capitol, 1973)

Its credit is open to debate. 'The drum lick and everything, that was my idea...' frontman Mark Farner griped to *Mojo*. 'Musically, that was my creativity. But I gave it to [drummer Don Brewer] because he came to me and said, "Listen man, I never wrote a song all by myself. Do you think I could just have this?"' Its influence, however, was certain. 'You wanted to go to a roadhouse bar where this band was playing,' David Lee Roth wrote. 'We must have learned ten songs by Grand Funk. This is where Van Halen cut a lot of its forceful identity.'

SAME OLD SONG AND DANCE
Aerosmith

🇺🇸

BY Steven Tyler, Joe Perry | PRODUCED BY Jack Douglas, Ray Colcord | FROM *Get Your Wings* (Columbia, 1974)

"Get Your Wings," Aerosmith is taking off.

They burst out of Boston heralded by the screams of thousands of their fans, won over by their first explosive album. Now after a cross-country tour, highlighted by devastating Steven Tyler performances, Aerosmith has combined their talents to make "Get Your Wings" bulge with all the compressed energy and drive one record can hold.

"Get Your Wings" is the album that's going to take Aerosmith and everyone else even higher.

'We relied on the drugs for recording, touring, partying, fucking – anything at all, really,' wrote Steven Tyler. 'But [in 1974] we already knew there was a dark side to all this, as in the lyrics to "Same Old Song and Dance".' The words spoke of cocaine and pain, but the music grooved in a way that spawned a thousand imitators. Its irresistible swing was aided by jazz stars Michael and Randy Brecker, and Stan Bronstein, saxophonist in John Lennon's backing band Elephant's Memory. Long a fan favourite, the song won new admirers via 2007's *Guitar Hero III*.

CAN'T GET ENOUGH
Bad Company

🇬🇧

BY Mick Ralphs | PRODUCED BY Bad Company | FROM *Bad Company* (Island, 1974)

'People said we took off in America because we were a supergroup,' sniffed guitarist Mick Ralphs to *Classic Rock*. 'But most people didn't know Free or Mott the Hoople. All they knew was what they heard on the radio.' This smash – based on a riff that Ralphs recycled from Mott's 'One of the Boys' – propelled Bad Company's debut to the top of the US chart. Being the first signing to Zeppelin's Swan Song label (on which the album was released Stateside) didn't hurt. 'Love us or not,' said singer Paul Rodgers, 'everybody would at least give us a listen.'

BURN
Deep Purple

🇬🇧

BY Ritchie Blackmore, Glenn Hughes, Jon Lord, Ian Paice, David Coverdale | PRODUCED BY Deep Purple | FROM *Burn* (Purple, 1974)

'Written in the dungeon of Clearwell Castle, in the Forest of Dean, Gloucestershire, UK,' recalled Glenn Hughes to themusic.com.au. Jon Lord – no stranger to borrowing a nifty riff (*see* 1970) – added a nod to George Gershwin's 'Fascinating Rhythm'. 'I had some problems in finding lyrics,' admitted David Coverdale, who sang it with Hughes (and reworked it for Whitesnake's *The Purple Album* in 2015). 'I wanted them to have a modern setting yet give a surrealist flavour.' Fortunately fans were too busy headbanging to worry about 'devil's sperm'.

STRUTTER
Kiss

BY Paul Stanley, Gene Simmons | PRODUCED BY Kenny Kerner, Richie Wise | FROM *Kiss* (Casablanca, 1974)

'One of the first songs I ever wrote for Kiss,' Paul Stanley recalled to *Guitar World*. Their debut album opener began with chords that Gene Simmons wrote for a song called 'Stanley the Parrot' – which, said his bandmate, 'had nothing to do with me. We sped the "Parrot" song up and gave it a Stones-ish strut, hence the name.' 'Our music is very honest, gut-level, straight-ahead stuff,' Simmons observed to Ken Sharp. 'When you're talking about a strutter, you're not talking about other levels of reality. I don't think we ever cared about that.'

PARASITE
Kiss

BY Ace Frehley | PRODUCED BY Kenny Kerner, Richie Wise | FROM *Hotter Than Hell* (Casablanca, 1974)

Ace Frehley, grumbled Gene Simmons, 'never showed up on time, never did his work, hardly ever showed up in the studio, and it was pulling teeth every step of the way. Having said all that, I wouldn't have had anyone else in the band.' The wayward guitarist wrote several of Kiss's greatest deep cuts, including this Sabbath-esque brute, which Simmons sang. 'One of the songs that I really dig is "Parasite",' Dave Mustaine told loudersound.com. 'Just the riff! It's so down and dirty – and, at the time, nobody was really doing that kind of stuff.'

WORKING MAN
Rush

🇨🇦 BY Geddy Lee, Alex Lifeson | PRODUCED BY Rush | FROM *Rush* (Moon Records, 1974)

'"Working Man" does sound like Zeppelin,' Kirk Hammett observed to writer Martin Popoff. 'From far away, it sounds like "Heartbreaker" [*see* 1969]... But it's a cool song with a great riff.' The song set the band on the path to success. '"Working Man" got picked up on a radio station in Cleveland,' Alex Lifeson told loudersound.com. That, said Geddy Lee, 'led to us signing with Mercury.' Listeners were especially struck by Lee's voice. 'I thought, "Man, people just don't sing like this,"' Dream Theater's John Petrucci noted. 'But that's what made it so appealing.'

ROCK BOTTOM
UFO

🇬🇧 🇩🇪 BY Michael Schenker, Phil Mogg | PRODUCED BY Leo Lyons | FROM *Phenomenon* (Chrysalis, 1974)

'Early songs, like "Rock Bottom", were very spontaneous,' Michael Schenker told songfacts.com. 'When I played "Rock Bottom", the riff, Phil [Mogg, singer] jumped up and said, "That's it!"' The cut became a staple of concerts by UFO and the Michael Schenker Group. '"Rock Bottom" has that piece, in the middle, of free expression...' the guitarist explained. 'It leaves a lot of space to come up with a whole bunch of creative ideas.' 'He'd come up with some stunning solos...' Mogg enthused to the *Guardian*. 'Not just a load of notes for the sake of it.'

STONE COLD CRAZY
Queen

🇬🇧 BY Freddie Mercury, Brian May, Roger Taylor, John Deacon | PRODUCED BY Roy Thomas Baker, Queen FROM *Sheer Heart Attack* (EMI, 1974)

'We'd all written "Stone Cold Crazy" together,' Roger Taylor told *Classic Rock*. 'That was our first proper song.' Queen rocked on their first two albums, but it was on their third that they blueprinted metal of the future. 'I loved this riff before I even started to play,' Slash raved to *Total Guitar*. 'That's how cool it is.' The song's reputation was sealed by Metallica's cover. 'I'm flattered that a class act should choose a bit of our material,' Brian May told Rockline. James Hetfield duly snarled it with Queen and Tony Iommi at 1992's Freddie Mercury Tribute Show.

SWEET F.A.
The Sweet

🇬🇧 BY Brian Connolly, Steve Priest, Andy Scott, Mick Tucker | PRODUCED BY Phil Wainman | FROM *Sweet Fanny Adams* (RCA, 1974)

'Sweet wrote some of the most influential music in history,' Annihilator's Jeff Waters told metalinsider.net, 'and people don't give them credit for it.' As Mike Portnoy told musicradar.com, the British glam rockers influenced acts on both sides of the Atlantic; Nikki Sixx, for example, hero-worshipped singer Brian Connolly. 'Behind the glitter and glamour were some great – and heavy – songs,' Portnoy explained. 'If you really want a few surprises that will blow you away, take a listen to "Sweet F.A.", "Set Me Free" and "Burn on the Flame".'

WORKIN' FOR MCA
Lynyrd Skynyrd

BY Ed King, Ronnie Van Zant | PRODUCED BY Al Kooper | FROM *Second Helping* (MCA, 1974)

Skynyrd's impeccable second album opens with 'Sweet Home Alabama'. The first side ends with the similarly wry 'Workin' for MCA' – the finest record company song until the Pistols' 'EMI' and the best biographical number until Aerosmith's 'No Surprize' (*see* 1979). 'I remember him really loving the way ['Workin' for MCA' co-writer] Ed King of Lynyrd Skynyrd played guitar,' Kirk Hammett told *Guitar World* of Metallica bassist Cliff Burton. 'He'd always ask me to show him Skynyrd licks, and then he'd end up saying, "Man, that's tricky. That's really tricky."'

IT'S A LONG WAY TO THE TOP...
AC/DC

BY Malcolm Young, Angus Young, Bon Scott | PRODUCED BY Harry Vanda, George Young | FROM *T.N.T.* (Albert Productions, 1975)

'I'm an AC/DC man,' Josh Homme revealed to ew.com. 'I like it primitive.' 'Primitive' fit AC/DC's debut *High Voltage*, issued earlier in 1975, to a tee. But its follow-up confirmed the band as a force to be reckoned with, wrongfooting listeners with bagpipes on 'It's a Long Way to the Top (If You Wanna Rock 'n' Roll)'. 'Watching the Youngs at work was like a Scottish Rubik's Cube, with added swearing and shouting,' wrote bassist Mark Evans. 'Perhaps it might have been an idea to hire a piper. If the track was in the right key for the bagpipes, which it wasn't.'

DOWN DOWN
Status Quo

BY Francis Rossi, Bob Young | PRODUCED BY Status Quo | FROM *On the Level* (Vertigo, 1975)

Quo's only UK number one single, in late 1974, propelled the following year's *On the Level* to the top in its first week of release. That triumph was appropriate for a song whose verses were rooted in defiance. 'In my mind I was speaking to my ex-wife and the British press at the time,' Francis Rossi recalled to songfacts.com. Less thought, however, went into the addictive chorus. 'Bob [Young, co-writer] said, "Well, we'll write 'down down',"' Rossi explained. 'I said, "Yeah, it sounds good. It makes no fuckin' sense at all, but it sounds great."'

SLOW RIDE
Foghat

BY Dave Peverett | PRODUCED BY Nick Jameson | FROM *Fool for the City* (Bearsville, 1975)

Best road tune? '"Slow Ride",' replied Dave Grohl. Why? 'Because it's fucking Foghat, dude!' The song began as an eight-minute epic on *Fool for the City*. 'The DJs would have to fade it out,' recalled drummer Roger Earl to lipulse.com. 'But later we acquiesced, and Nick [Jameson, bassist/producer] edited it down to four-and-a-half minutes. I love playing the song.' Tireless touring and hits such as 'Slow Ride' earned Foghat gold and platinum albums in the States – but, in their homeland, the British band never once charted.

SWEET EMOTION
Aerosmith

BY Steven Tyler, Tom Hamilton | PRODUCED BY Jack Douglas | FROM *Toys in the Attic* (Columbia, 1975)

'I remember showing Steven [Tyler] this riff a couple of times during the *Get Your Wings* sessions and he just didn't like it ,' recalled bassist Tom Hamilton. 'But one day we started the riff at a different point and it shed a whole new light on it... The rest is history.' The barbed lyric, said Tyler, concerned 'how pissed off I was at Joe [Perry]'s ex-wife, and all the other frustrations of the time'. The music was equally heavy, but with a monster groove. 'It's not heavy metal and it's still white...' Perry declared, 'but we're just funkier than the rest, man.'

BASTILLE DAY
Rush

BY Geddy Lee, Alex Lifeson, Neil Peart | PRODUCED BY Rush, Terry Brown | FROM *Caress of Steel* (Mercury, 1975)

'What is *this*?' wondered Gene Simmons on first hearing Rush. 'This is like Canadian Zeppelin.' 'With Kiss, we probably played fifty, sixty shows...' recalled Alex Lifeson. 'They were just this weird band from New York, and we got very, very close.' The legacy of their touring together through the spring of 1975 is this stormer, recorded in the summer, which begins with a riff reminiscent of Kiss's 'Parasite' (*see* 1974) before launching a fabulous one of its own. *Caress of Steel*'s liner notes, however, dutifully offer a 'special hullo' to 'Ape Friendly'.

COLD ETHYL
Alice Cooper

BY Alice Cooper, Bob Ezrin | PRODUCED BY Bob Ezrin | FROM *Welcome to My Nightmare* (Atlantic, 1975)

Just one cut on Alice's first solo album had the sleazy cool of the band that made him famous. It boasted sex sounds over a decade before 'Rocket Queen' and raised the ire of the *Chicago Sun-Times*'s advice columnist. 'I'm really sorry you found that old song of mine crude,' Alice wrote back. '"Cold Ethyl" is just a harmless number about necrophilia... The kids are not bothered by this – their parents are. The kids see the song and gruesome antics, like with the guillotine, for exactly what it is: satire, done with a sense of humour to a rock 'n' roll beat.'

SYMPTOM OF THE UNIVERSE
Black Sabbath

🇬🇧 BY Tony Iommi, Geezer Butler, Ozzy Osbourne, Bill Ward | PRODUCED BY Black Sabbath, Mike Butcher | FROM *Sabotage* (NEMS, 1975)

'The greatest ever riff,' Max Cavalera gushed to *Total Guitar*. 'It's so aggressive and brutal, man. Imagine hearing that in 1975!' Sludge has rarely sounded more thrilling than *Sabotage*'s 'Symptom of the Universe' and 'Hole in the Sky', and the former proved particularly influential. 'Everyone would know that riff if you played it on any setlist anywhere in the world,' Dave Grohl explained to *Q*. 'This is the swamp from whence much metal crawled.' But what did it *mean*? 'I can't really remember...' Geezer Butler confessed to uproxx.com. 'I think it's about love.'

DARK LADY
Scorpions

⬛ BY Uli Jon Roth | PRODUCED BY Dieter Dierks | FROM *In Trance* (RCA Victor, 1975)

'We tried out a lot of ideas when we were on the road,' Uli Jon Roth reflected to metalexpressradio.com. 'The songs weren't that complex.' Sure enough, 'Dark Lady' is as brutal as it is brainless – and Roth's shrieking guitar means Michael Schenker isn't missed. 'A song with absolutely no message,' Roth admitted to Scorps biographer Greg Prato. Nonetheless, it impressed Billy Corgan: 'I was like, "What the fuck is this guitar?!"... And, suddenly, I found myself obsessively listening to that album. Then I was like, "Who the hell is Uli Jon Roth?"'

DEUCE
Kiss

🇺🇸 BY Gene Simmons | PRODUCED BY Eddie Kramer | FROM *Alive!* (Casablanca, 1975)

'When people listen to Kiss's body of work and reflect on their forty-plus years, it can be a little embarrassing,' Phil Anselmo told *Metal Hammer*. 'But, honestly, that first live recording is a very powerful rock album that should not be overlooked.' The band's breakthrough boasted cool cuts like 'Cold Gin' and 'Got to Choose', and birthed a classic in 'Rock and Roll All Nite'. But the war was won in the first four minutes, with a storming version of Gene Simmons' goofily great rip of The Rolling Stones' 'Bitch'. (Check out the gonzoid take on 1993's *Alive III*, too.)

KISS ALIVE!

The album your customers are screaming for!

Kiss, the demons of Rock captured "Alive" on a specially priced 2-record set including an 8 page color booklet. Kiss, exclusively on Casablanca Records and Tapes.

Produced by Eddie Kramer

The image is Getting Clearer

IN MY TIME OF DYING
Led Zeppelin

 BY Robert Plant, Jimmy Page, John Paul Jones, John Bonham | PRODUCED BY Jimmy Page | FROM *Physical Graffiti* (Swan Song, 1975)

'It's so multidimensional and goes through so many twists and turns,' Corey Taylor told *Metal Hammer* of this epic. 'And I don't think it gets enough credit for how fucking gorgeous it is. It's a killer… and Bonham's backbeat on that tune is unrelenting!' 'Spectacular and monstrous,' agreed Robert Plant to *Rolling Stone*. 'It sped up, slowed down, went sideways, careened and spiralled – and I'm in the middle of it all.' Billy Corgan opined: '"In My Time of Dying" is as heavy as anything released.' But, as Jimmy Page noted, 'We're just doing what Led Zeppelin do.'

BLITZKRIEG BOP
Ramones

 BY Dee Dee Ramone, Joey Ramone, Johnny Ramone, Tommy Ramone | PRODUCED BY Craig Leon, Tommy Ramone | FROM *Ramones* (Sire, 1976)

'There were no standards after the Ramones,' explained Kirk Hammett. 'All you had to do was just be yourself.' The pioneers' legacy is illustrated by the cast of Rob Zombie's Ramones tribute *We're a Happy Family*, including the Chili Peppers, Metallica, Kiss, Marilyn Manson, Eddie Vedder, Garbage, Green Day, The Offspring and Rancid. 'Blitzkrieg Bop' kicks off their debut album and very little that follows in this book (okay, not 'Xanadu') wasn't in some way influenced by it. 'Groundbreakers,' marvelled Blink-182's Mark Hoppus. 'Heroes. Legends.'

VICTIM OF CHANGES
Judas Priest

 BY KK Downing, Rob Halford, Glenn Tipton, Al Atkins | PRODUCED BY Jeffrey Calvert, Max West, Judas Priest | FROM *Sad Wings of Destiny* (Gull, 1976)

Rob Halford, declared Armored Saint's John Bush to ranker.com, 'could weave in and out of styles and personalities… singing sometimes with a super falsetto or a down-in-the-bowels low tone.' The metal god's versatility was showcased on this brooding, multilayered epic and live staple – which, Halford's predecessor Al Atkins told mhf-mag.com, 'started out as my song "Whiskey Woman"… Rob added one of his slow songs to the end, called "Red Light Lady", Glenn [Tipton] added the intro and they retitled it. One of their biggest songs now.'

STARGAZER
Rainbow

 BY Ritchie Blackmore, Ronnie James Dio | PRODUCED BY Martin Birch | FROM *Rainbow Rising* (Oyster, 1976)

'"Stargazer",' Ronnie James Dio explained to *Circus*, 'is written from the standpoint of a slave in Egyptian times. He is serving the wizard, who observes the skies and stars and becomes obsessed with the idea of flying… Finally this wizard – this stargazer – attempts to fly and, of course, falls to his death.' 'That was a good tune,' Ritchie Blackmore observed to *Guitar World* of a song that routinely jostled 'Stairway to Heaven' in hard rock polls. 'I wrote that on the cello. I had given up on the guitar between '75 and '78. I completely lost interest.'

JAILBREAK
Thin Lizzy

BY Phil Lynott | PRODUCED BY John Alcock | FROM *Jailbreak* (Vertigo, 1976)

'Everything Thin Lizzy did has had an influence,' Cliff Burton assured *Rock Hard*. The band's breakthrough fifth album exploded thanks to the hit 'The Boys Are Back in Town', but its funky title cut is the connoisseurs' pick. 'The jailbreak thing is about youth and oppression,' Phil Lynott told *Melody Maker*. 'When you reach the age of fourteen or eighteen, you suddenly find strength that you've never had before. There's aggression, power and rebelliousness, and they want to exercise that power. It can be put to good use in the right position, where there is an oppressor.'

PROBLEM CHILD
AC/DC

BY Angus Young, Bon Scott, Malcolm Young PRODUCED BY Harry Vanda, George Young FROM *Dirty Deeds Done Dirt Cheap* (Albert Productions, 1976)

Truncated for the international version of 1977's *Let There Be Rock*, 'Problem Child' spits and snarls for nearly six minutes in its original *Dirty Deeds* incarnation. (Little wonder it returned to AC/DC's setlists when Axl took the helm.) 'It has a cool riff, cool lyrics and a great groove,' Kim Thayil noted to *Classic Rock*. 'Ozzy was over at my house in '76...' Glenn Hughes reminisced. 'We were watching the BBC and on comes this ballsy band, with a little lad in his school uniform. We both knew that they would go all the way, and this song stood out for me.'

CHERRY BOMB
The Runaways

BY Joan Jett, Kim Fowley | PRODUCED BY Kim Fowley | FROM *The Runaways* (Mercury, 1976)

'The Runaways recorded "Cherry Bomb" in a store room...' svengali and co-writer Kim Fowley declared to mixonline.com. 'We barely had equipment. But we had a plan: teenaged girls with guitars.' 'The Runaways were really the first all-girl band to really strut their stuff and say, "Fuck you,"' Lemmy noted to goldminemag.com. '"Cherry Bomb" was the best song for a girl band to sing. It was just outrageous at the time. There were American families sitting on the sofa watching television going, "Fuck me". It was great fun.'

DIRTY WOMEN
Black Sabbath

🇬🇧

BY Tony Iommi, Geezer Butler, Bill Ward, Ozzy Osbourne | PRODUCED BY Black Sabbath | FROM *Technical Ecstasy* (Vertigo, 1976)

'Black Sabbath fans generally don't like much of *Technical Ecstasy...*' Tony Iommi conceded to *Guitar World*. 'If we had stayed the same, people would have said we were still doing the same old stuff. So we tried to get a little more technical, and it just didn't work out very well.' But the patchy album was bookended by the gritty 'Back Street Kids' and sinister 'Dirty Women'. The latter – 'A reflection of what I've seen, watching dirty old men going into porno book stores and massage parlours,' Geezer Butler told *Circus* – was duly resurrected for the reunited Sabbath's final tours.

ACHILLES LAST STAND
Led Zeppelin

🇬🇧

BY Jimmy Page, Robert Plant | PRODUCED BY Jimmy Page | FROM *Presence* (Swan Song, 1976)

'The whole of that album, *Presence*, is absolutely wracked with pain,' Robert Plant shuddered to the *Guardian*. 'The fraternity of the band at the time was stretched to breaking point... If you want to know what I was like at the end of Zeppelin, really, this [song] was it.' Plant sang it from a wheelchair – the legacy of a car crash. Explaining the song's title to *Interview*, he said: 'I fell over when I was singing it... Pagey virtually carried me to the hospital. [Later] I was wheeled to the studio while the others were asleep and did the whole vocal track all over again.'

NOBODY'S FAULT
Aerosmith

🇺🇸 BY Steven Tyler, Brad Whitford | PRODUCED BY Jack Douglas, Aerosmith | FROM *Rocks* (Columbia, 1976)

Environmental apocalypse on an Aerosmith album? Goddam right. As Cinderella's Tom Keifer remarked, '"Nobody's Fault" was badass' – from the intro when, as Steven Tyler wrote, 'the band came in on a crashing E chord like Hitler was at the door.' The cut's admirers also include *Rocks* evangelist Slash, Vince Neil (who covered it), Kurt Cobain (who rated the album among his favourites) and Jeff Beck. 'When I heard that was Jeff's favourite Aerosmith song,' co-writer Brad Whitford beamed to songfacts.com, 'I just felt like I had arrived.'

(DON'T FEAR) THE REAPER
Blue Öyster Cult

Tattoo Vampire

BY Donald 'Buck Dharma' Roeser | PRODUCED BY David Lucas, Murray Krugman, Sandy Pearlman | FROM *Agents of Fortune* (Columbia, 1976)

'I wrote "Reaper" when I thought I was gonna croak,' guitarist Donald Roeser confessed to *NME*. 'I have a heart condition. Basically it's a great love song, with the dead boy coming back for his girl and finding she's waited for him.' Conceived as a Sabbath spoof, BÖC had harder songs than this, but none better and few darker. 'We were a parody of the heavy metal beast and then turned into it,' frontman Eric Bloom admitted to *Sounds*. Still, there were compensations: 'Since "The Reaper" was a hit, there are some ladies up front, which is nice.'

TIE YOUR MOTHER DOWN
Queen

BY Brian May | PRODUCED BY Queen | FROM *A Day at the Races* (EMI, 1a976)

'I actually performed this with Queen at the Freddie Mercury Tribute Concert,' Slash reminisced to *Total Guitar*. 'It's just one of the most instantly recognizable riffs.' It's also writer Brian May's favourite to play: 'People jump up when they hear it,' he told *Guitar World*. May, sometimes with Roger Taylor, has performed it with the Foos, The Darkness and Guns N' Roses. Of its sentiments, Freddie Mercury speculated, 'Maybe he was in one of his vicious moods. I think he's trying to outdo me after [*A Night at the Opera*'s] "Death on Two Legs".'

DETROIT ROCK CITY
Kiss

BY Paul Stanley, Bob Ezrin | PRODUCED BY Bob Ezrin | FROM *Destroyer* (Casablanca, 1976)

'A calling card of sorts for Kiss...' Paul Stanley suggested to loudersound.com. 'Albums, particularly ours, should start with a song that captures the spirit of what you're going to get on the rest of the album – and "Detroit Rock City" was very much that for *Destroyer*.' This flamenco-tinged tale of a fan killed en route to a show in North Carolina took on a life of its own. It inspired Pantera's 'Ride My Rock', bequeathed its title to a film and was performed by Stanley and the Foo Fighters in 2015. Joe Elliott's verdict: 'The best thing they ever wrote.'

2112
Rush

BY Geddy Lee, Alex Lifeson, Neil Peart | PRODUCED BY Rush, Terry Brown | FROM *2112* (Mercury, 1976)

'I heard that weird pedal effect at the beginning and thought, "Are you *kidding* me?!"' Dave Mustaine told thequietus.com. 'That was the opening of a whole new world.' A new world opened, too, for Rush – who, having seen their first three albums flounder, assumed the ambitious *2112* would be a last throw of the dice.

'The record company thought we were going down the tubes,' Alex Lifeson recalled to *Sounds*. 'We didn't get paid for months – and we got pissed off. We got angry and we fought back with *2112*. And after *2112* became a success,

there was a lot of back-slapping: "Yes, we knew you'd pull through!"'

The seven-part sci-fi epic ran to twenty minutes. 'We wrote the bits and pieces of "2112" while we were on the *Caress of Steel* tour,' Lifeson said. 'We'd play it in soundchecks and at every opportunity we got. So we were pretty well versed with it before we recorded it.'

'We had long songs before,' Geddy Lee noted, 'but "2112" was the first time we really pulled it off properly. It was so much more powerful and defined than [*Caress of Steel's* side-long] "The Fountain of Lamneth". That became the roadmap for how we would go forward.'

'I would get lost in this album,' Dream Theater's John Petrucci told musicradar.com. 'I wanted to know what they were talking about. "Who's this guy? What's happening?" It took you to another world… The way the tale evolves is astonishing, using the guitar as an actual part of the story.'

And the 'weird pedal effect' that blew Dave Mustaine's mind? 'Hugh Syme [the sleeve designer whose "starman" became a Rush icon] was also a musician, and played keyboards on *2112*,' Lifeson revealed. 'He made that spacey synth sound.'

FIGHT FROM THE INSIDE
Queen

BY Roger Taylor | PRODUCED BY Queen | FROM *News of the World* (EMI, 1977)

Queen, observed Anthrax sage Charlie Benante to songfacts.com, 'wrote some of the heaviest shit.' In the case of *News of the World*, that meant 'We Will Rock You' (see 1979), 'Sheer Heart Attack' ('Here were Queen saying to the punks, "We can be just as stripped-down and full-on as you!"' Taylor Hawkins told *Classic Rock*), 'Get Down, Make Love' (covered by Nine Inch Nails), the crashing 'It's Late' and, best of all, this bad-ass funk-metal prototype. Writer Roger Taylor sings, drums and plays bass and rhythm, leaving only the leads to Brian May.

BODIES
Sex Pistols

BY Johnny Rotten, Steve Jones, Paul Cook, Sid Vicious | PRODUCED BY Chris Thomas, Bill Price | FROM *Never Mind the Bollocks, Here's the Sex Pistols* (Virgin, 1977)

'No one ever had the guts to say what they said,' Billie Joe Armstrong noted to *Rolling Stone*. The punk heroes won over Jimmy Page ('I liked the Sex Pistols' music... it was superb', the *Guardian*), Axl Rose ('If I was stranded on a desert island, I might go with the Pistols, because maybe a boat would hear me if I played it', *Rolling Stone*) and Venom's Cronos ('Seeing the Sex Pistols for the first time was just one of the greatest things for me', *Guitar World*). AC/DC's Malcolm Young, however, was unmoved. 'They couldn't fucking play,' he grumbled to *Mojo*.

LIGHTS OUT
UFO

BY Michael Schenker, Phil Mogg, Andy Parker, Pete Way | PRODUCED BY Ron Nevison | FROM *Lights Out* (Chrysalis, 1977)

'My brother,' observed Rudolf Schenker of the Scorpions to *Classic Rock*, 'was very good on that album.' Michael Schenker's playing and *Lights Out*'s production made it a touchstone for Guns N' Roses: 'It was both outstanding and sounded amazing,' wrote Slash. And, as Dimebag Darrell noted to *Guitar World*, Pete Way and Andy Parker's rhythm section behind the lead in "Lights Out" is really driving: it's fire, it's guts, it's live, it's totally jamming!' In all, a song that, Tom Morello told musicradar.com, 'I would put toe to toe with just about any jam.'

DISSIDENT AGGRESSOR
Judas Priest

BY Glenn Tipton, Rob Halford, KK Downing | PRODUCED BY Roger Glover, Judas Priest | FROM *Sin After Sin* (CBS, 1977)

'It's about the Berlin Wall in 1970-something or other,' Rob Halford revealed to songfacts.com. 'I couldn't sleep, so I went out for a walk. I went to the Berlin Wall... and the East side was just dead. It was pitch black, no lights were on, and there were these Russian guys looking back at me in binoculars. That was the seed for what that song talks about.' Slayer covered it on 1988's *South of Heaven* because, Kerry King told *Rolling Stone*, 'it was super-heavy but very obscure. And, after we did, a lot of people still thought it was our own song.'

THE SAILS OF CHARON
Scorpions

BY Uli Jon Roth | PRODUCED BY Dieter Dierks | FROM *Taken by Force* (RCA Victor, 1977)

'My least favourite [Scorpions album],' guitarist Uli Jon Roth lamented to metalinsider.net, 'would have been *Taken by Force*, since I had virtually left the band in my head and was not giving my everything... [But it] had some of my best stuff... It still has "Sails of Charon".' The infectious cut became a guitar hero staple: it was quoted live by Kirk Hammett and, as Dave Ellefson told guitar.com, 'When [Shrapnel label boss] Mike Varney first brought Yngwie over, it was killer. He was playing the Scorpions' "Sails of Charon", just rippin' through this stuff.'

"Spectres." Blue Öyster Cult. On Columbia Records and Tapes.
Produced by Murray Krugman, Sandy Pearlman, David Lucas and Blue Öyster Cult.

DRAW THE LINE
Aerosmith

BY Steven Tyler, Joe Perry | PRODUCED BY Jack Douglas, Aerosmith | FROM *Draw the Line* (Columbia, 1977)

'*Draw the Line* was the lowest point,' Tom Hamilton despaired to *Classic Rock*. 'There was just too much decadence and destruction going on. We went from being this great, up-and-coming band to being this dilapidated shambles.' The frazzled title cut emerged from the wreckage. 'One of my favourite riffs that I ever wrote,' said Joe Perry. 'It's a simple thing, but so are most of the ones that stick.' It was influential, too: 'Our basic root is hard rock... in a vein like Aerosmith,' Axl Rose told *Rolling Stone*. '*Draw the Line*-type stuff. We love loud guitars.'

GODZILLA
Blue Öyster Cult

BY Donald 'Buck Dharma' Roeser | PRODUCED BY Murray Krugman, Sandy Pearlman, David Lucas, Blue Öyster Cult | FROM *Spectres* (Columbia, 1977)

'I was a big fan of the Raymond Burr Americanization of the [Japanese film company] Toho "Godzilla" films,' guitarist Donald 'Buck Dharma' Roeser told heraldtribune.com. 'When I came up with the guitar riff in a hotel room in Dallas, it made me think of Godzilla and the lyrics came quickly.' Brilliantly, when the song was omitted from the soundtrack of the 1998 *Godzilla* reboot, Roeser and singer Eric Bloom recorded 'Nozilla', poking fun at the acts who *did* make it and quipping, 'Millions spent on special effects but our tune just ain't gettin' no respect...'

NEW ROSE
The Damned

🇬🇧 BY Brian James | PRODUCED BY Nick Lowe | FROM *Damned Damned Damned* (Stiff, 1977)

'Brilliant songs,' Robert Plant enthused to the *Guardian*. 'They quite rightly kicked juggernauts like Pink Floyd into touch.' Bassist Captain Sensible recalled to *Rolling Stone*: 'Jimmy Page was such a fan... [He] saw something special in Brian [James]'s guitar style and writing.' Duff McKagan, who instigated GNR's version of the first British punk single, told thequietus.com: 'Rat [Scabies, drummer] said, "Thanks for covering that song – I got the biggest publishing cheque I ever got." But I didn't know what to say... These are my heroes.'

XANADU
Rush

🇨🇦 BY Neil Peart, Geddy Lee, Alex Lifeson | PRODUCED BY Rush, Terry Brown | FROM *A Farewell to Kings* (Anthem, 1977)

'Rush for me was a hard rock band,' Opeth's Mikael Åkerfeldt opined. 'But they were very odd.' Indeed, while punk raged, Neil Peart put poetry to eleven minutes of intricate yet thrilling music. 'I was trying,' he told the *Guardian,* 'to write a song inspired by the dark mood and subtle psychology of the film *Citizen Kane*, which features the opening lines of *Kubla Khan* by Samuel Taylor Coleridge. I looked up the poem and was overwhelmed by its imagery and emotional power... I portrayed Coleridge's idea of immortality as a grim curse.'

LET THERE BE ROCK
AC/DC

🇦🇺 BY Malcolm Young, Angus Young, Bon Scott | PRODUCED BY Harry Vanda, George Young | FROM *Let There Be Rock* (Albert Productions, 1977)

'Me and my buddies used to jam with this all day,' Scott Ian told musicradar.com. 'It was so much fun... This song was their first real anthem.' 'Great melody, huge drama, adrenaline-fuelled excitement...' Thunder's Danny Bowes raved to *Classic Rock*. 'Oh, and a fuck-right-off guitar riff.' Angus Young recalled that, by the end of two takes, smoke 'was pouring out of the fucking amp'. But for bassist Mark Evans, the star of the show was drummer Phil Rudd: 'Just absolutely out of this world... I thought the guy was gonna fucking explode.'

BARRACUDA
Heart

THE SPELLBINDING ROCK & ROLL OF "LITTLE QUEEN" IS ON PORTRAIT RECORDS AND TAPES.

BY Ann Wilson, Roger Fisher, Nancy Wilson, Michael Derosier | PRODUCED BY Mike Flicker | FROM *Little Queen* (Portrait, 1977)

'The female Led Zeppelin' stamped their boot on the seventies. The spark was an ad, placed in *Billboard* by record label Mushroom, that captioned a picture of Ann and Nancy Wilson, 'Sisters confess: It was only our first time.' The sapphic innuendo was compounded by a radio promotion guy who enquired of the whereabouts of Ann's 'lover'. Enraged, the singer began work on 'Barracuda'. The result, noted Nancy, 'addresses how much you want to call out somebody when they're an asshole... People can certainly relate to that.'

BAT OUT OF HELL
Meat Loaf

BY Jim Steinman | PRODUCED BY Todd Rundgren | FROM *Bat Out of Hell* (Epic, 197̶

'Blown-up and melodramatic and comical to the extent that it didn't seem as though anyone would take it seriously,' producer Todd Rundgren admitted to the BBC. 'Yet it involved a lot of humour and interesting things.' 'The imagery is heavy,' writer Jim Steinman observed. 'I'm tryin to incorporate the mythical imagery of metal with more of a variety of musical styles. I like a lot of the mythology, the resonance of heavy metal... Flamboyant fantasy qualities, too. I like adding Wagner to everything. A little bit of dramatic Gothic never hurt anyone.'

She said goodbye to innocence.
He said hello to paradise.
They knew it would never be like this again.

'Paradise by the Dashboard Light.'
One of seven spectacular tales on the Meat Loaf album "Bat Out of Hell."
On Epic/Cleveland International Records and Tapes.
Featuring "Two Out of Three Ain't Bad."

MEAT LOAF. "Bat Out of Hell."
Songs by Jim Steinman.

A Halloween tradition all year round.

CAT SCRATCH FEVER
Ted Nugent

BY Ted Nugent | PRODUCED BY Lew Futterman, Tom Werman, Cliff Davies | FROM *Cat Scratch Fever* (Epic, 1977)

'Obviously the number one guitar lick in the history of the world,' the Nuge declared to myglobalmind.com. 'Ted finally wrote a real single – a hit single,' co-producer Tom Werman told musicradar.com. 'This was the linchpin for his whole career – because, even though he was already successful, now he was on the radio... We had to change "pussy" to "kitty". I think everybody knew what he really meant.' But what was the Nuge's verdict on Pantera's cover, from 1999's *Detroit Rock City* soundtrack? 'No soul,' he grumbled. 'No balls, no feel.'

STOLE YOUR LOVE
Kiss

BY Paul Stanley | PRODUCED BY Kiss, Eddie Kramer | FROM *Love Gun* (Casablanca, 1977)

Love Gun's opener evoked both the rawness of Kiss's pre-*live!* days and the riff of Deep Purple's 'Burn' (*see* 1974). 'I was trying,' Paul Stanley admitted to writer Ken Sharp, 'to get closer to the things I liked in the British bands that were my influences.' Happily, Purple veteran Ritchie Blackmore told *Trouser Press*: 'Kiss I like because they don't care what people think of them. They take a chance and it's worked. They're the first ones to admit they're not good musicians.' 'I worked out all the parts,' Stanley said. 'If I didn't play them, I told someone else what to play.'

KILL THE KING
Rainbow

🇬🇧 🇺🇸

BY Ritchie Blackmore, Ronnie James Dio, Cozy Powell | **PRODUCED BY** Martin Birch | **FROM** *On Stage* (Oyster, 1977)

Rising, Ritchie Blackmore conceded to *Kerrang!*, 'is a very good album. I remember saying to Ronnie Dio at the time, "We're going to find it hard to follow that one up."' Rainbow bought time with a live set, which – after a delightful *Wizard of Oz* intro – opened with the explosive 'Kill the King' (held over from *Rising*, as was 'Long Live Rock 'n' Roll'). 'I have no idea what the lyrics to that song are about,' Blackmore confessed to the BBC. 'I didn't know too much about the lyrics, and they were very abstract; most of them talking about demons and devils.'

LONG LIVE ROCK 'N' ROLL
Rainbow

🇬🇧 🇺🇸

BY Ritchie Blackmore, Ronnie James Dio | **PRODUCED BY** Martin Birch | **FROM** *Long Live Rock 'n' Roll* (Polydor, 1978)

'Around the *Long Live Rock 'n' Roll* era, it was getting very tense,' Blackmore told thequietus.com. 'We were in a French chateau… and everybody was beginning to hate each other. You go through these periods of being with the same people for so long that their idiosyncrasies get magnified, including my own.' But Rainbow could still bring the noise, as this anthem attests. Asked by *Trouser Press* how he felt about the term heavy metal, Blackmore replied: 'It suits us fine. I know I can play a bloody concerto any day, so it doesn't bother me at all.'

SURRENDER
Cheap Trick

🇺🇸

BY Rick Nielsen | **PRODUCED BY** Ken Adamany | **FROM** *Cheap Trick at Budokan* (Epic, 1978)

'I remember being on the beach in Ocean City, Maryland,' Dave Grohl recalled, 'drunk as all hell, sitting on a lifeguard chair at three o'clock in the morning, staring out into the ocean and singing that song at the top of my lungs.' The track's popularity surprised guitarist Rick Nielsen, who explained its lyric to music.avclub.com: 'Every person I've ever met always thinks their parents are weird… The worst thing your parents can do is try to emulate you. And here's something that's like, "You got my Kiss records out." Oh my god! New lows.'

NICE BOYS
Rose Tattoo

🇦🇺

BY Geordie Leach, Angry Anderson, Dallas 'Digger' Royall, Peter Wells, Mick Cocks | **PRODUCED BY** Harry Vanda, George Young | **FROM** *Rose Tattoo* (Albert Productions, 1978)

'One of Australia's greatest rock bands,' wrote Slash, having met Rose Tattoo after Guns N' Roses unleashed a cover of 'Nice Boys' on *Live ?!*@ Like a Suicide*. '[Singer] Angry Anderson was everything I thought he'd be… he was every bit as real and honest as I'd hoped for.' 'I ain't no fuckin' Rose Tattoo rip-off,' Axl Rose assured a Sydney audience. 'They're just one of my favourite fuckin' bands, that's all. I put a Rose Tattoo song on our record because we wanted people in America to listen to some bitchin' Australian bands.'

BEYOND THE REALMS OF DEATH
Judas Priest

BY Les Binks, Rob Halford | PRODUCED BY Dennis MacKay, Judas Priest | FROM *Stained Class* (CBS, 1978)

I felt we needed to introduce some light and shade with a big rock ballad that started softly with acoustic guitar and built up to an explosive metal riff,' drummer Les Binks reflected to kkdowning.net of this ominous, near-seven-minute epic. 'I'd made a demo of a song which fitted the bill... They liked it, and Rob went away and wrote some lyrics for it, and came up with the title "Beyond the Realms of Death".' The result, KK Downing bragged to *Guitar World*, 'is Judas Priest's "Stairway to Heaven". It's a key song in the Priest repertoire.'

LA VILLA STRANGIATO
Rush

BY Geddy Lee, Alex Lifeson, Neil Peart | PRODUCED BY Rush, Terry Brown | FROM *Hemispheres* (Anthem, 1978)

'I see them as the high priests of conceptual metal,' Kirk Hammett said in the Rush biopic *Beyond the Lighted Stage*. 'Probably the hardest song that I ever learned how to play was "La Villa Strangiato",' laughed Vinnie Paul in the film. 'The drumming – it takes everything you've got to get through it.' Incredibly, the nine-and-a-half-minute conclusion to one of Rush's darkest albums was recorded in a single take – even though, as Geddy Lee admitted to the *Guardian*, 'That was a song where I would have to say our ideas exceeded our ability to play them.'

NEVER SAY DIE
Black Sabbath

BY Tony Iommi, Geezer Butler, Ozzy Osbourne, Bill Ward | PRODUCED BY Black Sabbath | FROM *Never Say Die!* (Vertigo, 1978)

It should've been called *I Wish I Was Dead*,' Ozzy sniped to *Rolling Stone* of his first Sabbath swan song. 'It was desperate,' Tony Iommi agreed to *Classic Rock*. 'The songs were all over the place.' *Never Say Die!*'s title cut, however, is among their best. 'We did some remarkable work...' said Ozzy, 'considering we were just full of cocaine and booze and on Quaaludes and Mandrax and Mogadons and Valium.' As Bill Ward told *Circus* in 1978: 'The band has been under such strain... but when you're up against the wall, you start kicking back.'

Never Say Die!

Their new album 9102 751

WHOLE LOTTA ROSIE
AC/DC

BY Angus Young, Bon Scott, Malcolm Young PRODUCED BY Harry Vanda, George Young FROM *If You Want Blood You've Got It* (Albert Productions, 1978)

If You Want Blood…, Malcolm Young reflected to writer Mark Blake, 'was recorded at one of the best gigs of that tour, at the Glasgow Apollo… "Whole Lotta Rosie" and "Let There Be Rock" were going down a treat by then.' The 'Angus!' chant (prompted by the preceding 'Problem Child') helped turn this into a standard. Its opening riff, Angus Young told *Sounds*, was 'our version of an old blues… like a classic Muddy Waters "Mannish Boy" or "I'm A Man" kinda thing. We were looking for something that might have that same sort of impact.'

BACK ON THE STREETS
Gary Moore

BY Gary Moore, Donna Campbell | PRODUCED BY Chris Tsangarides, Gary Moore | FROM *Back on the Streets* (MCA, 1978)

Gary Moore dismissed his early solo albums as 'feeble attempts at heavy rock' – but there's nothing feeble about 'Back on the Streets', featuring his Thin Lizzy comrade Phil Lynott on bass and vocals. Moore shared the writing credit with girlfriend Donna Campbell (inspiration for the album's 'Song for Donna') – who, having heard Moore's first band Skid Row on the BBC, 'hitchhiked from [South West England's] Bridgwater to London, got into the John Peel show, got backstage, and met Gary… He was underrated – definitely one of the best guitarists ever.'

RUNNIN' WITH THE DEVIL
Van Halen

BY Eddie Van Halen, Alex Van Halen, Michael Anthony, David Lee Roth | PRODUCED BY Ted Templeman | FROM *Van Halen* (Warner Bros., 1978)

'Van Halen was the very first band I saw in LA…' W.A.S.P.'s Blackie Lawless recalled. 'They were playing "Runnin' with the Devil"… I remember hearing that for the first time and thinking, "That's an okay song."' From an album full of standouts, the monstrous opener – first captured in faster, funkier form on a 1977 demo financed by Gene Simmons – proved one of the most enduring. 'You can sing along with most of our tunes,' Eddie Van Halen told *Guitar Player* in 1978, 'even though many of them do have the peculiar guitar and the end-of-the-world drums.'

THE ROCKER
Thin Lizzy

BY Phil Lynott, Brian Downey, Eric Bell | PRODUCED BY Thin Lizzy, Tony Visconti | FROM *Live and Dangerous* (Vertigo, 1978)

Initially, neither 'The Rocker' nor its parent album – 1973's *Vagabonds of the Western World* – made much impression outside Thin Lizzy's stomping ground of Ireland. But by 1976, when most of *Live and Dangerous* was taped, it had become a live staple – hence the audience demanding it as the album draws to a close. Nonetheless, drummer Brian Downey told *Hot Press* in 1978: 'A lot of people describe us as heavy metal, which surprises me. I wouldn't like to see the band get into a position where it had to depend on hard rock material to sell.'

N THE EVENING
Led Zeppelin

BY John Paul Jones, Jimmy Page, Robert Plant | PRODUCED BY Jimmy Page | FROM *In Through the Out Door* (Swan Song, 1979)

The singer's a bit of a bullshit artist,' Malcolm Young complained. 'There's too much echo and the fucking solos are too long.' But Led Zeppelin could still smack you around the head, even drenched in synths and in their dying days. 'I had gotten a brand new keyboard: a big Yamaha,' John Paul Jones explained to *Billboard*'s Craig Rosen of his unusually high rate of writing credits on *In Through the Out Door*. 'Basically, Robert [Plant] and I got to rehearsals first and, by the time Jimmy turned up, we had written a number of songs.'

OVERKILL
Motörhead

BY Lemmy, 'Fast' Eddie Clarke, Phil 'Philthy Animal' Taylor PRODUCED BY Jimmy Miller | FROM *Overkill* (Bronze, 1979)

'The double-bass drumming of Phil Taylor started the song,' Lars Ulrich recalled to *Rolling Stone* of this stepping stone to thrash. 'I had never heard anything that sounded like that. It blew my head off.' 'I had heard of other double-bass drummers,' Dave Lombardo observed in Sam Dunn's *Metal Evolution*, 'but I don't think they did anything like that.' Guitarist Eddie Clarke explained the creative process behind *Overkill* to *Classic Rock*: 'A bit of sulphate and some Special Brew, Phil would come up with a crazy drum beat, and we would all thunder along.'

ELL BENT FOR LEATHER
Judas Priest

BY Glenn Tipton | PRODUCED BY Judas Priest, Tom Allom | FROM *Priest in the East (Live in Japan)* (Epic, 1979)

Killing Machine (1978) blueprinted the razor-sharp sound that earned Priest's early eighties' domination. Three of its cuts wound up on an EP packaged with *Priest in the East*, the progenitor of *Unleashed in the East*. These included a storming take on the soon-to-be anthem 'Hell Bent for Leather'. (The song reappears on a 2001 reissue of *Unleashed...*) 'We had an idea of bringing a motorcycle on stage – and it made sense that, if I ride a bike, I should wear a biker's jacket,' Rob Halford told planetout.com. 'We finally looked like the music sounds.'

I LIKE TO ROCK
April Wine

BY Myles Goodwyn | PRODUCED BY Myles Goodwyn, Nick Blagona | FROM *Harder... Faster* (Aquarius, 1979)

'If you want to talk about April Wine, I am a giant fan,' Sebastian Bach raved to classicrockrevisited.com. '"I Like to Rock" is pure Sebastian Bach attitude that I learned when I was a little kid.' Opening with 'I Like to Rock' and closing with a pretty good take on '21st Century Schizoid Man' (*see* 1969), *Harder... Faster* eased April Wine's transition from Canadian heroes to international stars of sorts. A slot at the inaugural Castle Donington festival ensued, hence the live 'I Like to Rock' on Polydor's fine *Monsters of Rock* souvenir LP.

IN THE FLESH?
Pink Floyd

🇬🇧

BY Roger Waters | PRODUCED BY David Gilmour, Bob Ezrin, Roger Waters, James Guthrie | FROM *The Wall* (Harvest, 1979)

Bob Ezrin was introduced to Pink Floyd's music by Alice Cooper in 1970. 'I fell totally in love,' the producer recalled, 'and became a monster fan.' Nine years later, Ezrin helmed a Floydian monster of his own, which opens with this divebombing din – later covered in concert by Jane's Addiction, the Scorpions, Dream Theater and the Foo Fighters. 'Is he gonna be an opera singer?' mused Taylor Hawkins of Floyd frontman Roger Waters. 'No... but a lot of my favourite singers are not *good* singers. They know how to beat the shit out of a song.'

GETCHA ROCKS OFF
Def Leppard

🇬🇧

BY Rick Savage, Joe Elliott, Steve Clark, Pete Willis | PRODUCED BY Def Leppard | FROM *The Def Leppard E.P.* (Bludgeon Riffola, 1979)

'The first song we ever wrote...' Joe Elliott recalled to *Rolling Stone*. 'It was a Pete Willis riff... We were just a bunch of teenagers messing around, doing what we felt was right. But it did have a vibe about it that was above and beyond what everyone else seemed to be doing.' The industry agreed: DJs including the BBC's influential John Peel picked up on the band and, seven months after the release of their debut EP, Leppard were signed to Phonogram. They reworked the song as 'Rocks Off' in 1980, but the first version remains the best.

BEAUTIFUL GIRLS
Van Halen

🇺🇸

BY Eddie Van Halen, Alex Van Halen, Michael Anthony, David Lee Roth | PRODUCED BY Ted Templeman | FROM *Van Halen II* (Warner Bros., 1979)

'I remember hearing about this new band Van Halen, with David Lee Roth,' Steven Tyler groaned to *Rolling Stone*. 'Who does this fucking guy think he is? He's standing in my limelight!' So refreshing were Van Halen that it barely mattered their second album was patchier than DLR's pants. Of its highlights, the closing cut was quintessential. 'Whenever I think of "Beautiful Girls",' Steel Panther's Michael Starr told loudersound.com, 'I think about girls in jean shorts cut off... And there's really nothing better than short shorts, tanned skin and blonde hair.'

COAST TO COAST
Scorpions

🇩🇪

BY Rudolf Schenker | PRODUCED BY Dieter Dierks | FROM *Lovedrive* (Harvest, 1979)

'When [guitarist] Matthias Jabs joined the band,' Klaus Meine reflected to metalexiles.com, 'we found our style: fast riffs but great melodies.' But Jabs deferred to Michael Schenker – 'One of my favorite guitar players as far as melody goes' (James Hetfield, *Newsweek*) – on three *Lovedrive* cuts, including this soaring instrumental by Michael's brother, Rudolf. 'Great musicians...' noted Children of Bodom's Alexi Laiho to *Classic Rock*. 'The rhythm guitar parts especially, next to the melodies, played an important part. The riffs were super-catchy.'

WE WILL ROCK YOU (FAST VERSION)
Queen

🇬🇧
BY Brian May | PRODUCED BY Queen | FROM *Live Killers* (EMI, 1979)

'A cousin took me and [brother] Igor to see Queen in São Paulo in 1981...' Max Cavalera frothed to *Metal Hammer*. 'The next day I was like, "I got to get some of Queen's music!"... As it was a live album, it reminded me of the show, which was great.' *Live Killers* starts as it means to go on, with a turbocharged assault on Queen's greatest anthem, originally from *News of the World* (see 1977). Check out Guns N' Roses performing the slow *and* fast versions with Brian May at Wembley in 1992. 'Queen,' said Axl, 'has always been my favourite band.'

NO SURPRIZE
Aerosmith

🇺🇸
BY Steven Tyler, Joe Perry | PRODUCED BY Gary Lyons, Aerosmith FROM *Night in the Ruts* (Columbia, 1979)

'Most of the songs that we did that tell the true story of the band end up on some backburner album, so people didn't really hear 'em,' Steven Tyler lamented. 'This is one where I just spell it all out – and it's also a pretty damn good song.' 'One of the real good ones from *Night in the Ruts*,' agreed Joe Perry. 'If we'd been more together, that might have been the album where we took what we'd done on *Rocks*, but we were too fucked up.' 'Soon after that,' Slash sighed to *Rolling Stone*, 'they broke up, which to me marked the end of Seventies rock.'

HIGHWAY TO HELL
AC/DC

🇦🇺
BY Angus Young, Malcolm Young, Bon Scott | PRODUCED BY Robert John 'Mutt' Lange | FROM *Highway to Hell* (Albert Productions, 1979)

'After recording "Highway to Hell",' Joe Perry told *Blender*, 'AC/DC could have rested on their laurels.' Inspired by Angus Young's summary of life on tour, the song was demoed with Malcolm Young on drums, then polished by producer 'Mutt' Lange. 'Mutt said: "Sit here and I'll tell you what I want you to play,"' tour manager Ian Jeffery recalled. 'Angus was like, "You fucking will, will ya?"' The title worried the band's label, keen not to arouse ire in the American south. However, Angus told bravewords.com, 'Southern states were the first ones to play it!'

BACK IN BLACK
AC/DC

🇦🇺 🇬🇧

BY Angus Young, Malcolm Young, Brian Johnson | PRODUCED BY Robert John 'Mutt' Lange | FROM *Back in Black* (Albert Productions, 1980)

A riff that Malcolm Young toyed with on the *Highway to Hell* tour (and the first learned by a teenage Kurt Cobain) fuelled a memorial of sorts for the late Bon Scott. 'I just wrote what came into my head...' his successor Brian Johnson explained to *Rolling Stone*. 'The boys got it, though. They saw Bon's life in that lyric.' Judas Priest had supported AC/DC on five dates of that 1979 tour; 'So when the *Back in Black* album finally emerged,' KK Downing marvelled to *Classic Rock*, 'and I heard the title song, it was a moment of real emotion.'

RAPID FIRE
Judas Priest

🇬🇧

BY Glenn Tipton, Rob Halford, KK Downing | PRODUCED BY Tom Allom | FROM *British Steel* (CBS, 1980)

'Pure fucking heavy metal,' Phil Anselmo insisted to *Metal Hammer* of *British Steel*. 'Listen to "Rapid Fire" and the way Rob Halford delivers, the lyrics, the riffs... it's the epitome and blueprint for what Slayer would bring later.' 'You get *British Steel* and you find "Rapid Fire"...' Kerry King pointed out to phoenixnewtimes.com. 'Then you do your backwards homework... and you find "Hell Bent for Leather" [*see* 1979], *Sad Wings of Destiny* and all the original classic stuff, and you realise that there's way more to this band than "Living After Midnight".'

ANGEL WITCH
Angel Witch

🇬🇧

BY Kevin Heybourne | PRODUCED BY Martin Smith | FROM *Angel Witch* (Bronze, 1980)

'I'm a product of British metal,' Lars Ulrich declared to *Rolling Stone*. 'Iron Maiden, Saxon, Angel Witch...'. To uberrock.com, bassist Kevin Riddles described Ulrich as 'a lovely guy... We used to get him into the Marquee [club], just so he could be somewhere warm. For him to say what a great influence Angel Witch was on him and Metallica, that can only make you feel good!' The Blue Öyster Cultish 'Angel Witch' was the band's calling card; honed, Riddles recalled, by 'touring solidly for about eighteen months or two years before we got the deal with Bronze'.

NEON KNIGHTS
Black Sabbath

🇬🇧 🇺🇸

BY Geezer Butler, Ronnie James Dio, Tony Iommi, Bill Ward | PRODUCED BY Martin Birch | FROM *Heaven and Hell* (Vertigo, 1980)

'Could you picture Ozzy singing over that song?' Zakk Wylde asked songfacts.com. 'I can't either... It's a whole different band.' 'We needed one more to complete the album,' Ronnie James Dio explained to *Classic Rock*. 'We went in and knocked it out... Our feeling was, "Phew, thank God!"' The song became a banner-carrier for the new line-up. 'It took Sabbath quite a while to get anywhere remotely fast,' Kerry King observed to *Rolling Stone*. 'That happened probably in the Dio era with "Neon Knights"... that's thrashy to me.'

WHEELS OF STEEL
Saxon

BY Biff Byford, Paul Quinn, Graham Oliver, Steve Dawson, Pete Gill | PRODUCED BY Saxon, Pete Hinton | FROM *Wheels of Steel* (Carrere, 1980)

'Lars Ulrich is probably the biggest Saxon fan...' guitarist Graham Oliver informed the *South Yorkshire Times*. He told us that our 1980 album *Wheels of Steel*... was a benchmark for them.' Saxon's first top five album was studded with gems: the Metallica-covered 'Motorcycle Man', the soaring '747 (Strangers in the Night)' and the addictive title track – which, singer Biff Byford conceded to songfacts.com, 'has definitely got an AC/DC influence.' Their first hit, it put them alongside Iron Maiden as leaders of the New Wave of British Heavy Metal.

BAD REPUTATION
Joan Jett

BY Kenny Laguna, Ritchie Cordell, Joan Jett, Marty Kupersmith PRODUCED BY Kenny Laguna, Ritchie Cordell | FROM *Joan Jett* (Blackheart, 1980)

The opener on Joan Jett's first post-Runaways LP proved a self-fulfilling prophecy. 'We couldn't give it away,' she rued. '[Producer Kenny Laguna] offered it to people for free, just to put it out... nobody wanted it. It was Runaways backlash.' Eventually, a self-released copy found its way to Casablanca label boss Neil Bogart, who made Jett the figurehead of his new Boardwalk Records. *Joan Jett* was reissued as *Bad Reputation*, and its title cut became her anthem – covered by the Foo Fighters with Jett herself, and resurrected by the film *Kick-Ass*.

I DON'T KNOW
Ozzy Osbourne

BY Ozzy Osbourne, Bob Daisley, Randy Rhoads | PRODUCED BY Ozzy Osbourne, Bob Daisley, Lee Kerslake, Randy Rhoads | FROM *Blizzard of Ozz* (Jet, 1980)

'Ozzy told me that when he was in Black Sabbath, people tended to think of them as some kind of prophet...' laughed bassist and co-writer Bob Daisley to metalcrypt.com. 'They might know something about what's gonna happen with the world... But they were just a rock 'n' roll band who got the name from a Hammer Horror film. When Ozzy told me that, it's what I wrote "I Don't Know" about.' The star's secret weapon, of course, was his new guitarist. 'We'd turn everything up to ten,' Randy Rhoads told *Guitar World*. 'And, if it felt good, we'd play it.'

HELLO AMERICA
Def Leppard .

🇬🇧
BY Rick Savage, Steve Clark, Joe Elliott | **PRODUCED BY** Tom Allom | **FROM** *On Through the Night* (Vertigo, 1980)

'We had never even been to America...' Joe Elliott admitted to *Rolling Stone*. 'I had seen a TV show the night before – *Kojak* or *Starsky & Hutch*; something where they show the tree-lined boulevards of LA... You go, "Wow, this is a lot sexier than Sheffield!"' The resultant song – replete with sparkly synths – became a self-fulfilling prophecy for a band who filled Stateside arenas long before becoming heroes at home. Even Pantera's Dimebag was impressed, reminiscing to *Guitar World*, 'Man, that first Leppard album really jams.'

AM I EVIL?
Diamond Head

🇬🇧
BY Sean Harris, Brian Tatler | **PRODUCED BY** Diamond Head, Paul Robbins | **FROM** '*The White Album*' (self-released, 1980)

'My favourite riff at the time,' guitarist and co-writer Brian Tatler told *Classic Rock*, 'was Black Sabbath's 'Symptom of the Universe' [*see* 1975] and I wanted to beat that for relentless, mean riffage... The intro was inspired by "Mars" from Holst's *The Planets*.' Metallica covered the song – 'A little tougher and tighter,' Tatler acknowledged – for the b-side of 'Creeping Death', and it's an acknowledged influence on 'When', from Megadeth's *The World Needs a Hero*. 'We never really left that style of music,' Dave Mustaine admitted.

ANTISOCIAL
Trust

⬛ ⬛
BY Bernard Bonvoisin, Norbert Krief | **PRODUCED BY** Trust, Dennis Weinrich | **FROM** *Répression* (CBS, 1980)

Trust were friends with Bon Scott, whose 'Ride On' they covered, and their ranks included Maiden's Nicko McBrain and Clive Burr. But they energized metal with the vitality of punk – and, like Spain's Báron Rojo, they tackled sociopolitical issues while most metallers were singing about swords and sorcery. 'Antisocial' spotlighted both strengths, and became their defining song. Its longevity was boosted by a 1988 cover by Anthrax, who enlisted frontman and lyricist Bernard Bonvoisin for a live version on the 'Make Me Laugh' single.

WHITE KNUCKLES/ROCKIN' AND ROLLIN
G-Force

🇬🇧 🇺🇸
BY Gary Moore, Mark Nauseef | **PRODUCED BY** Gary Moore, Mark Nauseef, Tony Newton, Willie Dee | **FROM** *G-Force* (Jet, 1980)

'I don't particularly consider myself a heavy metal guitarist,' Gary Moore sniffed to *Ultimate Guitar*'s Steven Rosen. 'I consider myself a rock and roll guitarist. Sometimes I do play heavy metal guitar but I do have other things to say.' Of Eddie Van Halen – to whose 'Eruption' the blistering 'White Knuckles' was reportedly a response – he said: 'I don't think he was particularly responsible for making people aware of the guitar... He was like a second-generation player... For one album he did something fresh and after that he sort of went downhill.'

THE SPIRIT OF RADIO
Rush

🇨🇦

BY Geddy Lee, Alex Lifeson, Neil Peart | PRODUCED BY Rush, Terry Brown | FROM *Permanent Waves* (Anthem, 1980)

'The Spirit of Radio', Neil Peart told *Billboard*, was both 'a tribute to all that was good about radio' and 'an attack on the reality; on the formulaic, mercenary programming of most radio stations'. As Alex Lifeson rued to *Guitar World*, 'The station that we wrote that song about won't play our music.' Still, it has become one of Rush's greatest hits. 'A British band, Catherine Wheel... did a really a good version of "Spirit" – mixed it up a bit,' Peart told *Classic Rock*. 'I heard an interview with the guy, going, "The parts we left out were the ones we couldn't play."'

AND THE CRADLE WILL ROCK
Van Halen

🇺🇸

BY Eddie Van Halen, David Lee Roth, Alex Van Halen, Michael Anthony | PRODUCED BY Ted Templeman | FROM *Women and Children First* (Warner Bros., 1980)

'Al and I jammed on the basic riff for "And the Cradle Will Rock" two hours a day for two straight weeks,' Eddie Van Halen confessed to *Guitar World*. 'We were having fun because it just sounded so wicked. Then, out of nowhere, the chorus came to us.' The song also pointed a new way forward. 'Keyboards entered the mix,' Michael Anthony recalled to *Classic Rock*. 'But it didn't sound like a keyboard because Eddie played this cheap little Wurlitzer, just blazing through Marshalls... We heard it and said, "Wow, this was something different."'

ARMED AND READY
The Michael Schenker Group

🇩🇪 🇬🇧

BY Michael Schenker, Gary Barden | PRODUCED BY Roger Glover | FROM *The Michael Schenker Group* (Chrysalis, 1980)

Having bestowed stunning solos and riffs a-plenty on UFO and his brother Rudolf's Scorpions, the mad axeman struck out on his own with 'Armed and Ready'. This bar-room brawler *par excellence* later appeared, at Kirk Hammett's behest, on *Guitar Hero: Metallica*. 'Rudolf called me up from America in the early eighties,' Schenker recalled to forbassplayersonly.com. '"They're playing your guitar style over here!" I didn't know who Kirk Hammett was, but [Rudolf] was like: "Michael, this is incredible! It's your guitar style!" He couldn't believe it.'

ANIMAL MAGNETISM
Scorpions

🇩🇪

BY Rudolf Schenker, Klaus Meine, Herman Rarebell | PRODUCED BY Dieter Dierks | FROM *Animal Magnetism* (Harvest, 1980)

The steamy, sleazy 'The Zoo' – a singalong Scorps staple – is just a prelude to *Animal Magnetism*'s climactic title track. With divebombing guitars, anvil-like drums, pounding bass and spacey vocals, it's sinister yet sexy. (Testament's 2012 cover emphasizes the sinister, with none of the sexy.) As designer Storm Thorgerson remarked of the album's artwork, 'I don't think we figured it out. We just knew there was something rude.' Rudolf Schenker had the answer: 'Most of our audience is male – and they love thinking about girls.'

ACE OF SPADES
Motörhead

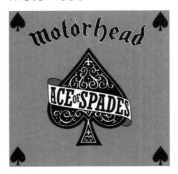

🇬🇧
BY Lemmy, 'Fast' Eddie Clarke, Phil 'Philthy Animal' Taylor | PRODUCED BY Vic 'Chairman' Maile | FROM *Ace of Spades* (Bronze, 1980)

'This is Metal DNA!' Dave Grohl raved to *Q*. 'It's the attitude... Dark and mean and intense as fuck.' As Duff McKagan informed *Esquire*, 'That was a real conjoining of punk, hard rock, rock 'n' roll, and some metal, and it was kind of a touchstone for everyone [in Guns N' Roses].' To Megadeth's Dave Ellefson, talking to phoenixnewtimes.com, it was 'the original thrash record.' However, as drummer Phil Taylor told *Trouser Press*, 'We don't like to be called heavy metal music. It's more like hard, fast, nasty, disgusting rock.'

PHANTOM OF THE OPERA
Iron Maiden

🇬🇧
BY Steve Harris | PRODUCED BY Will Malone | FROM *Iron Maiden* (EMI, 1980)

'One of the best pieces I've ever written...' Steve Harris told writer John Stix of Maiden's first epic. 'Certainly one of the most enjoyable to play. It's got all these intricate guitar lines, which keep it interesting. Then there's the slow middle part which creates quite a good mood. It's also got fast, heavy parts [and] areas for crowd participation.' As Bruce Dickinson said in 2005, 'This song really, is everything that Iron Maiden is all about.' And to a generation of British fans, it's the sound of a Lucozade advert starring decathlete Daley Thompson.

KILLER ON THE LOOSE
Thin Lizzy

🇮🇪 🇺🇸 🇬🇧
BY Phil Lynott | PRODUCED BY Thin Lizzy, Kit Woolven | FROM *Chinatown* (Vertigo, 1980)

'Chinatown is a seedy part of London late at night,' Phil Lynott explained to US TV's Robert Klein. 'I was there recording, so I got to meet many characters. A lot of the hookers were very paranoid about the killer who was on the loose [Peter Sutcliffe, 'The Yorkshire Ripper', convicted in 1981 of murdering thirteen women and attempting to murder seven others]. I wanted to write a warning song and the way I thought it could be most frightening was to become the part of the Ripper... Obviously I don't condone the rape of women.'

THE BIG BEAT
Billy Squier

🇺🇸

BY Billy Squier | PRODUCED BY Billy Squier, Eddy Offord | FROM *The Tale of the Tape* (Capitol, 1980)

Forget 'The Stroke'. *This* is the Zep-esque barnstormer that earns Billy Squier a place in rock legend. But while his vocals and guitar are fine, it's the wall-shaking percussion that makes it a classic. 'It's the most sampled song in history,' he declared to the *Boston Globe* (check out Jay-Z's '99 Problems' [*see* 2003] and Dizzee Rascal's 'Fix Up, Look Sharp', to name but two). 'They said that on MTV – so, even if I'm wrong, I'm not making it up. People sometimes write that "Billy is the king of hip-hop". I didn't even know what hip-hop was.'

RISE ABOVE
Black Flag

🇺🇸

BY Greg Ginn | PRODUCED BY Black Flag, Glen 'Spot' Lockett | FROM *Damaged* (Unicorn Records/SST, 1981)

'Was this the first Henry [Rollins] track?' Hüsker Dü's Bob Mould asked music.avclub.com. 'There were five members of Black Flag for that moment, when Dez Cadena went from singing to playing the second guitar… Black Flag were quite a band. That was always quite a sight, to see them on stage.' Slayer and Metallica, observed Minutemen's Mike Watt, 'wanted to build on the Flag vibe… [Slayer's 1988] *South of Heaven* album is the most massive fucking thing. Maybe that could never have existed without "Rise Above".'

Def Leppard's "High 'n' Dry." Hot as Summer.

LET IT GO
Def Leppard

🇬🇧

BY Pete Willis, Steve Clark, Joe Elliott | PRODUCED BY Robert John 'Mutt' Lange | FROM *High 'n' Dry* (Vertigo, 1981)

'It was so much more punchy than the first album, so we were going in the right direction,' Joe Elliott said on *High 'n' Dry*'s thirty-fifth anniversary. 'Bringin' on the Heartbreak' was the cut that broke Leppard in the States, thanks to rotation on the fledgling MTV, but 'Let It Go' is the album's most enduring rocker. 'It's a little more straightforward than anything we did on *Pyromania*,' reflected Steve Clark in 1984. 'But it's got some subtle things happening in it.' '"Let It Go" still gets played all the time…' Elliott noted. 'I still really enjoy doing [it] live.'

FOR THOSE ABOUT TO ROCK (WE SALUTE YOU)
AC/DC

BY Angus Young, Malcolm Young, Brian Johnson | PRODUCED BY Robert John 'Mutt' Lange | FROM For Those About to Rock (We Salute You) (Albert Productions, 1981)

'We had this chorus riff and we thought, "Well, this sounds rather deadly,"' Angus Young told Creem. 'And there's this book from years ago about the Roman gladiators called For Those About to Die We Salute You. So we thought, "For those about to rock"... It makes you feel a bit powerful and I think that's what rock 'n' roll is all about.'

'It's saying, "Maybe all of you have not rocked before – but in case you want to, we're going to prepare you for it,"' Dethklok's Brendon Small deadpanned to musicradar.com. 'It's an instruction manual on how to rock.'

The song's parent album had a messy conception. 'It took us forever to make...' Malcolm Young complained to writer Mark Blake. 'It doesn't flow properly like an AC/DC album should... There's only one song we like, and that's the title track. When we wrote it, we wanted another big song to play live, like "Let There Be Rock" [see 1977].

'"For Those About To Rock" has stood the test of time... But by the time we'd completed the album, it had taken so long, I don't think anyone, neither the band nor the producer, could tell whether it sounded right or wrong. Everyone was fed up.'

'"You Shook Me All Night Long" is probably the best song they've written...' Gene Simmons observed to thequietus.com, 'but it's not an anthem... because the lyrics aren't on that same level. They aren't big and bold. "For Those About to Rock (We Salute You)" means something. It's a connection. It's like nationhood.'

Or, as Twisted Sister's Eddie Ojeda suggested to Classic Rock, 'It's AC/DC's 1812 Overture.'

I'LL RIP YOUR SPINE OUT
Gillan

BY Ian Gillan, John McCoy, Mick Underwood | PRODUCED BY Steve Smith | FROM Double Trouble (Virgin, 1981)

Thanks to bruisers such as 'Unchain Your Brain' and 'Trouble', Gillan evolved from jazz-tinged oddballs into rockers who rivalled fellow post-Purple hit-makers Rainbow. And Double Trouble's opener 'I'll Rip Your Spine Out' demonstrated the influence of bassist John McCoy and drummer Mick Underwood. It's a thundering beast – or, as Underwood told dmme.net, one of 'the bad damn smasheroonies'. 'It was a resurgence,' Gillan reminisced to planetmosh.com, 'of uninhibited, balls-to-the-wall, new wave of British heavy metal.'

MOTÖRHEAD
Motörhead

BY Lemmy | PRODUCED BY Vic Maile | FROM No Sleep 'til Hammersmith (Bronze, 1981)

'I wrote that when I was in Hawkwind,' Lemmy told Rolling Stone. 'We put it on the b-side of "Kings of Speed". The song was about speed and it was an issue to Hawkwind, and that's why I got fired. I never asked them what they thought of "Motörhead" after that. I didn't care what they thought of it. I don't think of "Motörhead" as a defining song.' Others do, however. 'Fucking genius,' noted Graveyard's Axel Sjöberg. 'It's like Chuck Berry on speed.' The studio version on 1977's Motörhead is okay, but skip to this live version. It kills.

THE MOB RULES
Black Sabbath

'UNHOLY IN ITS SHEER AWESOMENESS'
TOM MORELLO

BY Geezer Butler, Ronnie James Dio, Tony Iommi | PRODUCED BY Martin Birch | FROM *Mob Rules* (Vertigo, 1981)

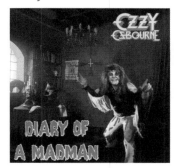

'Mob Rules" was great, really good,' Tony Iommi told the Sabbath fanzine *Southern Cross*. 'We done it at John Lennon's house... We used his gear he had floating around – we didn't use our equipment – and it was really good. It was all old gear but it was a great sound.'

'We wrote this song for the motion picture *Heavy Metal*, groundbreaking animated film,' Ronnie James Dio explained on 2003's *Stand Up and Shout* anthology. 'I was the only one in the band to see a prototype of the film, and I got it instantly. They wanted a song for a sequence where these people living behind a walled city are about to be attacked by barbarians. It was real science fiction, which I love, and the characters had horns coming out of their heads.'

Marilyn Manson cited the *Mob Rules* album as 'one of my favourite records' and Dio hailed the song as 'another one of my favourites'. Halestorm's Lzzy Hale, meanwhile, said, 'The title track might be my favourite, but the whole record has so much energy to it... The music feels young and reckless, but it's still Sabbath. The riffs are huge, the sound is massive – it's a rager, man.'

'That was the first thing we wrote together,' drummer Vinny Appice recalled to musicguy247.typepad.com. 'It was a really cool song. The energy level was great, and it worked well.'

TOM SAWYER
Rush

BY Geddy Lee, Alex Lifeson, Neil Peart, Pye Dubois | PRODUCED BY Rush, Terry Brown | FROM *Moving Pictures* (Anthem, 1981)

'We're beginning to appreciate staying in a groove,' Geddy Lee told *Sounds*, 'and then maybe just shading that groove a little... What we're doing makes for much better rock songs.' With lyrics that spoke of rebellion and instinct, the oddly funky "Tom Sawyer" became a rock radio and soundtrack staple. 'It changed our lives,' Geddy Lee told the *Guardian*. And in the *Beyond the Lighted Stage* film, Neil Peart admitted: 'I will never get tired of playing 'Tom Sawyer', because it's always difficult to play right. And any time I *do* play it right, I feel good!'

FLYING HIGH AGAIN
Ozzy Osbourne

BY Ozzy Osbourne, Randy Rhoads, Bob Daisley, Lee Kerslake | PRODUCED BY Max Norman, Ozzy Osbourne, Randy Rhoads | FROM *Diary of a Madman* (Jet, 1981)

'When I was a drug addict, I used to write things like "Flying High Again"...' Ozzy noted to *Spin*. 'That was where I was.' Its power owed much to the band. 'Randy [Rhoads] never met [bassist] Bob Daisley or [drummer] Lee Kerslake before...' Zakk Wylde marvelled to songfacts.com. 'If me and you took four complete strangers, stuck 'em in a room, and then they ended up coming out with two amazing records – what are the chances of that?' And a favourite? 'I love all the Randy Rhoads stuff,' he told Little Punk People. 'I guess I'll go with "Flying High Again".'

I LOVE ROCK 'N ROLL
Joan Jett & the Blackhearts

BY Jake Hooker, Alan Merrill | PRODUCED BY Ritchie Cordell, Kenny Laguna | FROM *I Love Rock 'n Roll* (The Boardwalk Entertainment Co, 1981)

When The Runaways split, Joan Jett decamped to the UK and cut "I Love Rock 'n Roll" with Sex Pistols Paul Cook and Steve Jones. Issued in Europe in 1979, that version won airplay in New York – but, Jett told *Sounds*, 'the record company weren't pushing it.' Convinced of the song's charms – 'I first saw The Arrows do it on a TV show when I was touring Britain and I loved it... so I thought other people would' – Jett tried again in 1981. The result? 'The most requested song on radio since "I Wanna Hold Your Hand"!' she marvelled. 'It's hard to comprehend.'

DEAD SOULS
Joy Division

BY Ian Curtis, Peter Hook, Stephen Morris, Bernard Sumner | PRODUCED BY Martin Hannett | FROM *Still* (Factory, 1981)

'Joy Division were a heavy metal band,' insisted Billy Corgan. '[Bassist] Peter Hook told me they were basically trying to make a primitive version of Black Sabbath and Led Zeppelin.' This book *isn't* claiming Joy Division were metal, but there's no questioning the heaviness of 'Dead Souls', even before Trent Reznor carbon-copied it for the *Crow* soundtrack. ('When I hear it,' Hook told wcpo.com of NIN's version, 'I think it's us.') Check out, too, the proto-doom 'Day of the Lords', the rifftastic 'Interzone' and the sludgy 'New Dawn Fades'.

LIVE WIRE
Mötley Crüe

BY Nikki Sixx | PRODUCED BY Mötley Crüe | FROM *Too Fast for Love* (Leathür, 1981)

'If we did have a message,' vocalist Vince Neil said to *Classic Rock* of primeval Mötley, 'it'd be about getting laid, having fun and getting drunk. Fuck philosophy.' The agenda was set by a song written at their first rehearsal, whose impact proved immense. 'Within the first minute-and-a-half of "Live Wire", I was like, "Oh shit, I can relate to this!"' recalled Chad Gray of Hellyeah. 'This was back in the Mötley Crüe dark leather days. I don't know what I would have done without that tape.' Tom Morello agreed: 'Jams like "Live Wire" are insanely wicked and still do the trick.'

UNCHAINED
Van Halen

BY Eddie Van Halen, David Lee Roth, Alex Van Halen, Michael Anthony | PRODUCED BY Ted Templeman | FROM *Fair Warning* (Warner Bros., 1981)

'Playing with Van Halen is like doing a solo album,' Eddie Van Halen told *Creem*. 'Complete freedom.' On *Fair Warning*, he confessed to *Guitar World*, freedom meant 'sneaking down in the studio around four o'clock in the morning... and re-recording things the way I wanted them.' Of 'Unchained', he said: 'It's rare that I can listen back to my own playing and get goosebumps, but that's one of them.' 'Probably the coolest heavy metal radio-friendly song ever,' Steel Panther's Michael Starr agreed to loudersound.com. 'It's fucking badass.'

C'MON LET'S GO
Girlschool

🇬🇧
BY Kim McAuliffe, Kelly Johnson | PRODUCED BY Vic Maile FROM *Hit and Run* (Bronze, 1981)

They have so many great songs, but this is my favourite,' Lita Ford told loudersound.com of this Runaways-meets-Motörhead monster. 'It grabs you by the throat and shakes you up. There's so much steel in this song. And it has a badass attitude… Whenever I hear this, it reminds me that Girlschool are a helluva band.' (Denise Dufort's drums in fact influenced Darkthrone's 2003 album *Hate Them*.) Guys would say about [guitarist] Kelly Johnson, "She's really good for a girl,"' Lemmy griped to *Crypt*. 'I'd say, "She's better than you, motherfucker!"'

DENIM AND LEATHER
Saxon

🇬🇧
BY Biff Byford, Steve Dawson, Pete Gill, Graham Oliver, Paul Quinn | PRODUCED BY Nigel Thomas | FROM *Denim and Leather* (Carrere, 1981)

'We wrote it for the fans back in the day…' Biff Byford declared to ramblinmanfair.com of a cut that, strangely, wasn't issued as a single in Saxon's homeland, yet became an anthem. 'It's a song for the people; a thank-you song. When we recorded it in '81, we got fans down to the studio to sing on the chorus. And wherever we play it, anywhere in the world, 'Denim and Leather' is the one that people love. Although there are only three notes in it, they're three of the most famous Saxon notes ever. The song is a hundred times bigger than the band.'

MURDERS IN THE RUE MORGUE
Iron Maiden

🇬🇧
BY Steve Harris | PRODUCED BY Martin Birch | FROM *Killers* (EMI, 1981)

'Murders in the Rue Morgue', Bruce Dickinson opined to *Spin*, 'basically could have been off of Deep Purple's *In Rock*.' It's hard to pick just one from *Killers*, but 'Murders in the Rue Morgue' (its title looted from an Edgar Allen Poe story) narrowly edges ahead of the likes of 'Wrathchild'. The song has a 'Speed King'-style intensity, but is quintessential Maiden in all their Grand Guignol glory. 'We wanted to create a mood,' Steve Harris explained of the much imitated, slow-intro-fast-song format, 'and then come in and hit people over the head.'

WELCOME TO HELL
Venom

🇬🇧
BY Cronos, Mantas, Abaddon | PRODUCED BY Keith Nichol, Venom FROM *Welcome to Hell* (Neat, 1981)

'One of those "holy shit!" records,' Scott Ian exclaimed to *Louder Than Hell*. 'Like, "Jesus Christ, listen to this. These guys are fucking insane"… It was so, so evil.' Venom, explained frontman Cronos, 'was all of our favourite bands thrown into a pot and mixed up: the stage show of Kiss, the lyrics of Sabbath, the speed of Motörhead, the look of Judas Priest.' Were it not for Venom, conceded Quorthon of Bathory, 'There wouldn't be any underground movement that would turn to death or black metal… you have to give a big respect to them.'

METAL ON METAL
Anvil

 BY Lips, Robb Reiner, Dave Allison, Ian Dickson | PRODUCED BY Chris Tsangarides | FROM *Metal on Metal* (Attic, 1982)

'When Anvil first showed up...' remarked Lars Ulrich, 'it was like, Fuck! This is cool! This is a statement! This is something that we're not used to... They had pushed it to a different level.' Twenty-six years before the *Anvil!* film, the band etched themselves into history – and a 2010 *Simpsons* episode – with this headbanger. 'I didn't want to be like Bon Jovi or Whitesnake,' Lips explained to eonmusic.co.uk. 'That is not metal. Anvil is metal; the *name* is metal. It should not be pop... The closest we ever came was "Metal on Metal".'

LIGHTNING STRIKES
Aerosmith

BY Richie Supa | PRODUCED BY Jack Douglas, Steven Tyler, Tony Bongiovi | FROM *Rock in a Hard Place* (Columbia, 1982)

Even broke and dope-sick, Aerosmith made one of their greatest albums – and the swaggering 'Lightning Strikes', noted *Rolling Stone*, boasted 'the sort of nasty glee that's always been an Aerosmith trademark'. It was conjured by Richie Supa ('My ally when shit would jump off in the band and I was fighting with Joe Perry,' wrote Steven Tyler) and featured guitar by newcomer Rick Dufay and the soon-to-be-gone Brad Whitford. 'I really like that song,' Joe Perry confessed to vanyaland.com. 'It rocks. It's like an Aerosmith record.'

SCREAMING FOR VENGEANCE
Judas Priest

BY Glenn Tipton, Rob Halford, KK Downing | PRODUCED BY Tom Allom | FROM *Screaming for Vengeance* (CBS, 1982)

'Not only Judas Priest's best LP,' raved *Kerrang!* in 1982, 'but one of the finest to emerge this century!' *Screaming for Vengeance* remains near-flawless; if you buy only one Priest album, make it this. Its classics include 'The Hellion/ Electric Eye' and 'You've Got Another Thing Coming', the hit that helped make *Screaming* their biggest seller. But the greatest is the title cut. 'It's not quite thrash,' observed Rob Halford, 'but it's got that attitude about it.' 'Rob's vocal is unbelievable,' said producer Tom Allom. 'I will never know how he fitted the words in at that speed.'

HALLOWED BE THY NAME
Iron Maiden

🇬🇧

BY Steve Harris | PRODUCED BY Martin Birch | FROM *The Number of the Beast* (EMI, 1982)

'THAT SONG, AND THE WHOLE ALBUM, TOOK MAIDEN TO A DIFFERENT LEVEL'
BRUCE DICKINSON

The terrifying title cut and riotous 'Run to the Hills' were the hits, but *Number of the Beast*'s theatrical climax is its ace in the hole. Covered by Dream Theater and Machine Head, it rarely left Maiden's setlists (until a dispute over the writing credits) and showcases what Dimebag hailed in *Guitar World* as Dave Murray and Adrian Smith's ability to 'shred with the best when it was appropriate'.

'We're trying to create a mood with the build-up of the song,' Steve Harris told John Stix, the year after its unleashing. 'The classical-guitar-like opening was Dave building the mood, with bells in the background... In concert, the end part of this one takes off.'

The lyrics, he conceded to *Night Rock News*, are 'a bit morbid, but it's about a prisoner who is in the death cell. He's had these real strict beliefs all through life, and then, with about two hours to go, he's not really sure. There's one line in it that says, "If there's a God, then why does he let me die?" It's just conflicting ideas in your mind.'

(With fittingly grim gallows humour, a live version was issued as a single with Bruce-Dickinson-skewering artwork, after the air-raid siren's exit in 1993.)

The result, noted Lars Ulrich to *Rolling Stone*, is 'one of those metal epics, along with [Judas Priest's] "Beyond the Realms of Death" [*see* 1978] and [Deep Purple's] "Child in Time" [*see* 1970], that are almost a blueprint for songs like "Fade to Black" [*see* 1984].'

JULY 1982: THE BEASTIE BOYS DEBUT WITH THE *POLLY WOG STEW* EP

CHINA WHITE
Scorpions

BY Rudolf Schenker, Klaus Meine | PRODUCED BY Dieter Dierks | FROM *Blackout* (Harvest, 1982)

Sixteen years and eight albums into their career, *Blackout* confirmed the Scorpions as Germany's greatest rock export, earning their first top ten placings at home and in the US. The title cut became a live staple and 'No One Like You' their first *Billboard* Rock Tracks chart-topper – but *Blackout*'s secret weapon was this 'Kashmir'-esque crusher, with vicious leads by Rudolf Schenker. The song's title nods to heroin, but the incongruously wide-eyed lyrics call for world peace and an end to 'senseless wars'. Who needs 'Wind of Change'?

LOS ROCKEROS VAN AL INFIERNO
Barón Rojo

BY José Luis Campuzano, Carolina Cortés | PRODUCED BY Vicente Romero, Barón Rojo | FROM *Volumen Brutal* (Chapa Discos, 1982)

Unafraid to criticize their country's eventful politics, Barón Rojo ('Red Baron' – with 'Rojo' pronounced, fittingly, 'rokko') ploughed a less polemical but equally determined furrow with this Spanish anthem. Written by the band's bassist and his wife, it was recorded at Ian Gillan's Kingsway Studios in London, while Bruce Dickinson reportedly assisted with its translation into the Anglicised 'Rockers Go to Hell'. Spanish metal's only international stars until Mägo de Oz, Barón Rojo were later cited as an influence by Fenriz of Darkthrone.

FAST AS A SHARK
Accept

BY Wolf Hoffmann, Stefan Kaufmann, Udo Dirkschneider, Peter Baltes | PRODUCED BY Accept | FROM *Restless and Wild* (Brain, 1982)

The first speed metal song? 'Maybe...' mused guitarist Wolf Hoffmann, 'but at the time we just had fun and didn't think it was anything dramatically new.' Double-bass drum fury signalled otherwise, the song exploding after a take on the folk song 'Ein Heller und ein Batzen' by Scorpions producer Dieter Dierks. '"Fast as a Shark" set the bar,' said Scott Ian. 'Hearing it for the first time, I lost my mind... and thought, "How is that even possible? Am I really hearing what I think I'm hearing?"' 'One of the great metal songs of all time,' agreed Billy Corgan.

IRON FIST
Motörhead

BY Lemmy, 'Fast' Eddie Clarke, Phil 'Philthy Animal' Taylor PRODUCED BY 'Fast' Eddie Clarke, Will Reid-Dick | FROM *Iron Fist* (Bronze, 1982)

'Here's the latest example of vinyl shrapnel, guys and gals,' wrote Lemmy in *Iron Fist*'s sleevenotes. 'Hope you are standing to attention. We had a great time making this fab opus. Listen to it wrapped in barbed wire.' Behind the jollity, Motörhead's sixth album – celebrated for its brutal title cut – proved the last by the classic Lemmy-Eddie-Phil lineup. Of his producer role, Eddie Clarke told headbanger.ru, 'That was the beginning of the end... Phil was very happy about it, Lemmy wasn't... That's when things started to go wrong between us.'

TEARING AND TEARING
Led Zeppelin

🇬🇧

BY Jimmy Page, Robert Plant | PRODUCED BY Jimmy Page | FROM *Coda* (Swan Song, 1982)

Rockabilly with sinister sex in mind, this 1979 offcut was turbocharged into latterday Zep's most brutal rocker. 'It was like an assault,' Jimmy Page marvelled to *Classic Rock*. Robert Plant explained to *Guitar World*: 'We wanted to put it out on a different label under the name of a different artist, alongside The Damned and The Sex Pistols, because it was so vicious and so emphatically fresh. And if you hadn't known it was us, it could have been anybody at all who was young and virile and all the things that we were then not supposed to be.'

BANNED IN D.C.
Bad Brains

🇺🇸

BY H.R., Darryl Jenifer, Dr Know | PRODUCED BY Jay Dublee | FROM *Bad Brains* (ROIR, 1982)

Bad Brains spat in the face of trends, birthing a legacy that extends from Agnostic Front ('Untouchable. They are one of the best and most influential hardcore bands,' Roger Miret, noisecreep.com) to System of a Down ('So influential, and not just musically. They paved the way for artists to not give a fuck,' Shavo Odadjian, *Louder Than Hell*), and from Anthrax ('When we're writing... one of us will look up and say, "What would Bad Brains do?"' Scott Ian, thequietus.com) to Mark Tremonti ('It was like Bob Marley on punk steroids').

CREATURES OF THE NIGHT
Kiss

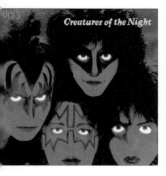

BY Paul Stanley, Adam Mitchell | PRODUCED BY Michael James Jackson | FROM *Creatures of the Night* (Casablanca, 1982)

We had become rich, fat and lazy,' Paul Stanley admitted to Ken Sharp, '[and] enamoured with the idea of having our peers think we were smart and musical... When we did *Creatures*, it was that step of us declaring that we were back.' Mission accomplished: this barnstormer opened their heaviest and greatest album. However, while Stanley sang and Eric Carr drummed up a Bonhamesque storm, the guitar solo was by future Mr Mister man Steve Farris – one of the candidates to replace Ace Frehley – and the bass was by Toto's Steve Porcaro.

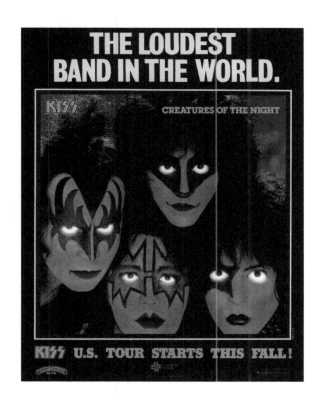

BLACK METAL
Venom

BY Abaddon, Mantas, Cronos | PRODUCED BY Venom, Keith Nichol | FROM *Black Metal* (Neat, 1982)

'I WOULDN'T CALL IT THRASH, BUT DEFINITELY FASTER METAL. SHIT, IT'S "BLACK METAL" THEY COINED THE PHRASE

KERRY KING

'Every aspect of that band was exaggerated to the point where you couldn't focus on just one thing,' Dave Grohl enthused to *Metal Hammer*. 'It was all just so fucking loud and crazy.' The title track of Venom's second album duly opened with a chainsaw cutting through a metal door – designed, as sulphur-throated frontman Cronos gloated, to panic listeners: '"Oh fuck, my stereo's broken!"'

The taboo-busting band stumbled on a term that rapidly outgrew them. 'Not much black metal,' Emperor's Ihsahn pointed out, 'sounds like Venom.' 'Our music is power metal, Venom metal, black metal…' Cronos cackled to *Kerrang!* 'Not heavy metal, 'cos that's for the chicks.' ('It's always nice to hear that we came up with the phrase "black metal"…' he concluded to *Louder Than Hell*. 'There are millions of people around the world who also like that style of music… that's just the most amazing thing.')

Venom were hailed by *Sounds* as 'Sabbath on angel dust, Motörhead for zombies', and their disciples include most of the Big Four. James Hetfield and Dave Mustaine, the latter told *Metal Hammer*, 'would drive sixty miles an hour up and down the Pacific Coast Highway in the fog, drunk and listening to Venom.' 'The best shitty band ever,' Kerry King opined to *Rolling Stone*.

'The first time I heard it, I felt sick inside,' Phil Anselmo told musicradar.com of the *Black Metal* album. 'But it was a sickness I didn't mind revisiting.'

COLD SWEAT
Thin Lizzy

BY John Sykes, Phil Lynott | PRODUCED BY Thin Lizzy, Chris Tsangarides | FROM *Thunder and Lightning* (Vertigo, 1983)

'"Cold Sweat" is a favourite of mine…' said Dave Mustaine, who covered it on Megadeth's *Super Collider*. 'John Sykes' guitar-playing in that particular song is over the top… so fast and so many notes – although it's very melodic and very beautiful.' Sykes earned his sole Lizzy writing credit for this beast, but he's the star of their last and heaviest album. Phil Lynott, the guitarist told metalexpressradio.com, 'asked if I had any riffs and I started playing the "Cold Sweat" riff… About twenty minutes later it was pretty much all there.'

DIE HARD THE HUNTER
Def Leppard

BY Robert John 'Mutt' Lange, Steve Clark, Rick Savage, Joe Elliott | PRODUCED BY Robert John 'Mutt' Lange | FROM *Pyromania* (Vertigo, 1983)

'Mutt Lange said, "We can make another *High 'n' Dry* or we can try and create a hard rock version of *Sgt. Pepper*,"' Joe Elliott recalled to *Mojo*. If not quite 'A Day in the Life', 'Die Hard…' earned Phil Collen's verdict: 'Sort of an epic.' Its title inspired by the film *The Deer Hunter*, the song is, Elliott told David Fricke, 'about a guy who comes home from war and can't adjust… I wanted to write about something other than sex, drugs, women backstage and Jack Daniels. I wanted to deal with a serious subject that I didn't necessarily have to be a big expert on.'

BARK AT THE MOON
Ozzy Osbourne

BY Ozzy Osbourne | **PRODUCED BY** Ozzy Osbourne, Bob Daisley, Max Norman | **FROM** *Bark at the Moon* (Epic, 1983)

The title for this song actually came from a joke I used to tell where the punchline was "Eat shit and bark at the moon",' Ozzy recalled in *The Ozzman Cometh*'s liner notes. 'I'd had the vocal line for this and Jake [E. Lee] came up with the riff. It was the first song we wrote together.' Lee and bassist Bob Daisley, paid a lump sum for playing and writing, were omitted from the credits.) 'There's some great fucking guitar playing in there,' noted Alexi Laiho of Children of Bodom. 'I think Jake E. Lee is so underrated, but he's kicking some ass on this one.'

ZERO THE HERO
Black Sabbath

BY Tony Iommi, Geezer Butler, Ian Gillan, Bill Ward | **PRODUCED BY** Robin Black, Black Sabbath | **FROM** *Born Again* (Vertigo, 1983)

In the rock 'n' roll dictionary under 'skull-crushing', 'Zero the Hero' is Sabbath's heaviest song, and the highlight of their most unfairly maligned album. '*Born Again*,' Ozzy told *Circus* in 1984, 'is the best thing I've heard from Sabbath since the original group broke up.' The album is notorious for its 'dust-on-the-needle' production – but, as Ian Gillan observed to Australian radio station 2MMM, 'If you can hear under the muffle, under the blanket of bass, there's some great songs.' And there's the 'Zero the Hero' riff that reappeared in 'Paradise City'...

STAND UP AND SHOUT
Dio

BY Ronnie James Dio, Jimmy Bain | **PRODUCED BY** Ronnie James Dio | **FROM** *Holy Diver* (Vertigo, 1983)

'HE HAD A GREAT VOICE. A LOT OF PEOPLE GOT A LOT OF IDEAS FROM DIO'
OZZY OSBOURNE

I never ever disbelieved in myself,' Ronnie James Dio told *Music Connection* of his post-Sabbath venture, 'but I had only worked in bands. So, once I got out of that security blanket, I began to feel more confident with myself... With the people I put around me, especially Vinny [Appice], I just knew that it was going to work.'

Holy Diver's opening salvo was a blistering statement of intent. 'One of those inadvertent anthems,' Dio wrote in a reissue's liner notes. 'Because of the dissatisfaction of no longer being in Black Sabbath, I had to do something.

I wasn't about to quit rock 'n' roll and be a plumber. I went back to basics. Alone, in my garage in our house in Tarzana, California, with some low-tech Radio Shack equipment, I started writing and demoing, just like in the beginning.'

Even legendary rivals found kind words. 'Ronnie Dio's band's good,' Ritchie Blackmore conceded to *Sounds*. Later fans included Dave Grohl: 'I'll never forget seeing "Stand Up and Shout" on [US TV show] *Don Kirschner's Rock Concert* for the first time,' he recalled to *Q*. 'For a little guy he had a commanding stage presence. Vinny Appice is a great drummer on this, too.'

Not everyone was convinced. 'What does Ronnie *mean* when he writes stuff like "Holy Diver"?' Gene Simmons asked *Kerrang!* 'A rabbi with swimming trunks?'

MALIBU BEACH NIGHTMARE
Hanoi Rocks

🇫🇮

BY Andy McCoy | PRODUCED BY Dale 'Buffin' Griffin, Pete 'Overend' Watts | FROM *Back to Mystery City* (Johanna, 1983)

Finland's finest, wrote Slash in his autobiography, 'were an influence on Guns N' Roses, and are still an undervalued rock-and-roll institution.' Make that *the* influence on Guns N' Roses, above even Aerosmith and Iggy. 'They were influenced in the best possible way,' singer Michael Monroe allowed to thequietus.com. 'They got the point and the attitude.' That attitude is encapsulated by Hanoi's madcap glam punk classic – think crashing drums and tootling sax – spawned from their 1981 calypso pastiche 'Malibu Nightmare'.

READY TO BURN
Krokus

➕

BY Fernando Von Arb, Chris Von Rohr, Marc Storace, Butch Stone, Mark Kohler | PRODUCED BY Tom Allom | FROM *Headhunter* (Ariola, 1983)

Krokus's *raison d'être* was to mark time between AC/DC albums, their stock-in-trade being variations on the Bon Scott era. But what they lacked in originality they made up in gung-ho, which sailed them high in transatlantic charts. *Headhunter* had Judas Priest producer Tom Allom at the helm and – bar the hit ballad 'Screaming in the Night' – sounded precisely like Priest and AC/DC. None of this need detain you longer than the four-minute duration of 'Ready to Burn', whose place in this book is sealed by backing vocals from metal god Mr Halford.

SEEK AND DESTROY
Metallica

🇺🇸

BY James Hetfield, Lars Ulrich | PRODUCED BY Paul Curcio | FROM *Kill 'em All* (Megaforce 1983)

'The idea for "Seek" came from a Diamond Head song called "Dead Reckoning",' James Hetfield admitted to *Guitar World*. 'I used to work in a sticker factory in LA, and I wrote that riff in my truck outside work.' Twinned with lyric that were, he told *Playboy*, 'just about smashing shit up,' an anthem was born. 'That's the song that has the most life,' Lars Ulrich told theringer.com in 2017. 'It's always different there are different raps, different things. It's loose; it's crazy It's a little loopy. So, to some extent, it is the quintessential live Metallica song.'

EBEL YELL
illy Idol

🇬🇧 🇺🇸
BY Billy Idol, Steve Stevens | PRODUCED BY Keith Forsey | FROM *Rebel Yell* (Chrysalis, 1983)

/ithout axe-man Steve Stevens, this would be pop. *With* m, it's pop-rock *par excellence*. 'The intro part got put n as the last element...' he told musicradar.com. 'Billy ecided we needed to let people know the cavalry is oming. I said, "Gimme an hour!" and it seems to have orked.' Classic status was secured by Jeff Stein's deo. 'I put the hot-looking girls with the big tits up front,' e director recalled. 'Billy went from playing to fifteen undred people to playing the Oakland Coliseum in six eeks. That was the power of MTV.'

BLACK MAGIC
Slayer

🇺🇸
BY Kerry King, Jeff Hanneman | PRODUCED BY Slayer | FROM *Show No Mercy* (Metal Blade, 1983)

'This is crap, pure unadulterated junk,' complained *Kerrang!* at the time. 'NOT what Magick is all about!' But history has been kind to *Show No Mercy*, and it's aged better than most formative thrash albums. The pummelling 'Black Magic', in fact, endured in setlists all the way to Slayer's final tour. 'I'd rather sing about the devil than sing about God,' Kerry King told *Kerrang!* in 1985. 'It's interesting, you know? I like to read up on it because it's something I want to know about. But we don't sacrifice babies or burn churches or anything.'

HOUT AT THE DEVIL
Mötley Crüe

🇺🇸
BY Nikki Sixx | PRODUCED BY Tom Werman | FROM *Shout at the Devil* (Elektra, 1983)

Before we recorded *Shout at the Devil*, we played all the ongs at the US Festival,' Nikki Sixx recalled to *Blender*. remember watching 300,000 people going, "Shout! hout! Shout!" That was a moment of clarity.' 'Everybody as singing along,' agreed Vince Neil, 'which was st incredible, being that it was the first time anybody eard it outside of the band.' The lyrics, Sixx told *Creem*, ncouraged fans to 'shout at your teachers, police, oliticians, anybody that's an authoritative figure that puts ou down or doesn't let you achieve what you want'.

MUSIC TO ENRAGE THE SAVAGE BEAST. MOTLEY CRÜE'S NEW ALBUM, "SHOUT AT THE DEVIL" IS FUELING THE FIRE.

MESSIAH
Hellhammer

BY Tom G. Warrior, Martin Ain | PRODUCED BY Tom G Warrior, Martin Ain | FROM *Satanic Rites* (Prowlin' Death Records, 1983)

'I couldn't make a top ten of what I consider to be black metal without putting Hellhammer in it,' Primordial singer AA Nemtheanga told loudersound.com. The seeds sown by Venom were cultivated by future Celtic Frost founders Tom G. Warrior, aka 'Satanic Slaughter', and Martin 'Slayed Necros' Ain. Like their British forefathers, they had a sense of humour, and proficiency so limited that, while traditionalists were appalled, fans realized they could do it too and formed the next wave of death metal (Mayhem's drummer even named himself Hellhammer).

GUNS FOR HIRE
AC/DC

FLICK OF THE SWITCH

BY Angus Young, Malcolm Young, Brian Johnson | PRODUCED BY AC/DC | FROM *Flick of the Switch* (Albert Productions, 1983)

'I've always admired AC/DC,' Ritchie Blackmore admitted to *Kerrang!* in 1984. 'They've stuck steadfastly to their own brand of straightforward music through thick and thin.' As *Rolling Stone* wrote of *Flick of the Switch*, 'There is still something perversely reassuring about the brute, Godzilla-like stomp of AC/DC's rhythm section, the industrial guitar crunch of Angus and Malcolm Young and the macho bark of singer Brian Johnson.' The album has a handful of highlights, of which 'Guns for Hire' stands comparison with its Mutt Lange-produced predecessors.

EVIL
Mercyful Fate

BY Hank Shermann, King Diamond | PRODUCED BY Henrik Lund | FROM *Melissa* (Roadrunner, 1983)

'We were all looking for the most extreme stuff...' Kirk Hammett recalled in Rick Ernst's metal documentary *Get Thrashed*. 'Back then, the most popular music was Mercyful Fate, Venom, Motörhead...'

The quintet earned their place in such company thanks to the glass-shattering shrieks of King Diamond. 'It's just so insane, what he does...' Arch Enemy's Angela Gossow enthused to music.avclub.com. 'He has to be the only guy who can sing the word "grandma" and make it sound frightening. It's like, *"GRANDMA!"* "Oh, holy shit!"'

> **'KING DIAMOND IS A NUT. HE SANG ABOUT BLACK MASSES AND RITUALISTIC SACRIFICE LIKE OTHERS SING ABOUT GOING TO THE PROM'**
> DAVE GROHL

Essentially a Priest for a new generation, Mercyful Fate entranced future stars. 'Super prog, amazing guitar performances, and King Diamond's heaven-to-hell vocal work is incredible,' Billy Corgan told musicradar.com.

At the time, Kerry King said the *Melissa* album 'has some of the hottest riffs ever written'. Thirty years later, when Slayer toured with King Diamond, King guested on 'Evil'. 'If you told teenage Kerry that someday I would be on stage with King Diamond playing Mercyful Fate songs,' he admitted to *Rolling Stone*, 'I'd go, "Fuck right off."'

'The guitar playing in Mercyful Fate has my favourite riff of all time,' Mark Tremonti raved. 'The *Melissa* record, *Don't Break the Oath*... everything.'

Not everyone was smitten, however. 'We hate Mercyful Fate,' Venom's Cronos complained to *Kerrang!* 'We just want to kill 'em.'

HERE EAGLES DARE
on Maiden

🇬🇧 BY Steve Harris | PRODUCED BY Martin Birch | FROM *Piece of Mind* (EMI, 1983)

'THEY WERE INTO STORYTELLING... THERE WAS A LOT OF VIVID IMAGERY GOING ON'
JOHN PETRUCCI, DREAM THEATER

'Where Eagles Dare" is a white hats and black hats adventure, *Boys' Own* paper romp,' Bruce Dickinson told *reem*. 'Killing the jolly old Nazis and all the rest of it... It's great: picturing yourself in the cockpit, big scarf sticking out and everything. It's fun.'

Inspired by a 1968 World War II film of the same name, 'Where Eagles Dare' features a machine-gun-style breakdown. 'It's not very loud in the mix,' Steve Harris told John Stix, ' but we wanted it that way so people who listened to it a couple of times would say, "What's that?"'

The song 'was done in two takes' and is notable for what Tom Morello hailed as the 'cavalry charge' drumming of Nicko McBrain. 'His playing is very different than Clive [Burr, his predecessor] and changed the flavour of the band,' Harris told *Bass Player*. 'We did experiment with a few things, like the "Where Eagles Dare" drum pattern. I tapped that out on my legs for him, and I can't play drums to save my life.'

'Making *Piece of Mind* was one big adventure...' McBrain marvelled to *Classic Rock*. 'And of course we had all these epic tracks – "The Trooper", "Revelation", "Flight of Icarus" and, best of all for me, "Where Eagles Dare". The intro in that track – that drum riff – is right up there with the likes of Phil Collins and Neil Peart. It's still one of my favourite Maiden songs.'

DANCING ON YOUR GRAVE
Motörhead

🇬🇧

BY Lemmy, Phil 'Philthy Animal' Taylor, Brian Robertson | PRODUCED BY Tony Platt | FROM *Another Perfect Day* (Bronze, 1983)

'I hate Motörhead,' Brian Robertson complained while he was in the band. 'But I respect them for playing shit for so many years and making money at it.' The union with the ex-Thin Lizzy guitarist might have been the most bad-tempered in 'headstory, but it yielded this classy gem – and, according to Max Cavalera, bequeathed a name to Sepultura (which is Portuguese for 'grave'). 'I'm proud of the record because it's so different...' Robertson admitted to sleazeroxx.com. 'The guys were at the pub, so they left me alone working with the producer.'

GIMME ALL YOUR LOVIN'
ZZ Top

🇺🇸

BY Billy Gibbons, Dusty Hill, Frank Beard | PRODUCED BY Bill Ham | FROM *Eliminator* (Warner Bros., 1983)

'We had dabbled with the synthesizer,' Billy Gibbons observed to *Rolling Stone*, 'and then all this gear was showing up from manufacturers. We threw caution to the winds. This was one of the first tracks that started unfolding.' As he expanded to musicradar.com, 'The heaviness of the synthesizers created a nice platform that allowed the guitar to stand on its own.' The song's danceability even won favour from fans of old. 'Being from Texas,' Vinnie Paul noted to *Louder Than Hell*, 'we were always fans of ZZ Top and bands that had big grooves.'

METAL HEALTH (BANG YOUR HEAD)
Quiet Riot

🇺🇸

BY Carlos Cavazo, Kevin DuBrow, Frankie Banali, Tony Cavazo | PRODUCED BY Spencer Proffer | FROM *Metal Health* (Pasha, 1983)

'We were huge fans of AC/DC, so we wanted something that had a very simple, straightahead groove,' drummer Frankie Banali told songfacts.com. 'Kevin [DuBrow, singer] just ran with the lyrics.' 'It's not a take-off of a metal song,' DuBrow pointed out to *NME*. 'It's just a metal song with a funnier lyric.' But Quiet Riot's defining anthem was almost lost. 'The tape was shedding oxide when we were mixing it,' DuBrow told writer Craig Rosen. 'I remember thinking, "This was the best thing we ever recorded and now it's being turned into magnetic dust."'

TURN UP THE RADIO
Autograph

BY Steve Plunkett, Randy Rand, Steve Isham, Steve Lynch, Keni Richards | PRODUCED BY Neil Kernon | FROM *Sign In Please* (RCA, 1984)

'It was a last-minute song that RCA didn't even want on the album because they thought it had no commercial value,' guitarist Steve Lynch told fullinbloom.com. 'We insisted on it until we finally got our way… We were all accustomed to how things worked – or didn't work – in the music industry.' '"Turn Up the Radio" is such a radical song and the chorus is mega slammin',' Steel Panther's Satchel enthused to *Classic Rock*. 'It's a testament to how good that song was – they were one of the uglier hair metal bands. I wouldn't fuck any of those guys.'

METAL THRASHING MAD
Anthrax

BY Dan Lilker, Scott Ian, Neil Turbin, Dan Spitz, Charlie Benante | PRODUCED BY Carl Canedy | FROM *Fistful of Metal* (Megaforce, 1984)

'I was listening to this song from Accept, called "Flash Rockin' Man", and I just thought, Wow, that really flows,' singer Neil Turbin told truemetal.org. 'I came up with "Metal Thrashing Mad". From that song title, that's where "thrash metal" came from. [The media] started terming things metal thrashing bands and thrashing metal bands and thrash metal bands. Suddenly, *voila! Voi-fucking-la!*' 'It didn't need to be four or five minutes,' drummer Charlie Benante noted to songfacts.com. 'It was a short song and just pretty much got to the point.'

ROCK YOU LIKE A HURRICANE
Scorpions

BY Rudolf Schenker, Klaus Meine, Herman Rarebell | PRODUCED BY Dieter Dierks | FROM *Love at First Sting* (Harvest, 1984)

'Nobody else could come up with "Rock You Like a Hurricane",' opined Mötley manager Doc McGhee. 'You have to be German to come up with shit like that.' 'The funny thing is,' Rudolf Schenker noted to songfacts.com, 'the girls say, Oh, I love your song "Rock Me Like a Hurricane".' Inspired by touring America, it soundtracks Marilyn Manson's cameo in the film *Jawbreaker*. 'I have a moustache, I'm having doggy-style sex, and the music they're playing is "Rock You Like a Hurricane"…' he gloated to *Metal Edge*. 'That's as metal as it gets!'

ROCK HARD
Beastie Boys

BY Ad Rock, MCA, Mike D, Rick Rubin | PRODUCED BY Rick Rubin, Beastie Boys | FROM 'Rock Hard' (Def Jam, 1984)

'If you're not gonna have as much equipment as AC/DC,' Mike D opined, 'you really shouldn't play instruments.' Instead, the Beasties looted 'Back in Black' (see 1980) and hollered over it, with glorious results. 'Rick [Rubin] played it on a Walkman for Angus and Malcolm Young,' Def Jam's George Drakoulis recalled to *Select*. 'They weren't upset about it, just intrigued. It was like, "Ah, interesting! I see what you've done there. But aren't the drums very loud?"... I don't think they paid much attention to it...' *(But later they had to be paid a lot of money?)* 'Yeah.'

INTO THE CRYPTS OF RAYS
Celtic Frost

BY Tom G. Warrior | PRODUCED BY 'Mad' Horst Müller, Martin Ain, Tom G. Warrior | FROM *Morbid Tales* (Noise, 1984)

Born from the ashes of Hellhammer (*see* 1983), Tom G. Warrior's avant-garde Swiss quartet never quite fitted into the nascent black/death/thrash metal movement. Their blend of punk and metal even made fans of Nirvana, who had a tape with the Smithereens on one side and Celtic Frost on the other. 'That tape was always getting played, turned over and over again,' Krist Novoselic told writer Michael Goldberg. 'They had so many progressive ideas,' Mark Tremonti observed, 'and when they made dark, atmospheric music, it was *really* dark.'

KNOCKING AT YOUR BACK DOOR
Deep Purple

BY Ritchie Blackmore, Roger Glover, Ian Gillan | PRODUCED BY Roger Glover, Deep Purple | FROM *Perfect Strangers* (Polydor, 1984)

'*Perfect Strangers* was a good enough album,' Roger Glover equivocated to *Rock Express*, 'but it really hung on the strengths of two or three great tracks – and the rest, yeah, they could have been better.' Among those two or three was the singalong opener. 'Great riff!' Glover noted to *Guitarist*. 'Ritchie [Blackmore] really is the riff king! We'd had that one for a couple of years – I've got tapes of us jamming over that riff in Rainbow – but we couldn't write anything over it that was satisfactory at that time. Best to save them for another day.'

SACRIFICE
Bathory

BY Quorthon | PRODUCED BY Quorthon, Börje 'The Boss' Forsberg | FROM *Bathory* (Black Mark Production, 1984)

'Just about the most diabolically nasty that metal is likely to get,' *Kerrang!* predicted of Bathory's superb debut. 'I wanted to combine the energy and speed of Motörhead with the evil sound and heaviness of Black Sabbath,' Quorthon explained. Sabbath's influence was evident in the introductory atmospherics of 'Storm of Damnation', but thereafter it was lo-fi black metal for anyone who found Venom too polished. Hearteningly, for all the rampant evil, it was co-produced by the then seventeen-year-old Quorthon and his dad, Börje Forsberg.

ETAL CHURCH
Metal Church

BY David Wayne, Kurdt Vanderhoof, Craig Wells | PRODUCED BY Metal Church, Terry Date | FROM *Metal Church* (Ground Zero Records, 1984)

utting black metal and thrash in an old-school blender, etal Church were manna for adolescents in their native eattle; Kurt Cobain took to spelling his name 'Kurdt' in bute to guitarist Kurdt Vanderhoof. 'With this track,' Dave ohl told *Q*, 'it just comes down to the riff. It reminds me of king acid... I learnt to play the drums to this.' Later, Flotsam Jetsam's Michael Gilbert told phoenixnewtimes.com, '[It] as probably the biggest influence on me while I wrote me of the music on *Doomsday for the Deceiver*. Great uitar playing. Killer dark vibe.'

CHEMICAL WARFARE
Slayer

BY Jeff Hanneman, Kerry King | PRODUCED BY Slayer | FROM *Haunting the Chapel* (Metal Blade, 1984)

'The intro to "Chemical Warfare" sounds like termites boring their way to the centre of hell,' Scott Batiste of Saviours noted to noisecreep.com. 'I actually held Dave [Lombardo]'s drum kit together while he recorded "Chemical Warfare",' Gene Hoglan – then a Slayer roadie – shuddered to *Decibel*. 'During the first few takes, the kit was going all over the place... I just remember looking up through the clear drumheads on the toms, thinking, "I hope he does this in one or two takes, because this is rough." That was the start of my hearing loss.'

OWERSLAVE
on Maiden

BY Bruce Dickinson | PRODUCED BY Martin Birch | FROM *Powerslave* (EMI, 1984)

ower is always in the hands of a few privileged people...' uce Dickinson explained to *Enfer*. 'The power gives em a certain status, and this status makes them slaves their power.' That weighty theme is matched by the axe tack. 'I turned up at the studio really hungover,' Adrian mith admitted to *Classic Rock*. 'There's Martin [Birch, oducer] still up from the night before, and beside him is obert Palmer, who lived next door... I had the shakes, but I st went, Fuck it. I pulled off a solo and Robert Palmer was ping, "That's fucking great!"'

FADE TO BLACK
Metallica

🇺🇸

BY James Hetfield, Lars Ulrich, Cliff Burton, Kirk Hammett | PRODUCED BY Metallica, Flemming Rasmussen, Mark Whitaker | FROM *Ride the Lightning* (Megaforce, 1984)

'HAVE YOU EVER HEARD A SLOW METALLICA SONG? IS THERE ONE YOU COULD DANCE TO AT A PROM? IF YOU ASKED THEM, THEY'D GO, "WHY WOULD WE?"'
STEVEN TYLER

Few bands made greater leaps to a second album than Metallica. Their evolution peaked with what James Hetfield hailed as 'one of those pivotal songs where we had the hardcore fans that said, "Screw you. You sold out. You did a ballad"... Then you had the other people that said, "Wow, I totally relate to that and it has helped me"'.

'I was really proud of the fact that we had the guts to do it,' Lars Ulrich told MTV. 'People were shocked because it was melodic, it had acoustic guitars and picking guitars... At that time me and James spent a lot of time talking about

death... I don't want to say [*Ride the Lightning* is] the death album, but there's a lot of elements about the fear of death and the process of dying.'

'Fade to Black' was a rare group-credited effort. 'The super-melodic outro – that was all stuff [Cliff Burton] brought to the table,' Ulrich explained to Chris Jericho.

'For the extended solo at the end, I wasn't sure what to play,' Kirk Hammett admitted to *Guitar World*. 'We had been in Denmark for five or six months, and I was getting really homesick. We were also having problems with our management. Since it was a sombre song, and we were bummed out anyway, I thought of very depressing things while I did the solo, and it really helped.'

'I got addicted to that song,' Axl Rose told *Musician*. 'It was the only thing I could put on at the end of the day, which was usually around dawn. It's a song about suicide but I would put it on before I went to sleep and it would make me relax... It made me want to try harder. I'd think, "Yeah, I can get up and face tomorrow."'

FREEWHEEL BURNING
Judas Priest

🇬🇧

BY Glenn Tipton, Rob Halford, KK Downing | PRODUCED BY Tom Allom | FROM *Defenders of the Faith* (CBS, 1984)

Defenders of the Faith's opening salvo, Rob Halford noted to classicrockrevisited.com, 'is all metal.' Of his rapid-fire vocals, he recalled: 'I wanted this kind of semi-automatic delivery... That is what I love about Priest: you might have the most ridiculous-sounding ideas but we never kill it.' *Defenders* was hardly the band's finest ('Judas Priest really sold out!' Kerry King complained to *Kerrang!*), but 'Freewheel Burning' is – as KK Downing told *Guitar World* – 'a killer song... There's a few neat guitar tricks in it, especially the skidding sounds.'

THE GREAT SUZUKI COMPETITION
WIN ONE OF 3 GS125 MOTORBIKES
PLUS ONE OF A LEATHERETTE TOUR JACKETS
GET THE ALBUM & CASSETTE FOR DETAILS

NEW ALBUM & CASSETTE
DEFENDERS OF THE FAITH
FEATURING THE SINGLE 'FREEWHEEL BURNING'

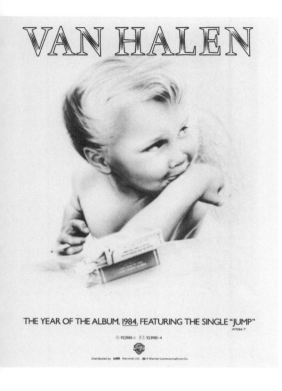

THE YEAR OF THE ALBUM. 1984. FEATURING THE SINGLE "JUMP"

HOUSE OF PAIN
Van Halen

BY Eddie Van Halen, Alex Van Halen, Michael Anthony, David Lee Roth | PRODUCED BY Ted Templeman | FROM *1984* (Warner Bros., 1984)

'House of Pain' was envisaged by Gene Simmons as the opener for Van Halen's debut: the 'Zero' demo version ends with car horns that were to segue into 'Runnin' with the Devil' (*see* 1978). Instead, the song wound up closing *1984*. But it was worth the wait: what *Rolling Stone* hailed as an 'unhinged' demo (produced by Simmons) became one of the band's most awesome skullcrushers. 'The only thing that's the same is the main riff,' Eddie noted to *Guitar World*. 'The intro and verses are different... Nobody really liked it the way that it originally was.'

WANNA ROCK
Twisted Sister

BY Dee Snider | PRODUCED BY Tom Werman | FROM *Stay Hungry* (Atlantic, 1984)

Metal is an outlet for negative emotion,' singer Dee Snider suggested to *Record*. 'You punch your fist in the air. You want to stomp on somebody; you stomp on the floor. You want to scream at your parents; you scream into the air.' Sophisticated? No. Timeless? Yes. 'Twisted Sister is a little cult legend...' Twiggy Ramirez observed to *Seconds*. 'But they had a lot to offer.' Of 'I Wanna Rock', Snider told songfacts.com: 'I thought that if I could combine the drive of a Maiden song with the anthemic quality of an AC/DC song, I'd have a fucking huge hit. I was right.'

ROUND AND ROUND
Ratt

🇺🇸 BY Warren De Martini,
Stephen Pearcy,
Robbin Crosby |
PRODUCED BY Beau Hill
FROM *Out of the Cellar*
(Atlantic, 1984)

The multimillion-selling *Out of the Cellar*, Dave Grohl noted to *Classic Rock*, is 'an iconic album. There were *hits* on that record.' The greatest of those hits was 'Round and Round', penned at the band's scuzzy LA apartment, Ratt Mansion West. 'We were even on the Mars rover,' singer Stephen Pearcy marvelled to *Classic Rock*. 'It was voice-activated and, to get the arms going, they played "Round and Round". So that song went beyond these shores. It went beyond this world.' Check out Pearcy's splendid remake of the song, from 2008, with The Donnas.

LET'S GO CRAZY
Prince and the Revolution

🇺🇸 BY Prince | PRODUCED
BY Prince and the
Revolution | FROM
Purple Rain (Warner
Bros., 1984)

Purple Rain's irresistible opener was Prince's most over-the-top rocker since his debut album *For You*'s 'I'm Yours'. The press – including *Kerrang!*, who put him on their cover, much to readers' consternation – duly revived the comparisons to Jimi Hendrix. 'If they really listened to my stuff, they'd hear more of a Santana influence...' Prince observed to *Rolling Stone*. 'I don't know what these people are thinking – they're usually non-guitar-playing mamma-jammas saying this kind of stuff. There are only so many sounds a guitar can make.'

KILLED BY DEATH
Motörhead

🇬🇧 BY Lemmy, Würzel,
Phil Campbell, Pete
Gill | PRODUCED BY Guy
Bidmead, Vic Maile |
FROM *No Remorse*
(Bronze, 1984)

With Phil Taylor and Brian Robertson exiting, the best-of *No Remorse* might have formed Motörhead's epitaph. Instead, with Lemmy joined by ex-Saxon drummer Pete Gill and guitarists Phil Campbell and Würzel, it was a rebirth. Each of its four sides closed with a cut by the new lineup: the thrashing 'Snaggletooth' and 'Locomotive', the Maidenesque 'Steal Your Face' and the live-staple-to-be 'Killed By Death'. 'That's from [comedian] Spike Milligan,' Lemmy explained to *Spin*. '"How'd you die?" "Oh, you know, killed by death." It's an English thing.'

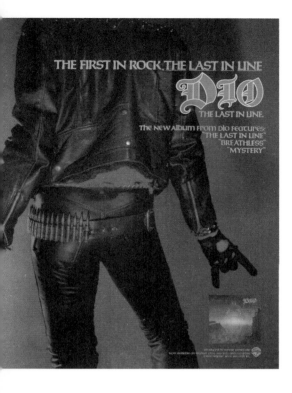

THE LAST IN LINE
Dio

BY Ronnie James Dio, Vivian Campbell, Jimmy Bain | PRODUCED BY Ronnie James Dio | FROM *The Last in Line* (Vertigo, 1984)

'You could be the last in line, meaning, "Oh shit, all the good stuff is already gone,"' Ronnie James Dio remarked on a 2003 anthology. 'Or you could be the last: the strongest... To me, it's always been that: the perseverance that comes from going through challenges in life. And when you get to the end, and you're the last one standing, and you ask yourself, "Was it worth it?", you better say yes.' The equal of anything Dio cut with Rainbow or Sabbath, 'The Last in Line' became the name of a tribute act, led by Vivian Campbell, after the star's death.

ANIMAL (FUCK LIKE A BEAST)
W.A.S.P.

BY Blackie Lawless | PRODUCED BY Mike Varney | FROM 'Animal (Fuck Like a Beast)' (Music for Nations, 1984)

This isn't a normal song...' complained W.A.S.P.'s label Capitol. 'It's a song about "animal sex" with no emotional or love commitment, which can be corrupting to young people.' Unleashed instead by Music for Nations, 'Animal Fuck Like a Beast)' became a sensation – especially when PMRC founder Tipper Gore found her son playing it. 'She's hinking, "We are *not* having that!"' Blackie Lawless told *Kerrang!* 'So there were people coming at us with fiery orches like Frankenstein's monster... It did, of course, nake us household names.'

CATHOLIC SCHOOL GIRLS RULE
Red Hot Chili Peppers

BY Anthony Kiedis, Cliff Martinez, Flea, Jack Sherman | PRODUCED BY George Clinton | FROM *Freaky Styley* (EMI America, 1985)

Thanks to P-Funk producer George Clinton, *Freaky Styley* is the Chili Peppers' most straightforwardly funky album. Yet its most notorious cut is this slice of punk filth, inspired by a young lady that Anthony Kiedis 'met' on tour. 'The attitude of rock was in hip-hop,' Clinton explained. 'That's where it was naturally headed – that attitude the Red Hot Chili Peppers were representing. Then you had Fear and the punk rockers. Those dudes were rocking and funky. It wasn't metal, it wasn't alternative; it was serious bangin' shit. "Knucklehead music", I call it.'

THE EXORCIST
Possessed

BY Mike Torrao | PRODUCED BY Randy Burns | FROM *Seven Churches* (Combat, 1985)

So death metal that they wrote a song called 'Death Metal' to stake their claim as pioneers, Possessed conjured one of *the* thrash debuts with *Seven Churches*. All of it is spectacular, so if you don't like the opening 'The Exorcist' (with a 'Tubular Bells'-looting introduction by producer Randy Burns), you're probably reading the wrong book. Vocalist and bassist Jeff Beccara later remade the track with fellow Californian death metallers Sadistic Intent – the mundane result suggesting that Possessed really may have been, er, possessed with genius of sorts.

MECHANIX
Megadeth

BY Dave Mustaine | PRODUCED BY Dave Mustaine, Karat Faye | FROM *Killing Is My Business... and Business Is Good!* (Combat, 1985)

'To be able to get kicked out of Metallica...' Scott Ian noted to *Louder Than Hell*, 'and then come back with *Killing Is My Business... and Business Is Good!* – churn out all those great riffs and songs – is no small accomplishment.' One of those great songs had, however, already appeared as *Kill 'Em All*'s rather less remarkable 'The Four Horsemen'. 'I wrote "Mechanix" long before I was in Metallica,' Dave Mustaine explained to *Rolling Stone*. 'The lyrics are about a horny gas-station attendant because I *was* a horny gas-station attendant.'

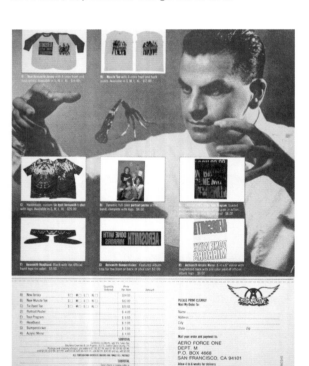

MY FIST YOUR FACE
Aerosmith

BY Steven Tyler, Joe Perry | PRODUCED BY Ted Templeman | FROM *Done with Mirrors* (Geffen, 1985)

'What I always liked about them,' Axl Rose enthused to *Sounds*, 'was that they weren't the guys you'd want to meet at the end of an alley if you'd had a disagreement.' *Done with Mirrors* is Aerosmith's most vicious album, with this cut shooting from their druggy depths. 'I wound up at East House, a rehab facility...' Steven Tyler recounted. 'I put it in a song called "My Fist Your Face" ("East House pinball wizard").' Cliff Burton duly instructed *Rock Hard* in 1986 that his influences included 'a lot of the old Aerosmith; the new Aerosmith shit, too'.

A.I.R.
Anthrax

BY Charlie Benante, Frank Bello, Scott Ian, Dan Spitz, Joey Belladonna | PRODUCED BY Carl Canedy, Anthrax | FROM *Spreading the Disease* (Megaforce Worldwide, 1985)

felt it was missing something,' Charlie Benante told oisey.vice.com of Anthrax's second album. 'I had this one ong that was "A.I.R." and I did a demo of it, sent it to the uys in Ithaca, and they all loved it... and it ended up being he first song on the record.' The result was extraordinary. That was huge for me,' marvelled Dimebag. 'It was ke somebody hit you with a two-by-four across the ace.' As Flotsam & Jetsam's Michael Gilbert told hoenixnewtimes.com, 'Thirty years later, that opening ack, "A.I.R.", still stands monumental.'

AT DAWN THEY SLEEP
Slayer

BY Tom Araya, Jeff Hanneman, Kerry King PRODUCED BY Brian Slagel, Slayer | FROM *Hell Awaits* (Metal Blade, 1985)

At Dawn They Sleep" was always my favourite track off hat album,' Dave Lombardo told *Decibel*. 'It was kind of low and grungy, but then it had that double-bass part n the middle.' Phil Anselmo told *Louder Than Hell* about laying it for Dimebag: 'That big curly head started to nove a little and groove. And, by the end of the song, he's ke, "Damn, son, that's badass!"' 'The half-time feel on "At Dawn They Sleep" is really cool...' Dime noted to *Guitar World*. 'I like how they just start and stop out of nowhere, sing no time to build up or wind down.'

(BEYOND THE) NORTH WINDS
Celtic Frost

BY Tom G. Warrior | PRODUCED BY Horst 'The One & Only' Müller, Tom G. Warrior FROM *To Mega Therion* (Noise, 1985)

'Metal to us was still hilarious...' Justin Broadrick (Godflesh/ Napalm Death) recalled to *Louder Than Hell*. 'We literally picked up the Celtic Frost sleeve and were laughing at the way they looked. Next thing you know, [Napalm drummer] Mick Harris actually bought one of these records, played it to me, and I was like, "Fucking shit, this is amazing."' Celtic Frost's second album was as splendid as it was ludicrous, and yielded a classic in the form of the pummelling 'Circle of the Tyrants'. However, the zippy '(Beyond the) North Winds' is its most infectious moment.

WE CARE A LOT
Faith No More

BY Roddy Bottum, Bill Gould, Jim Martin, Chuck Mosley | PRODUCED BY Matt Wallace | FROM *We Care A Lot* (Mordam Records, 1985)

'It goes to the borders of what you would and wouldn't care about,' lyricist and keyboardist Roddy Bottum told *Sounds* of the anthem that skewered the Live Aid generation. 'It's what I cared about, at that time.' Was it, songfacts.com enquired, the first rap rock song? 'The Chili Peppers were rapping over funk,' singer Chuck Mosley noted, 'and the Beastie Boys were rapping over beats... So yeah.' 'It all started off with Faith No More...' Jonathan Davis agreed in *Louder Than Hell*. 'They had groove... they were heavy and weird.'

KING OF ROCK
Run-D.M.C.

BY Larry Smith, Run, D.M.C. | PRODUCED BY Russell Simmons, Larry Smith | FROM *King of Rock* (Profile, 1985)

Faith No More get the kudos, but Run-D.M.C. had been fusing rap and metal since 1984's 'Rock Box'. 'The rock-rap sound,' D.M.C. noted, 'was [producer] Larry Smith's vision, not Rick Rubin's.' The result was as heavy as anything outside death metal in 1985. 'I went through kind of a rap phase back then, because it was totally new,' Jeff Hanneman told *Decibel*. 'It's boring as hell now – but, at the time, I liked LL [Cool J] and Run-D.M.C.' The latter, Scott Ian admitted to thequietus.com, 'moved me in the same way Motörhead and Iron Maiden moved me.'

BONDED BY BLOOD
Exodus

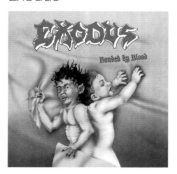

BY Gary Holt, Paul Baloff | PRODUCED BY Mark Whitaker | FROM *Bonded by Blood* (Torrid, 1985)

'When Kirk [Hammett] left, it put me in the driver's seat,' guitarist Gary Holt recalled to *Louder Than Hell*. 'I was able to point the band in the direction Paul [Baloff, singer] and I wanted, which was much more violent and brutal and faster.' Mission accomplished: *Bonded by Blood*, admitted Scott Ian, 'might be better than all the rest of our debut records.' 'Scary guitar playing... and catchy, fast, choppy rhythms,' said Flotsam & Jetsam's Michael Gilbert. 'There's nothing on here to skip,' Kerry King raved to *Rolling Stone*. 'I will listen to that entire record from top to bottom.'

ROCK THE NIGHT
Europe

BY Joey Tempest | PRODUCED BY Europe | FROM 'Rock the Night' (Epic, 1985)

Before 'The Final Countdown', Europe were credible rockers. They had scored two top twenty albums in their homeland – possibly aided by Sweden's fondness for the band's most obvious inspiration, Deep Purple – and birthed a classic in the form of 1984's 'Scream of Anger'. The original, addictive 'Rock the Night' graced the soundtrack of the film *On the Loose* and gave them a top five Swedish hit. Sadly, its better known incarnation is the *Final Countdown* version that damps John Norum's guitars so cruelly that he ultimately quit the band.

YOU'RE IN LOVE
Ratt

BY Stephen Pearcy, Juan Croucier | PRODUCED BY Beau Hill FROM *Invasion of Your Privacy* (Atlantic, 1985)

'I remember Cliff [Burton] asking this girl why she was wearing a Ratt t-shirt,' wrote James Hetfield. 'Her reply was, "Duh, cause they're so hardcore"... We just looked at each other and felt like shoving her head into the tour bus speakers while Discharge crushed her tiny groupie brain!' Dave Mustaine was more forgiving: 'Stephen [Pearcy] is a unique guy,' he told *RIP*. 'Warren [DeMartini] is a great guitar player, Robbin [Crosby, guitarist] was pretty cool and Juan [Croucier, bassist]... seemed like a nice guy.' And they conjured a few classics, like 'You're in Love'.

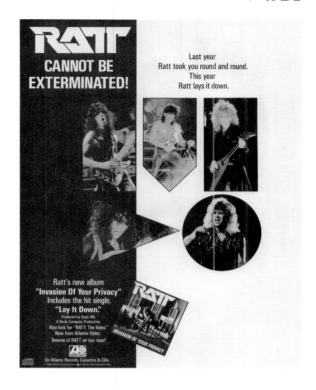

NO SLEEP TILL BROOKLYN
Beastie Boys

BY Mike D, Ad Rock, MCA, Rick Rubin | PRODUCED BY Rick Rubin, Beastie Boys | FROM *Licensed to Ill* (Def Jam, 1986)

'The Beasties' music,' Jeff Hanneman observed to *NME* in 1987, 'is very much like ours, in that it's real extreme.' But his bandmate Kerry King did the honours on 'No Sleep...'. '[Rick] Rubin was like, "This song needs a lead,"' King told *Decibel*. 'So he paid me a couple hundred bucks to come into the studio. I certainly wasn't a virtuoso at that time, but that was a lot of money to me.... In the video, they originally wanted the gorilla to knock me off the stage, but I was like, "If there's gonna be any knocking off stage, it'll be me knocking the gorilla." So that's what we did.'

KEROSENE
Big Black

BY Dave Riley, Jeff Pezzati, Santiago Durango, Steve Albini | PRODUCED BY Big Black, Iain Burgess | FROM *Atomizer* (Homestead, 1986)

'A song Jerry Lee Lewis wrote,' frontman Steve Albini deadpans on Big Black's live *Pigpile*, 'before he killed one of his wives.' But as bassist Dave Riley told *Melody Maker*, 'In actual fact, the song is about American small towns where life is so boring, there's only two things to do: go blow up a whole load of stuff for fun, or have a lot of sex with the one girl in town who'll have sex with anyone. "Kerosene" is about a guy who tries to combine the two.' Stick with Big Black's abrasive original and skip the blah Burn the Priest (aka Lamb of God) cover.

YOU GIVE LOVE A BAD NAME
Bon Jovi

 BY Jon Bon Jovi, Richie Sambora, Desmond Child | PRODUCED BY Bruce Fairbairn | FROM *Slippery When Wet* (Mercury, 1986)

'We got together [with Desmond Child] to write a song for Loverboy,' Jon Bon Jovi recalled to *Billboard*'s Craig Rosen. 'We wrote "You Give Love a Bad Name" and I said, "I think we'll keep that one for ourselves."' At the cutting edge of nothing, Bon Jovi nonetheless redefined rock in 1986. '*Slippery When Wet* was our *Thriller, Born in the USA* and *Back in Black*,' JBJ noted to *Q*. 'The radio stations were like, "What is this? Is this top forty pop or rock?" So we actually changed radio and MTV. At one point we were selling a million records a month.'

A TRIUMPH OF ARTISTRY

BON · JOVI

SLIPPERY WHEN WET
Produced By Bruce Fairbairn
LP – VERH 38 ◆ CHROME TAPE – VERHC 38 ◆ CD – 830 264-2

**Includes The Rock Classic
'YOU GIVE LOVE A BAD NAME'**

DARKNESS DESCENDS
Dark Angel

 BY Jim Durkin, Gene Hoglan | PRODUCED BY Randy Burns, Dark Angel | FROM *Darkness Descends* (Combat, 1986)

'We always tried to make the drums as heavy as possible,' hammer god Gene Hoglan explained to tempecarnivore.blogspot.com, 'the beats as heavy as possible and the riffs as heavy as possible.' That's the greatest understatement in this book: with the exception of Slayer, no one in 1986 was faster or nastier than Dark Angel. '*Darkness Descends* is one of the most relentless records in the history of fucking relentlessness,' Phil Anselmo told *Metal Hammer*. 'There's a power within old-school thrash that I don't think is better exemplified than on this record.'

DEMON'S GATE
Candlemass

BY Leif Edling | PRODUCED BY Candlemass, Ragne 'Valhalla Warrior' Wahlquist | FROM *Epicus Doomicus Metallicus* (Black Dragon, 1986)

It's 1986. You're a Black Sabbath fan. You could invest in Tony Iommi's solo-album-in-all-but-name *Seventh Star*. Or you could do the right thing and get Candlemass's doom metal blueprint, *Epicus Doomicus Metallicus*. Johan Längqvist's vocals and Klas Bergwall's guitar vie for attention, but the thundering bass of Leif Edling and drums of Mats Ekström steal the honours. The opening 'Solitude' is the best-known track, but skip that – especially if operatic vocals ain't your bag – and head straight for 'Demon's Gate'. Doom shake the room!

SEA OF MADNESS
Iron Maiden

🇬🇧
BY Adrian Smith | PRODUCED BY Martin Birch | FROM *Somewhere in Time* (EMI, 1986)

Nineteen eighty-six yielded a tired album by a tired band. 'I was very messed up in the brain department,' Bruce Dickinson admitted to *Hard Force*. 'Even [Steve Harris] had a lot of head problems after the *Powerslave* tour, and nobody had really resolved them by the time we came to do *Somewhere in Time*.' This creative malaise opened the door for Adrian Smith, who birthed the album's best cuts: the single 'Wasted Years' and this chunky gem, whose Faith No More-esque bassline could have been the pointer to a more rewarding new direction.

GIMME THE PRIZE (KURGAN'S THEME)
Queen

🇬🇧
BY Brian May | PRODUCED BY Queen, David Richards | FROM *A Kind of Magic* (EMI, 1986)

Wherever Queen strayed in the eighties, Brian May could be counted on to bring the noise: 'Dragon Attack' on *The Game*, 'Battle Theme' on *Flash Gordon*, 'Put Out the Fire' on *Hot Space*, 'Tear It Up' on *The Works* and this monster on *A Kind of Magic*. Director Russell Mulcahy – in whose *Highlander* it originated – loathed it, as did John Deacon and Freddie Mercury (the latter possibly because it leans on his own 'Princes of the Universe'). But it's got gonzoid guitars, sandpaper singing, decapitated heads, swords and bagpipes. *'There can be only one!'*

THE ELIMINATOR
Agnostic Front

🇺🇸
BY Rob Kabula, Roger Miret, Peter Steele | PRODUCED BY Norman Dunn | FROM *Cause for Alarm* (Combat Core, 1986)

Music by New York hardcore heroes, with lyrics by Peter Steele (then of Carnivore, later of Type O Negative)? Sounds heavy, and so 'The Eliminator' is. (Not least because it owes a debt to 'A Lesson in Violence' by Exodus.) 'Everybody that listened to Black Sabbath, metal or any hardcore was definitely an outcast, and wasn't socially acceptable,' singer Roger Miret recalled to songfacts.com. 'The biggest difference between [metal and hardcore] was lyrically… But [the music] was out of step from society.'

WE GOTTA KNOW
Cro-Mags

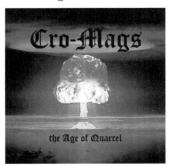

BY Parris Mitchell Mayhew, Harley Flanagan, John Joseph | PRODUCED BY Christopher Williamson | FROM *The Age of Quarrel* (Profile, 1986)

'For sheer brutality, it doesn't get much heavier than the Cro-Mags,' Scott Ian told thequietus.com. 'You put on "We Gotta Know" and if the intro doesn't make you want to throw a chair through a window then there's something wrong with you.' 'They started as a hardcore band...' Dave Grohl explained to *Q*. 'Scary-looking skinheads who were actually all Krishna devotees.' But their roots were metal. 'If it were not for Venom and Motörhead,' bassist Harley Flanagan told *Louder Than Hell*, 'the Cro-Mags would not have sounded the way we did.'

WAKE UP DEAD
Megadeth

BY Dave Mustaine | PRODUCED BY Dave Mustaine, Randy Burns | FROM *Peace Sells... But Who's Buying?* (Capitol, 1986)

'This track was amazing,' Dave Grohl frothed to *Q*, 'and the video was killer: the band playing in a cage in stretch pants, hi-tops and mullets... It was a headbanger's fantasy.' 'There are probably a dozen riffs there, and a lot of them are really good, but they just fly by so fast...' Dave Mustaine told *Guitar World*. 'That was motivated by a will to succeed and prove to doubters that I was a capable guitarist.' The song's star, however, is drummer Gar Samuelson. 'Gar gave it this flow...' guitarist Chris Poland told *Guitar*. 'It kind of lifts you up to the next level.'

ORGASMATRON
Motörhead

BY Lemmy, Würzel, Phil Campbell, Pete Gill | PRODUCED BY Bill Laswell, Jason Corsaro | FROM *Orgasmatron* (GWR, 1986)

Motörhead's renaissance was crowned by this classic. 'One verse was about organized religion, one verse about politicians, and one verse about war...' Phil Campbell recalled to songfacts.com. 'It had nothing to do with Woody Allen [whose film *Sleeper* features a device called an orgasmatron]. Even though we did love Woody Allen.' 'Got up in a hotel room at about four in the morning,' Lemmy recalled in 1999, 'wrote it down and got back into bed! Didn't even remember doing it. Probably my best set of lyrics, too – which might say a lot!'

DISPOSABLE HEROES
Metallica

🇺🇸 BY James Hetfield, Lars Ulrich, Kirk Hammett | PRODUCED BY Metallica, Flemming Rasmussen | FROM *Master of Puppets* (Elektra, 1986)

'The best Metallica song ever...' Corey Taylor frothed to *Rolling Stone*. 'That fucking song is a clinic... I can't play it and I can play almost anything. That's how good it is.' '"Disposable Heroes" is also the most intense epic since "In My Time of Dying" (*see* 1975). 'I couldn't believe it,' Dave Grohl recalled to *Q*. 'I'd heard Motörhead and some punk but not a band as fast and tight and as metal.' 'I love the rhythm and timing on this one,' Slash noted to *Paste*, 'and it's got a real sinister drive to it, too. Like you just know something bad's about to happen.'

DEATH IS YOUR SAVIOUR
Kreator

BY Mille Petrozza, Rob Fioretti, Jürgen 'Ventor' Reil | PRODUCED BY Harris Johns | FROM *Pleasure to Kill* (Noise, 1986)

'We were just young kids full of enthusiasm, who wanted to sound like the bands they listened to,' Kreator mainman Mille Petrozza reminisced to udiscovermusic.com. 'We were tape-traders: we would listen to all kinds of stuff from the metal underground – Hirax, Sepultura, Possessed, Death... We just wanted to be part of that scene – and when I listen to our album *Pleasure to Kill* now, that's what I hear.' What the rest of us heard was, as *Kerrang!* noted, 'enjoyably painful' – or, as Gene Hoglan told *Louder Than Hell*, 'the hyper-blur thing that was really cool.'

LET THERE BE DEATH
Onslaught

🇬🇧 BY Sy Keeler, Nige Rockett, Jase Stallard, Paul Mahoney, Steve Grice | PRODUCED BY Onslaught, Dave 'Death' Pine | FROM *The Force* (Under One Flag, 1986)

'With England, we are good at inventing something,' guitarist Nige Rockett mused to metal-temple.com. 'Then, in most cases, everyone else does it better – i.e. football, cricket...' So it proved for Onslaught: perfectly positioned to soak up the influences of the New Wave of British Heavy Metal and speed metal, but lacking the allure of more far-flung acts. However, *The Force* holds its head high among the class of '86 – and Onslaught had the decency to later cover the inspiration for its opener, AC/DC's 'Let There Be Rock' (*see* 1977).

CRY TOUGH
Poison

🇺🇸 BY Bobby Dall, CC DeVille, Bret Michaels, Rikki Rockett | PRODUCED BY Ric Browde | FROM *Look What the Cat Dragged In* (Enigma, 1986)

'That was our very first single,' Rikki Rockett recalled to theaquarian.com, 'and it wasn't a very successful one.' In fact, 'Cry Tough' didn't chart at all in the US. 'The song got more popular after the band broke,' Rockett explained. 'It reminds me of the struggle when we just really couldn't get much traction. We wrote that song when we were living in downtown LA in a pretty nasty section.' 'We're the kind of band that was voted the best and worst band in every magazine...' Bret Michaels admitted to *Kerrang!* 'At least they have an opinion on us.'

GET UP
Van Halen

🇺🇸 BY Edward Van Halen, Sammy Hagar, Michael Anthony, Alex Van Halen | PRODUCED BY Van Halen, Mick Jones, Donn Landee FROM *5150* (Warner Bros., 1986)

'I've never heard anything like that in my life,' producer Mick Jones (of Foreigner) told the second incarnation of Van Halen when they played him the demo of 'Get Up'. 'It sounds like four guys fighting inside the speaker cabinets, beating the shit out of each other.' Amid *5150*'s hits, the breakneck piledriver maintained the band's metal credentials. '*5150* will always remain the most exciting album I made since the first Montrose album [*see* 1973],' Sammy Hagar declared to *Billboard*'s Craig Rosen. 'It was a great, high-energy record.'

GONNA GET CLOSE TO YOU
Queensrÿche

🇺🇸 BY Lisa Dalbello | PRODUCED BY Neil Kernon | FROM *Rage for Order* (EMI America, 1986)

Canadian chanteuse Lisa Dalbello's *whomanfoursays* (1984) provided rich rock pickings: Heart covered its 'Wait for an Answer', German rockers Heaven's Gate covered 'Animal' and Queensrÿche – metal's nuttiest pre-Tool prog-rockers – adopted the sinister 'Gonna Get Close to You'. 'Lisa was a friend of mine,' Geoff Tate explained to sleazeroxx.com. 'That song was one I was playing around with. I let our manager at the time, Diane Harris, hear it. She said, "You should record that." Lisa's version is somewhat different. We mechanized it. We made it us.'

BIG TROUBLE
David Lee Roth

🇺🇸 BY David Lee Roth, Steve Vai | PRODUCED BY Ted Templeman | FROM *Eat 'Em and Smile* (Warner Bros., 1986)

No relation to a song of the same name on Van Halen's first demo (reworked as 'Big River' on *A Different Kind of Truth*), 'Big Trouble' epitomises the creativity of its writers. Roth's evocatively weird lyrics are, Steve Vai suggested to examiner.com, 'influenced by his like of Tom Waits.' Vai himself is characteristically superb. 'He is absolutely brilliant,' Ritchie Blackmore marvelled to writer Dave Ling. 'Not just because he can play any style, but especially because he can write. His solos are all written down carefully and are all small masterpieces.'

ANGEL OF DEATH
Slayer

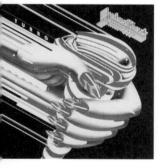

'WHEN I HEARD THE BRIDGE RIFF FROM "ANGEL OF DEATH", MY HEAD SPUN SIMILAR TO REGAN IN THE MOVIE THE EXORCIST. THIS WAS EVIL, IT WAS SCARY, IT WAS AMAZING'

MARK HUNTER, CHIMAIRA

BY Jeff Hanneman | PRODUCED BY Rick Rubin, Slayer | FROM *Reign in Blood* (Def Jam, 1986)

'Angel of Death', Jeff Hanneman protested to *NME*, 'is like a history lesson. But as soon as we released it, everybody was calling us Nazis. Our singer's a dark-skinned Chilean; there's no way we're fascists. I'd read a lot about the Third Reich and was absolutely fascinated by the extremity of it all: the way Hitler had been able to hypnotize a nation and do whatever he wanted; a situation where Mengele could evolve from being a doctor to being a butcher.'

'Yeah, "Slayer are Nazis, fascists, communists" – all that fun shit,' Kerry King groaned to *Decibel*. 'And of course we got the most flak for it in Germany. I was always like, "Read the lyrics and tell me what's offensive about it. Can you see it as a documentary, or do you think Slayer's preaching fucking World War II?"'

'If I truly believed that Jeff Hanneman was a Nazi, then I might have had problems with it,' Scott Ian observed to thequietus.com. 'But I knew Jeff, we were friends and they were certainly aware that I was a Jewish kid from New York City, so I never once thought that Jeff was writing those lyrics because he hated Jews.'

The song is a gleefully glorious introduction to *Reign in Blood*. 'Best opening metal song ever!' Max Cavalera raved to *Metal Hammer*. 'Just a great roaring cacophony' Rob Halford noted to thequietus.com. 'But there are some really strong hooks and melodies in there, which is really difficult to do with that type of music.'

TURBO LOVER
Judas Priest

BY Glenn Tipton, Rob Halford, KK Downing | PRODUCED BY Tom Allom | FROM *Turbo* (CBS, 1986)

With vocals evoking the Stones' "Play with Fire" (a cover which Priest mooted for *Ram It Down*), this *Eliminator*-esque ode to – as Rob Halford put it – 'fun in the back seat' initially appalled fans. However, as Glenn Tipton noted to *Guitar World*, 'When we played some of the songs from that album live... as soon as I cranked up the old synth-guitar, the crowd went berserk.' 'Ah, those guitar synths!' producer Tom Allom recalled to classicrockrevisited.com. 'I don't think they made many friends among the Priest faithful, but hopefully all is forgiven now.'

WELCOME TO THE JUNGLE
Guns N' Roses

BY Axl Rose, Slash, Duff McKagan, Izzy Stradlin, Steven Adler | PRODUCED BY Mike Clink | FROM *Appetite for Destruction* (Geffen, 1987)

'That intro is almost symphonic,' Gene Simmons noted to thequietus.com, 'and it just defined the band.' 'Welcome to the Jungle' showcased the talents that put GN'R ahead of the pack, including the riffing ('Slash plays what's needed for the song,' Joe Perry told *Rolling Stone*, 'as opposed to trying to make the tune a showcase for his technique') and Axl's imagery. 'You could feel where they came from,' Corey Taylor observed to musicradar.com. 'You could hear it, but you felt it too. There was so much aggression, yet it was so dirty and groovy.'

I AM THE LAW
Anthrax

BY Joey Belladonna, Frank Bello, Charlie Benante, Dan Lilker, Scott Ian, Dan Spitz | PRODUCED BY Anthrax, Eddie Kramer | FROM *Among the Living* (Megaforce, 1987)

'I remember Charlie [Benante] coming in with the riff...' Scott Ian recalled to *Louder Than Hell*. 'I was like, "Oh my god – fucking *huge*."' There are finer cuts on *Among the Living* ('Efilnikufesin (N.F.L.)' and 'A.D.I./Horror of It All', for example) but none more iconic. It originated, Benante explained to revolvermag.com, from 'a few riffs I had during the *Spreading the Disease* time... It sounded like the soundtrack to a horror movie. And we were so big on comic books at the time, especially Judge Dredd, that we decided to write that song about him.'

ENTER THE ETERNAL FIRE
Bathory

BY Quorthon | PRODUCED BY Börje 'Boss' Forsberg, Quorthon | FROM *Under the Sign of the Black Mark* (Under One Flag, 1987)

'On *Under the Sign...* we had one song called "Call From The Grave" and one called "Enter The Eternal Fire",' Quorthon noted to *Backstage*. 'Those two were different due to the fact that they were not fast. They were slow and a bit different musically. When that album was released, we got loads of letters from fans all over the world who wanted us to continue in that way and asked if we could do more songs like that.' Little wonder: 'Call of the Grave' is a great song, and the swelling, soaring 'Enter the Eternal Fire' is a black metal milestone.

OUR SOME SUGAR ON ME
ef Leppard

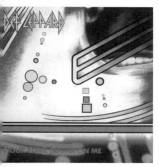

BY Steve Clark, Phil Collen, Joe Elliott, Robert John 'Mutt' Lange, Rick Savage | PRODUCED BY Robert John 'Mutt' Lange | FROM *Hysteria* (Bludgeon Riffola, 1987)

be [Elliot] was playing around on the acoustic guitar, nging, "Pour some sugar on me,"' Phil Collen recalled *Billboard*. 'Mutt said, "What's that?" Within an hour or , [they'd] formed a song and we recorded that song ten days, which was the quickest thing we did... Mutt id it should almost be like a rap song. Even the vocal as based on a rap thing, like Public Enemy.' 'We tested at rock radio,' Elliott told *Rolling Stone*, 'and it flopped agnificently. But then some guy requested it at a strip bar Florida... and then it spread like The Walking Dead.'

MR. SCARY
Dokken

BY George Lynch, Jeff Pilson | PRODUCED BY Neil Kernon | FROM *Back for the Attack* (Elektra, 1987)

'I tried to write this heavier track,' guitarist George Lynch recalled to songfacts.com of his signature jam. 'All the Dokken records had to have this balance: a ballad, a mid-tempo song, a fast song or two. And a heavy song balanced the light. We intended Don [Dokken] to sing on it, but he just wasn't feeling it, which I can understand – you can't really sing over that song.' *Kerrang!* dismissed the feuding foursome's bewilderingly successful output as 'pretty unadventurous melodic metal', but 'Mr. Scary' is the exception that proves the rule.

ILD SIDE
Mötley Crüe

BY Nikki Sixx, Vince Neil, Tommy Lee | PRODUCED BY Tom Werman | FROM *Girls, Girls, Girls* (Elektra, 1987)

'Wild Side" started out as a bastardized version of the ord's Prayer,' Nikki Sixx explained to *Rolling Stone*. It rolved into one of Mötley Crüe's grittiest and greatest ongs, inspired by Sixx's visits to Sunset Boulevard dealers, n the corners with Persian heroin in balloons that they buld keep in their mouth.' A thrilling live video helped rn it into a hit, but not everyone was impressed. 'When I as sixteen [in 1987], the priests made my dad burn all of y Mötley Crüe posters and tapes,' Korn's Jonathan Davis tched to *Kerrang!* 'That sucked!'

LOVE REMOVAL MACHINE
The Cult

BY Ian Astbury, Billy Duffy | PRODUCED BY Rick Rubin, George Drakoulias | FROM *Electric* (Beggars Banquet, 1987)

'I first thought, "What the fuck is this AC/DC stuff going on here?"' John Garcia of Kyuss admitted to thequietus. com of the reborn paisley goth gods. 'But I was such a fan at that point – and had seen their transitions from Southern Death Cult to Death Cult and so on – that I gave it a chance.' 'We had *Back in Black* playing in the studio,' Ian Astbury confessed to songfacts.com. 'Rick [Rubin] was listening to it every day... "Love Removal Machine" was that AC/DC influence where you're getting down to things in their very elemental form, instead of waxing lyrical.'

STILL OF THE NIGHT
Whitesnake

'THE FIRST PART I WROTE WAS THE MIDDLE SECTION. ALL THAT WAS WRITTEN ON GUITAR IN MY MUM'S KITCHEN'
John Sykes

🇬🇧

BY David Coverdale, John Sykes | PRODUCED BY Mike Stone, Keith Olsen | FROM *1987* (EMI, 1987)

'A hybrid of "Jailhouse Rock" by Elvis Presley [and] The Jeff Beck Group's "Rice Pudding",' David Coverdale revealed of his magnum opus. 'But, of course, the Zeppelin overtones... It's one of my favourite songs to perform. It's one of the audience favourites because, as soon as I stop singing, they just take over for me. It's really cool.

'I had a scrubby little riff... and John [Sykes]'s contribution to that guitar lick is just astonishing. It's a unique piece that every single one of the guitar players that I've worked with can't wait to play.'

The song inaugurated Whitesnake's US pomp – thanks in part to the first of three iconic videos. 'The band you see in that video wasn't a band,' A&R guru John Kalodner noted to the authors of *I Want My MTV*. 'David had fired the rest of Whitesnake, so I assembled a great bunch of musicians for his new band. That video was the first time they met one another.'

'Coverdale had marched through my house the previous Saturday night with a girl named Tawny Kitaen,' director Marty Callner recalled, 'who at the time was having an affair with OJ Simpson... I asked if she wanted to be in a music video, and she said yes.'

'I've played that song all over the world,' Coverdale told *Classic Rock*, 'and nobody had a problem with it other than Robert Plant... A couple of years later [Jimmy] Page is playing it with me and going, "This is fucking hard!"'

DUDE (LOOKS LIKE A LADY)
Aerosmith

🇺🇸

BY Steven Tyler, Joe Perry, Desmond Child | PRODUCED BY Bruce Fairbairn | FROM *Permanent Vacation* (Geffen, 1987)

'They wrote this about Vince Neil,' Alice Cooper noted to *Rolling Stone*. 'Mötley Crüe were a bunch of good-looking girls then.' 'These fucks pulled up in a limo,' Steven Tyler cackled to *FHM*. 'Every other word out of their mouths was "dude". You know, "Yo dude! Your dude is really dude, dude."' Tyler's title 'Cruisin' for the Ladies' became 'Dude (Looks Like a Lady)' at writer Desmond Child's insistence. 'Joe [Perry] stepped in and said, "I don't want to insult the gay community,"' Child told songfacts.com. 'I said, "Okay, I'm gay, and I'm not insulted. Let's write this song."'

HELPLESS
Metallica

🇺🇸

BY Sean Harris, Brian Tatler | PRODUCED BY Metallica | FROM *The $5.98 E.P. – Garage Days Re-Revisited* (Elektra, 1987)

'We have been very lucky to have four songs covered by the biggest metal band of all time,' Diamond Head's Brian Tatler told rocknrolljournalist.com. 'It has done so much for myself and the band.' 'Helpless' was the second of those covers; after the 'Creeping Death' b-side 'Am I Evil?', before the 'One' b-side 'The Prince' and *Garage Inc.*'s 'It's Electric' and excluding the unreleased 'Sucking My Love'. It's also the best. 'If it hadn't been for Metallica...' Tatler conceded to *Classic Rock*, 'we'd have probably slipped into obscurity along with Angel Witch.'

BACKWOODS
Red Hot Chili Peppers

BY Anthony Kiedis, Jack Irons, Flea, Hillel Slovak | PRODUCED BY Michael Beinhorn | FROM *The Uplift Mofo Party Plan* (EMI America, 1987)

'We're probably one of the most influential bands in terms of... funk and rock being together, and rapping and all that shit,' Flea noted. 'But at the time I don't think we captured it in vinyl or were very consistent with our songwriting.' Yet *The Uplift Mofo Party Plan* is awash in highlights, from the whimsical 'Behind the Sun' to the walloping 'Fight Like a Brave', 'Me and My Friends' and, best of all, 'Backwoods'. And, bar Lemmy and Keith Richards, who else was paying tribute to Chuck Berry, Little Richard, Bo Diddley and Howlin' Wolf in 1987?

1000 MORE FOOLS
Bad Religion

BY Brett Gurewitz | PRODUCED BY Bad Religion | FROM *Suffer* (Epitaph, 1988)

'Many similar-sounding bands have taken Bad Religion's patented sound further chartwise,' says the Epitaph label website, as snootily as it can without adding 'Green' and 'Day'. In 1988, *Suffer* was as good as punk-pop got, and '1000 More Fools' has both a killer lyrical hook and distinctive backing vocals that Bad Religion dubbed the 'Oozin' ahs'. 'We were the quintessential Californian punk band,' Brett Gurewitz told *Total Guitar*, 'because we started putting in harmonies that were clearly inspired by the surf sounds of the region.'

DON'T CHANGE THAT SONG
Faster Pussycat

BY Greg Steele, Taime Downe | PRODUCED BY Ric Browde | FROM *Faster Pussycat* (Elektra, 1987)

'Faster Pussycat was a lot of fun,' producer Ric Browde recalled to metalsludge.tv. 'The day we started recording, the bigwigs from Elektra came to the studio and wanted to drop the band. But because the label had given me $50,000 upfront... Elektra was too cheap to drop them until the album was finished. This motivated everyone from Pussycat to work their asses off.' The result was low-slung good-time glam, epitomised by 'Bathroom Wall' and the opening 'Don't Change That Song', which summed up Pussycat's sleazily self-mocking charm.

POWER METAL
Pantera

BY Phil Anselmo, Diamond Darrell, Vinnie Paul, Rex Rocker | PRODUCED BY Jerry 'The 'Eld'n' Abbott, Pantera | FROM *Power Metal* (Metal Magic, 1988)

Behold: Phil Anselmo transforms Pantera from jokes to giants. 'I wanted to make sure if I joined that we would be going in a heavier direction...' he told *Louder Than Hell*. 'They played me these demos and, sure, it is more aggressive... [especially] 'Power Metal'... I went in there and nailed that motherfucker.' They even played it with Kerry King. 'There was a breakdown part where Dime and Kerry went into this creepy, Slayeresque, anti-melodic harmony part...' Anselmo reminisced to talkingmetal.com. 'It was very spontaneous but still cool as hell.'

LAY YOUR HANDS ON ME
Bon Jovi

BY Jon Bon Jovi, Richie Sambora | PRODUCED BY Bruce Fairbairn | FROM *New Jersey* (Mercury, 1988)

If anyone can be forgiven for a line as messianic as 'Lay Your Hands on Me' (apart from Peter Gabriel, who wrote it first), it's Jon Bon Jovi, at the time rock's biggest star. The song – 'A big audience favourite,' he noted to *Request* – is a grandiose introduction to his band's greatest albaum and just the right side of self-congratulatory. 'A lot of that arrogance, in retrospect, was out of fear of the success not being there forever,' Jon admitted to *Interview* ten years later. 'People who have to tell you how successful they are aren't really successful.'

GYPSY ROAD
Cinderella

BY Tom Keifer | PRODUCED BY Andy Johns, Tom Keifer, Eri Brittingham | FROM *Long Cold Winter* (Mercury, 1988)

No one did AC/DC better in the late eighties than Bon Jovi protégés Cinderella, and the proof is 'Gypsy Road' – successor to the 'DCish 'Shake Me' on *Night Songs* (1986). They had a nifty line in ballads – 'Nobody's Fool', 'Don't Know What You Got (Till It's Gone)' – but, for all the glam trappings, Cinderella were raunchy rockers. 'It goes back to the Stones, Zeppelin and the Eagles...' Tom Keifer told thevinyldistrict.com. 'The bands that I grew up on really embraced, and were inspired by, American roots music, from the blues to country to R&B to gospel.'

MOTHER
Danzig

BY Glenn Danzig | PRODUCED BY Rick Rubin | FROM *Danzig* (Def American, 1988)

'You've got to check out Samhain,' James Hetfield and Cliff Burton insisted to Rick Rubin. The producer was duly impressed by onetime Misfit Glenn Danzig's writing; less so by Samhain, who he remodelled into Danzig. 'I remember calling Rick Rubin in the middle of the night,' the singer recalled to *Flex*, 'and telling him that I wrote an incredible song... The first time we played it, people went crazy.' 'It was so much fun hearing him sing it...' Rubin told *Rolling Stone*. 'That song [remixed to hitmaking effect in 1993] has got such a great vibe.'

MOUNTAIN SONG
Jane's Addiction

BY Perry Farrell, Eric Avery, Dave Navarro, Stephen Perkins | PRODUCED BY Dave Jerden, Perry Farrell | FROM *Nothing's Shocking* (Warner Bros., 1988)

'*Nothing's Shocking*, man: everything changed,' Devin Townsend marvelled to thequietus.com. 'Jane's Addiction made hard rock interesting lyrically again...' Taylor Hawkin explained to *Rolling Stone*. 'They were esoteric and they made you think.' They *rocked*, too. 'We'd say, "How should these guitars sound?"' frontman Perry Farrell recalled to *Classic Rock*, 'and [producer] Dave Jerden would go, "Like a Panzer division in your face, man!" We'd say, "What do these drums sound like, Dave?" and he'd go, "Like a fucking Panzer division in your face!"'

LEPROSY
Death

BY Chuck Schuldiner | PRODUCED BY Dan Johnson | FROM *Leprosy* (Combat, 1988)

'*Leprosy* is the most consistent and brutal of all seven Death albums...' Chuck Schuldiner's manager Eric Grief opined to metalunderground.com. 'It is the first of so many albums recorded in Tampa at what became the mecca of extreme metal, Morrisound... Like *Reign in Blood* or *Ride the Lightning*, it is a new chapter in brutality... And with it sounding less raw than its predecessor [1987's influential] *Scream Bloody Gore*, and with a stronger production, it is heavy as hell.' *Kerrang!* agreed: 'If raw death metal is what you crave, then this is a feast.'

I WANT OUT
Helloween

BY Kai Hansen | PRODUCED BY Tommy Hansen, Tommy Newton | FROM *Keeper of the Seven Keys Part II* (Noise International, 1988)

'*Keeper of the Seven Keys Part I* hooked me first, but the follow-up was even better,' Fozzy's Chris Jericho told musicradar.com of the pumpkin-crazed power metallers' best-loved albums. 'M. Shadows from Avenged Sevenfold and I are good friends. Helloween brought us together. We even got matching Helloween tattoos.' 'I heard "I Want Out" at a tattoo shop...' Shadows recalled to *Rolling Stone*. 'The songs are so well crafted, they could be pop songs.' 'I Want Out' proved a self-fulfilling prophecy: writer Kai Hansen quit Helloween the following year.

EYES OF A STRANGER
Queensrÿche

BY Chris DeGarmo, Geoff Tate | PRODUCED BY Peter Collins | FROM *Operation: Mindcrime* (EMI-Manhattan, 1988)

'Somewhere down the line, where we're at and where public tastes are at will mesh,' Chris DeGarmo predicted to *Kerrang!* in 1988. 'The stars will open up and we'll have that one really big album.' *Mindcrime* initially fared little better than *Rage for Order* (see 1986), but the *2112*-for-eighties-kids sealed Queensrÿche's reputation, and its closer is a classic. 'The message of some of our songs might be cold and quite bleak...' Geoff Tate admitted, 'but I still want the way we portray ourselves and the music to have a certain warmth and sincerity.'

CULT OF PERSONALITY
Living Colour

BY Vernon Reid, Will Calhoun, Corey Glover, Muzz Skillings | PRODUCED BY Ed Stasium | FROM *Vivid* (Epic, 1988)

'They play with feeling and conviction,' rock 'n' roll pioneer Little Richard evangelized to *Rolling Stone*. 'The same thing that started in the fifties with me, they are taking it through the nineties...They are keeping it alive.' On this smart, Grammy-winning hit – the first and best from their debut album – 'keeping it alive' was mainly down to Vernon Reid's relentless riffing and extraordinary soloing. 'I came from funk and jazz and crazy stuff,' he explained to metalsucks.net, 'yet I wound up here because I love Led Zeppelin as much as the next dude.'

HOOK IN MOUTH
Megadeth

BY Dave Mustaine, Dave Ellefson | PRODUCED BY Paul Lani, Dave Mustaine | FROM *So Far, So Good… So What!* (Combat, 1988)

'I don't know why that didn't become a huge hit,' 'deth guitarist Chris Poland told machinemusic.wordpress.com of *So Far*'s thrashiest cut. 'It had everything going for it. You know what it was: it was that those guys were fucked up. Music wasn't the main goal then… When they spell the chorus out? That's fucking genius. It's like a total anthem.' To ultimate-guitar.com, Poland's replacement Jeff Young took credit for the guitar solo: 'I thought, "Okay, I'll do this kind of Michael Schenker, 'Flight of the Bumblebee', with a Russian twist to it."'

AND JUSTICE FOR ALL
Metallica

BY James Hetfield, Lars Ulrich, Kirk Hammett | PRODUCED BY Metallica, Flemming Rasmussen FROM *…And Justice for All* (Elektra, 1988)

Mercyful Fate and Diamond Head, James Hetfield told *Guitar World*, 'taught us that there were more than three parts to a song… *…And Justice for All* [was] where we really started to go over the top.' 'We were always telling 'em, "Dude, you've got seven parts in this song… and the tempo changes ten times,"' Eerie Von of the Misfits told *Louder Than Hell*. '"Why don't you take each riff and write a good song?"' The album's nine-minute title track, however, proved the sum of its parts. 'We were,' said Hetfield, 'into packing songs with riffs.'

RAM IT DOWN
Judas Priest

BY Glenn Tipton, Rob Halford, KK Downing | PRODUCED BY Tom Allom | FROM *Ram It Down* (CBS, 1988)

'It's a lot like "Freewheel Burning" [*see* 1984] in that it's very fast and energetic,' KK Downing enthused to *Guitar World* of *Ram It Down*'s title cut. 'It features some serious playing from Glenn [Tipton] and I… Some of the rhythm parts in that song are just absolutely scary. Doing that song in the middle of a live set will just annihilate an audience.' After 1986's *Turbo*, ultimateclassicrock.com noted, 'Old-school fans were relieved to hear *Ram It Down*'s potent title track… quickly achieving speed-metal velocity [and] ignited by a paint-peeling scream.'

GHOSTS OF WAR
Slayer

BY Kerry King, Jeff Hanneman | PRODUCED BY Rick Rubin, Slayer | FROM *South of Heaven* (Def Jam, 1988)

'That album was a late bloomer…' Tom Araya conceded to *Decibel*. 'It didn't have that *Reign in Blood* effect.' In fact, the *Blood* effect kicked in halfway through *South of Heaven*. 'Everybody always wants to hear "Ghosts of War",' Kerry King lamented to knac.com, 'and I'm just not a big fan of that song. I like the ending… the big heavy part. And I always say, "Let's put the heavy ending at the end of 'Chemical Warfare' and just do the last half." But I could never make that fly.' Check out Hatebreed's 2009 cover, which niftily recreates the original's lo-fi opening.

ONE IN A MILLION
Guns N' Roses

BY Axl Rose, Steven Adler, Slash, Duff McKagan, Izzy Stradlin PRODUCED BY Mike Clink | FROM *GN'R Lies* (Geffen, 1988)

d been fucking around with this little riff,' Axl Rose told vriter Mick Wall. 'It was the only thing I could play on uitar… [The lyrics were] to fuck with [writer/friend] West Arkeen]'s head… The chorus came about because I was etting really far away, like "Rocket Man" Elton John… like, n my head. Getting really far away from all my friends and amily in Indiana.' The result was GN'R's most notorious ong. 'I can't sit here with a clear conscience and say it's kay that it came out…' Slash admitted to *Select*. 'All I can ay, really, is that it's a lesson learned.'

CAN I PLAY WITH MADNESS?
Iron Maiden

BY Adrian Smith, Bruce Dickinson, Steve Harris PRODUCED BY Martin Birch | FROM *Seventh Son of a Seventh Son* (EMI, 1988)

Maiden's jolliest hit was, Bruce Dickinson told *Hard Force*, 'a real collaborative effort'. The singer brought the lyrics and riffs, Adrian Smith the chords (from his unreleased 'On the Wings of an Eagle') and Steve Harris 'the Zeppelin-y bit'. The result was among an embarrassment of riches on Maiden's strongest album. 'The singles [were] catchy, like "Can I Play With Madness?",' Dickinson reflected to *Billboard*. 'People listen to the catalogue and go, "Oh, it's Maiden, not a lot of melody." It's like, "Just a minute! All of our songs are stuffed full of tunes."'

NOTHIN' BUT A GOOD TIME
Poison

BY Bobby Dall, CC DeVille, Bret Michaels, Rikki Rockett | PRODUCED BY Tom Werman | FROM *Open Up and Say… Ahh!* (Enigma, 1988)

No one brought clichés to life with more pep than Poison, nd 'Nothin' but a Good Time' was less an anthem, more manifesto. 'We wrote that song around the time we were ving in a warehouse in downtown LA,' Rikki Rockett told xs.com. '[It] spoke to people… people doing their best to rind it out. It was just like us when we were a band back n Pennsylvania. We all had second jobs so that we could uy PA equipment or drum heads. That's what the song s for. It's for the working class and the wish that you can ave a good time among all that.'

DISCIPLES OF THE WATCH
Testament

BY Alex Skolnick, Eric Peterson, Chuck Billy | PRODUCED BY Alex Perialas | FROM *The New Order* (Megaforce, 1988)

The New Order, singer Chuck Billy told theaquarian.com, 'was basically about all Nostradamus predictions about the planet, the greenhouse effect and things like that… We kind of got away from our first record, [1987's] *The Legacy*, which was more like ghoulies and goblins and demons; almost like stereotypical heavy metal lyrics… We decided to write about things that actually were real.' However, the album's best-loved cut took inspiration from another fabled writer: Stephen King – specifically, his 1977 short story 'Children of the Corn'.

MAKE ME LAUGH
Anthrax

BY Joey Belladonna, Frank Bello, Charlie Benante, Scott Ian, Dan Spitz | PRODUCED BY Anthrax, Mark Dodson | FROM *State of Euphoria* (Megaforce, 1988)

Nearly every cut on *State of Euphoria* is a 'fuck you' to someone. In 'Make Me Laugh', it's televangelists. 'There's this preacher looking out at you through the camera with this imploring expression,' Charlie Benante explained to *Melody Maker*, 'and he goes on about the will of God, and "We really need the money"… The unfunny part is that people believe in all this shit because they have nothing else to believe in. And the evil part is that this guy is sucking the lost and lonely in; brainwashing them to send in money and then everything will be beautiful.'

CHAPEL OF GHOULS
Morbid Angel

BY Trey Azagthoth, Mike Browning | PRODUCED BY Digby 'Dig' Pearson, Morbid Angel | FROM *Altars of Madness* (Combat/ Earache, 1989)

Initial reactions to these death dealers were far from favourable. 'One label,' vocalist/bassist David Vincent told *Louder Than Hell*, 'went so far as to say, "You do for music what King Herod did for babysitting."' But, as Behemoth's Nergal observed, 'I don't believe that you can find one death metal band nowadays that has not been influenced by either Morbid Angel or Deicide.' Arch Enemy's Angela Gossow confessed that Vincent 'was a big influence on me', but 'Chapel of Ghouls' is essentially a spooky showcase for guitar hero Trey Azagthoth.

ALICE IN HELL
Annihilator

BY Jeff Waters, John Bates | PRODUCED BY Jeff Waters | FROM *Alice in Hell* (Roadracer, 1989)

'It was actually based on a true story about a young girl…' guitarist Jeff Waters told songfacts.com of his first album's title track. 'She had a mental disorder and her parents would lock her in her room because she was waking up with these nightmares about the boogeyman and things like that. And the parents did this for a few years. The kid was really young, and she went into some kind of full-on mental breakdown.' Disturbing lyrics plus what *Kerrang!* called 'skilfully schizoid metal' added up to the Canadian stars' biggest song.

'TIL DEATH
Obituary

BY John Tardy, Allen West, Trevor Peres, Donald Tardy | PRODUCED BY Scott Burns | FROM *Slowly We Rot* (RC, 1989)

'Everybody wanted to record with Scott [Burns],' Deicide's Glen Benton told *Louder Than Hell* of the death producer. 'He's the George Martin of fuckin' death metal.' Burns made his production debut with a band who set out to be the heaviest on the planet. 'I knew the Tardy brothers [vocalist John, drummer Donald] because they had been coming to the [Morrisound] studio,' he explained to voicesfromthedarkside.de. 'The producer tag was a kind gesture… We were just friends.' And how better to celebrate friendship than with ''Til Death'?

THE REAL ME
W.A.S.P.

BY Pete Townshend | PRODUCED BY Blackie Lawless | FROM *The Headless Children* (Capitol, 1989)

'No one has ever done a Who song the way you did,' Pete Townshend told Blackie Lawless of his thunderous take on the *Quadrophenia* cut. The W.A.S.P. man's Who fandom began, he told metalcrypt.com, with Keith Moon's drumming on *Live at Leeds*: 'It just killed me.' For 'The Real Me', drummer Frankie Banali recalled to joelgausten.com, 'I said to myself, "This has to be in the spirit of Keith Moon." I drank a half a pint of really, really cheap bourbon... played the track top to bottom one time and hoped that it was good because I didn't have another one in me.'

LOVE IN AN ELEVATOR
Aerosmith

BY Steven Tyler, Joe Perry | PRODUCED BY Bruce Fairbairn | FROM *Pump* (Geffen, 1989)

'I was talking to Rick Rubin once about writer's block,' Joe Perry told *Total Guitar* of the origins of 'Love in an Elevator'. 'He said, "Make a CD of all the songs that you fell in love with and made you love rock 'n' roll. Listen to that over and over again and it'll start the wheels going." So I was listening to a lot of Hendrix, and it was one of those riffs that just played itself.' The result was Aerosmith's greatest single since their seventies heyday. 'I listened to "Love in an Elevator", going, "Whoops! This is gonna be a hit!"' recalled Steven Tyler. 'I *knew*.'

DR. FEELGOOD
Mötley Crüe

BY Mick Mars, Nikki Sixx | PRODUCED BY Bob Rock | FROM *Dr. Feelgood* (Elektra, 1989)

'They sent me a demo...' Bob Rock told musicradar.com. 'The first song was "Dr. Feelgood", and I went, "Whoa!"' Heavier than Mötley had been since *Shout at the Devil*, the song also had a chunky Aerosmith groove. 'That's a compliment...' Nikki Sixx told *Billboard*'s Craig Rosen. 'I really like those down and dirty riffs that Aerosmith does.' The monster sound entranced Metallica, who recruited Rock but met his first suggestions, Lars Ulrich recalled, with, '"Why don't you go fuck yourself and... just get us that bass sound like the Mötley Crüe album."'

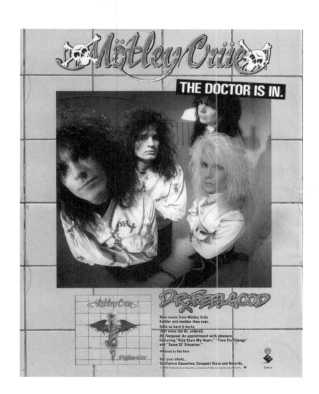

NEGATIVE CREEP
Nirvana

BY Kurt Cobain | PRODUCED BY Jack Endino | FROM *Bleach* (Sub Pop, 1989)

'Nirvana were picking up where Black Flag and GBH had left off,' Josh Homme mused to *Spin*. 'I didn't want my band to sound anything like Nirvana because they had set the bar so high.' *Bleach* edged towards metal in its second half, especially on 'Negative Creep' – 'which,' Kim Thayil noted to *Rolling Stone*, 'would be amazing as a hardcore song or as sort of a metal-grunge song.' Marilyn Manson also enthused to *Rolling Stone* about *Bleach*: 'There was something really dark and alluring... You can hear a tear in his voice; the pain going on there.'

THIEVES
Ministry

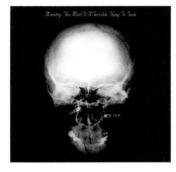

BY Al Jourgensen, Paul Barker, Chris Connelly, Kevin Ogilvie | PRODUCED BY Al Jourgensen, Paul Barker | FROM *The Mind Is a Terrible Thing to Taste* (Sire, 1989)

'My entire career was basically launched by applying the cut-up methods of writers like William Burroughs to music,' Al Jourgensen explained to comingsoon.net. 'I love film as well. There's the samples and all that.' The *Full Metal Jacket* samples in 'Thieves' prompted a call from its director Stanley Kubrick (hence Jourgensen's appearance in Kubrick and Spielberg's *A.I.*), while the song confirmed Ministry's evolution from pop to mindmangling industrial noise. 'If anyone ever asks me about influences,' Trent Reznor admitted to MTV, 'I always say Ministry.'

WHEN DEATH CALLS
Black Sabbath

BY Tony Martin, Tony Iommi, Geoff Nicholls, Cozy Powell | PRODUCED BY Tony Iommi, Cozy Powell | FROM *Headless Cross* (I.R.S., 1989)

'That was the first album I wrote with [drummer] Cozy Powell, even though we had known each other for almost twenty years,' Tony Iommi recalled to *Guitar World*. 'I like *Headless Cross* very much.' Others did, too: 'Iommi writes giant powerchord anthems,' *Kerrang!* noted, 'and [Tony] Martin wraps a colossal vocal around them.' Nowhere was that better realised than on 'When Death Calls', complete with a solo by Brian May. Sabbath, the Queen man marvelled, 'have struck more unforgettable riffs into the hearts of man than any group on the planet.'

YOUTH GONE WILD
Skid Row

BY Rachel Bolan, Dave 'The Snake' Sabo | PRODUCED BY Michael Wagener | FROM *Skid Row* (Atlantic, 1989)

'When Skid Row wanted me to join...' Sebastian Bach told *Guitar International*, 'they sent me a cassette with a bunch of songs on it and that song was probably my favourite... I got "Youth Gone Wild" tattooed on my arm when we were a club band. So I'm the one who brought that shit to the planet.' Producer Michael Wagener explained to tapeop.com: '"Youth Gone Wild" was a thousand voices... There were about ten or fourteen people in the studio singing. We would record a whole bunch of tracks and bounce them down to one, then record a bunch more.'

ȮUD ĻȮVE
oundgarden

BY Chris Cornell, Kim Thayil, Hiro Yamamoto, Matt Cameron | PRODUCED BY Terry Date, Soundgarden | FROM *Louder Than Love* (A&M, 1989)

Many people have told me that that specific song was big influence,' Chris Cornell told *Classic Rock*. 'It made erfect sense to hear it on the radio, even though it ounded huge and was unlike anything else they played... felt vital and exuberant.' 'Enter Sandman' was its best nown descendant, as befits the near title track of *Louder han Love* (which replaced the mooted *Louder Than uck*). 'It's sort of making fun of heavy metal bravado,' ornell confessed to *Sounds*. 'Metal bands would say ouder Than Thunder... What *is* louder than love?'

TERRIBLE LIE
Nine Inch Nails

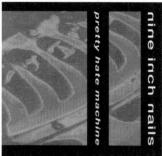

BY Trent Reznor | PRODUCED BY Flood, Trent Reznor | FROM *Pretty Hate Machine* (TVT, 1989)

'There are just some things that don't seem very fair,' Trent Reznor complained to *Alternative Press*. 'Like this fucking hypocrisy of organized religion. I just don't understand how people can blindly believe a bunch of the shit they're fed... so that they don't think too hard about other issues – "Be a good boy and you'll go to heaven"... It doesn't work for me. And that pisses me off because I kind of wish it did.' The result was the heaviest cut on an album that, as David Bowie noted, 'birthed the first real mainstream breakthrough for industrial rock.'

PIƧ
aith No More

BY Mike Bordin, Roddy Bottum, Billy Gould, Jim Martin, Mike Patton | PRODUCED BY Matt Wallace, Faith No More | FROM *The Real Thing* (Slash, 1989)

Ve did videos for "From Out of Nowhere" and "Falling to eces", and they didn't go anywhere,' Billy Gould recalled *Louder Than Hell*. 'We wanted a video for "Epic", which e all thought was the best-sounding song on the album... blew up and we were on the road for a year and a half.' he result became an albatross for newbie Mike Patton. hat kind of adolescent, bratty thing he did was absolutely ght...' producer Matt Wallace told mixonline.com. 'He was nging the way young people thought of the world, like, Jo one understands us."'

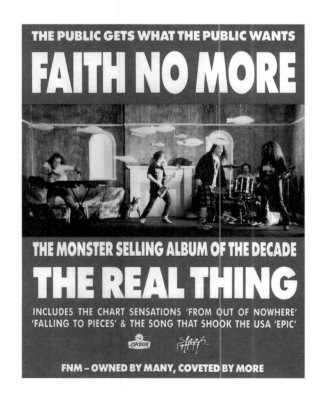

LIKE RATS
Godflesh

🇬🇧

BY Justin Broadrick, GC Green | PRODUCED BY Godflesh | FROM *Streetcleaner* (Earache, 1989)

'Godflesh is misinterpreted as an attacking thing,' former Napalm Deathster Justin Broadrick told trebuchet-magazine.com, 'where it's more of a defensive thing… It's about trying to communicate this sense of frustration; living in urban hell, in council estates, growing up in the seventies in Birmingham. My own upbringing was pretty confused and chaotic… so it was all part of the process that went into making that album.' The result: industrial horror so seething that the monolithic 'Like Rats' qualifies as one of *Streetcleaner*'s most singalong cuts.

GOOD TIME BOYS
Red Hot Chili Peppers

🇺🇸

BY Flea, John Frusciante, Anthony Keidis, Chad Smith | PRODUCED BY Michael Beinhorn | FROM *Mother's Milk* (EMI USA, 1989)

'Michael Beinhorn, the producer, wanted a lot of Les Paul-sounding, chugging metal,' Chad Smith complained. 'We got labelled as funk metal and all that bullshit.' But funk metal was rarely better than on the sensational 'Good Time Boys', which pays tribute to Fishbone, Thelonious Monster, X and fIREHOSE. 'A hardcore crunching funk song,' observed Anthony Keidis, 'that sounds like twenty-five garbage trucks being pushed off the Capitol tower and landing onto the naked rear end of President Bush, filling his entire anal orifice with garbage.'

AUSGEBOMBT
Sodom

▬▬▬

BY Tom Angelripper, Frank Blackfire, Chris Witchhunter | PRODUCED BY Harris Johns | FROM *Agent Orange* (Steamhammer, 1989)

'We liked Sodom,' drum master Gene Hoglan smirked to *Louder Than Hell*, 'because they were so bad and could barely play their instruments – kind of like Venom.' By their third album, however, the trio could compete with thrash's leading lights. *Agent Orange* is dedicated 'to all people – soldiers and civilians – who died by senseless aggressions of wars all over the world' and the punky 'Ausgebombt' ('bombed') is the best of its killer cuts. Tom Angelripper's lyrics rage against the arms trade, furthering a war theme that became a Sodom trademark.

INNER SELF
Sepultura

🇧🇷

BY Max Cavalera, Andreas Kisser, Paulo Jr., Igor Cavalera | PRODUCED BY Scott Burns, Sepultura | FROM *Beneath the Remains* (RC, 1989)

'No one wanted to go to Brazil over Christmas to record a death metal band for very little money,' producer Scott Burns recalled to voicesfromthedarkside.de. 'I said, "Hell yeah." Sometimes it is better to be lucky than good.' Sepultura's third album was their first true classic – and 'Inner Self', Max Cavalera told *Metal Hammer*, 'was the first Sepultura song that had its own identity… It's really almost like an autobiography of my life and my experiences living in Brazil… The Brazilian streets were dirty back then and there was trash and bombs and shit everywhere.'

.IVE
irvana

BY Kurt Cobain,
Krist Novoselic |
PRODUCED BY Butch
Vig | FROM 'Sliver'
(Sub Pop, 1990)

rvana's first session with Butch Vig yielded eight songs: a
over of The Velvet Underground's 'Here She Comes Now'
nd the originals 'In Bloom', 'Polly', 'Pay to Play', 'Lithium',
nmodium', 'Sappy' and 'Dive'. The latter – among the
est of their post-*Bleach* songs – was relegated to the
side of the excellent 'Sliver'. Two years later, it received
e attention it deserved, opening *Incesticide*. 'A lot of the
ooks in the songs, Krist was writing on bass,' Vig recalled.
hink that Kurt basically let him come up with his own
arts. They're great hooks.'

GOT THE TIME
Anthrax

BY Joe Jackson |
PRODUCED BY Anthrax,
Mark Dodson | FROM
Persistence of Time
(Megaforce/Island,
1990)

'Fucking Anthrax covering a fucking Joe Jackson song!'
exclaimed Dave Grohl at the time. 'It's like, What the hell?!'
Jackson himself was equally unimpressed, but 'Got the
Time' was a welcome reminder of Anthrax's playful side
amid the darkness of *Persistence of Time* (best of the rest:
'H8 Red'). NASA used it to wake up the Mars rover in 2016,
making Anthrax the first metal band to be played on that
planet. 'Holy shit, this is résumé stuff!' Frank Bello told
axs.com. 'If I make it to ninety, I am going to be sitting there
thinking about how I have a song on Mars.'

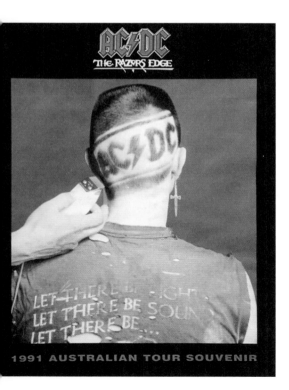

1991 AUSTRALIAN TOUR SOUVENIR

THUNDERSTRUCK
AC/DC

BY Angus Young,
Malcolm Young |
PRODUCED BY Bruce
Fairbairn | FROM *The
Razors Edge* (Albert
Productions, 1990)

'It started off from a little trick I had on guitar,' Angus
Young recalled. 'AC/DC equals power. That's the basic
idea.' Its title was inspired by a toy: a hydrofoil called
ThunderStreak. The result? '*The* AC/DC song for me,'
Thin Lizzy's Scott Gorham enthused to *Classic Rock*.
'Great guitar playing, cool groove and tight production.'
'"Thunderstruck" is unique...' Joe Satriani explained. 'The
two main guitar riffs are syncopated yet bone-crunching.'
And, as Malcolm Young put it to Mark Blake, 'It's one of
those songs that sounds great on stage.'

CIVIL WAR
Guns N' Roses

BY Slash, Axl Rose, Duff McKagan, Izzy Stradlin PRODUCED BY Guns N' Roses, Mike Clink | FROM *Nobody's Child* (Warner Bros., 1990)

'When I hear "Civil War" on the radio, it's like leftfield to me,' Slash told *Musician*. 'Everybody else seems to be doing something completely different; pushing the nice pop single.' The song began as an instrumental before Australian shows in 1988. 'Axl started writing lyrics... and we worked it up into a proper song at soundcheck in Melbourne,' Slash recalled. 'It's pretty indicative of where my head is at,' he told *Guitar World*. 'I'm trying to spend more time getting my head and fingers to connect with the guitar neck, as opposed to just wailing.'

TATTOOED MILLIONAIRE
Bruce Dickinson

BY Bruce Dickinson, Janick Gers | PRODUCED BY Chris Tsangarides | FROM *Tattooed Millionaire* (EMI, 1990)

'I fucked his wife, and I think he was upset...' Nikki Sixx told *Blender*. 'She was his wife, but I didn't know that. I don't think Bruce found out about it until [2001's] *The Dirt*.' But 'Tattooed Millionaire' was clearly aimed at the Crüe. 'The whole vibe about that scene is it's nothing to do with music!' Dickinson complained. "We want to ride round in limos, and do all the garbage, and we want to get chicks, man." He subsequently admitted to metal-rules.com: 'A lot of this album is kind of generic... [but] "Tattooed Millionaire" is actually a really good pop metal track.'

THREE DAYS
Jane's Addiction

BY Perry Farrell, Eric Avery, Dave Navarro, Stephen Perkins | PRODUCED BY Dave Jerden, Perry Farrell | FROM *Ritual de lo Habitual* (Warner Bros., 1990)

Jane's Addiction, Marilyn Manson enthused to *Rolling Stone*, 'infused all of the imaginative elements of cinema and literature into rock 'n' roll... in a way that made me want to do something.' 'It always seems brand new,' Axl Rose told *Hit Parader*, 'no matter how many times I hear it.' 'Three Days' – 'A fucking amazing song' (Devin Townsend, thequietus.com) – was their peak, inspired by Perry Farrell's time with two girlfriends. 'Just imagine that for yourself, with two people you love,' he suggested to *Classic Rock*. 'It would make anybody smile.'

CEMETERY GATES
Pantera

BY Dimebag Darrell, Vinnie Paul, Phil Anselmo, Rex Brown | PRODUCED BY Terry Date, Pantera | FROM *Cowboys from Hell* (Atco, 1990)

'They'd play "This Love" and "Cemetery Gates" on big rock stations,' Hatebreed's Jamey Jasta marvelled to *Louder Than Hell*, 'and I remember thinking, "Damn, that's *huge* for metal."' It was huge for Pantera, too: the subtly Maidenesque 'Cemetery Gates' confirmed their extraordinary evolution from poodle-haired Kiss wannabes into the genre's most influential act of the nineties. 'That to me is the best metal...' Evanescence's Amy Lee told *Metal Hammer*. 'It's Dime. He was just incredible. There was something very special about that man.'

WAR ENSEMBLE
Slayer

BY Jeff Hanneman, Tom Araya | PRODUCED BY Rick Rubin, Andy Wallace, Slayer | FROM *Seasons in the Abyss* (Def American, 1990)

'Before I die, I'd like to see World War III,' Jeff Hanneman confessed to *Kerrang!* 'I'm so into the war thing.' The first and best five minutes of *Seasons in the Abyss* (which emerged during the Gulf War) certified this obsession, and inspired Tom Araya too. 'I read all sorts of stuff...' he told *Kerrang!* 'Stuff on the strategies of war and the games behind it. If, for example, Jeff comes to me like he did with "War Ensemble" and tells me it's about the chess games behind war, then I'll go and get a book about it and read up on it so as I can really understand it.'

STARDOG CHAMPION
Mother Love Bone

BY Andrew Wood, Stone Gossard, Jeff Ament, Greg Gilmore, Bruce Fairweather | PRODUCED BY Terry Date, Mother Love Bone | FROM *Apple* (Polydor, 1990)

'A kinda fake, kinda patriotic rock anthem,' singer Andrew Wood told *RIP* of one of his band's best loved songs. (Its name was attached to a Polydor imprint created for their 1989 debut EP *Shine*.) 'Mother Love Bone was the first grunge band inspired by Led Zeppelin,' Rudolf Schenker observed to *Louder Than Hell*, 'but they also had this more kind of fucked-up kind of feeling – very dark.' Credited to the whole band, 'Stardog Champion' was largely the work of Wood and Stone Gossard. 'Me and Stoney are a team,' the singer said. 'Partners in crime.'

GET THE FUNK OUT
Extreme

BY Nuno Bettencourt, Gary Cherone | PRODUCED BY Michael Wagener | FROM *Extreme II: Pornograffiti* (A&M, 1990)

'We weren't a metal band, we weren't a funk band, but we had all of these elements,' guitarist Nuno Bettencourt explained to *Classic Rock*. 'All of that came to fruition with that song... [It] is a great calling card.' 'We were doing this sound before it got popular,' bassist Pat Badger protested to *M.E.A.T.* 'We're more a traditional funky rock band, like Aerosmith, Led Zeppelin or Van Halen.' But not everyone was convinced. '"Get the Funk Out" is a huge Chili Pepper rip-off,' Flea grumbled to *Guitar Player*. 'It's the most unfunky shit I ever heard.'

HANGAR 18
Megadeth

'THIS TUNE WAS ACTUALLY MUCH LONGER, BUT GOT SERIOUSLY EDITED. I REMEMBER WALKING INTO THE STUDIO AND WADING THROUGH THE MILES OF TWO-INCH TAPE'
MARTY FRIEDMAN

BY Dave Mustaine | PRODUCED BY Mike Clink, Dave Mustaine | FROM *Rust in Peace* (Combat/Capitol, 1990)

'"Hangar 18" was something I had from the band I was in before Metallica...' Dave Mustaine told *Rolling Stone*. 'It was called "N2RHQ" and it was about an environment that was up on another planet.' From these interplanetary origins sprang a song that, he explained to the *New York Review of Records*, 'is about military intelligence – two words combined that don't make sense. I can't understand why they're hiding stuff from us. It's our country too.'

The result – written, he recalled to *Kerrang!*, 'once I decided to straighten myself out. Everything else we'd

done inebriated' – is one of *the* Megadeth songs. It even spawned a sequel: 'Return to Hangar' on 2001's *The World Needs A Hero*.

But what turned it into a classic was a smorgasbord of solos, traded between Mustaine and Marty Friedman. 'When we go to the first extended solo section, it's a very Spanish, "jazzy" kind of part...' Mustaine noted to musicradar.com. 'When the guitar duel takes over, it's no-holds-barred, get the fuck out of the way!'

'One of the greatest guitar duel recordings...' latterday 'deth man Al Pitrelli told metalupdate.com. 'The solos are ferocious and the rhythm guitar parts underneath the solos are equally as ferocious.'

As for chords shared with 'The Call of Ktulu', Mustaine who co-wrote the Metallica song – was unruffled: 'You can go on the internet and look up the four-chord songs and you'll find three hundred or four hundred of them.'

SILENT LUCIDITY
Queensrÿche

BY Chris DeGarmo | PRODUCED BY Peter Collins | FROM *Empire* (EMI America, 1990)

'It started out as simply just acoustic guitar and voice,' Geoff Tate told songfacts.com. 'Our producer didn't really want to put it on the record because he didn't think it was that well developed... It inspired Chris DeGarmo and I to really buckle down and finish the song.' The result, he conceded to noisecreep.com, 'has a Pink Floyd vibe', thanks in large part to orchestrator and Floyd collaborator Michael Kamen. 'He has his own signature sound and his style of melody composition,' observed Tate, 'and that definitely comes through on "Lucidity".'

WE DIE YOUNG
Alice in Chains

BY Jerry Cantrell | PRODUCED BY Dave Jerden | FROM *Facelift* (Columbia, 1990)

'I was riding the bus to rehearsal and I saw all these nine, ten, eleven-year-old kids with beepers...' Jerry Cantrell recalled of his band's formative days in Seattle. 'The sight of a ten-year-old kid with a beeper and cellphone dealing drugs equalled "We Die Young" to me.' What might have been a dirge was made explosive by Cantrell's pyrotechnic guitar and Layne Staley's scary delivery. 'We don't stuff our personal demons inside us, we get them out,' the singer told *Rolling Stone*.' [But] I'm sure I'll never be completely, one hundred per cent, at peace with myself.'

IE DYE ON THE HIGHWAY
obert Plant

BY Robert Plant, Chris Blackwell | PRODUCED BY Robert Plant, Phil Johnstone, Mark Stent FROM *Manic Nirvana* (Es Paranza, 1990)

spent so much time pretending I wasn't the singer with ed Zeppelin,' Robert Plant admitted to *Kerrang!*, 'and oking at David Coverdale and wondering where I was. hought, What a wanker, I could do that. In fact, I *do* do at. That's me! I want my money back!' *Manic Nirvana* was e result, peaking with the hippified lyrics, grinding guitars nd Woodstock samples of 'Tie Dye on the Highway'. ven though "Tie Dye" does harken and gesture [to eppelin],' he told *Musik Express,* 'there's also a sense of umour and parody, which make it perfect for me.'

EXHORDER
Exhorder

BY Chris Nail, Vinnie LaBella, Jay Ceravolo, Kyle Thomas | PRODUCED BY Scott Burns, Exhorder | FROM *Slaughter in the Vatican* (RC, 1990)

'One of my favourite bands of all-time,' producer Scott Burns told voicesfromthedarkside.de. His enthusiasm couldn't save Exhorder, whose chief legacy is an undying debate about their influence on Pantera. They didn't even like their own debut. 'We didn't want our record to sound like Sepultura, Death and so on – and it did,' guitarist Vinnie LaBella complained. 'Even the fuckin' snare sound was sampled off of [Sepultura's] *Beneath the Remains*.' But for all the controversy, 'Exhorder' is as extraordinary an anthem as 'Motorhead' (*see* 1981).

AINKILLER
udas Priest

BY Glenn Tipton, Rob Halford, KK Downing | PRODUCED BY Chris Tsangarides, Judas Priest | FROM *Painkiller* (CBS, 1990)

hey decide, Okay, we're going to try selling out and see if at works,' Axl Rose complained to *Kerrang!* 'They toned eir music down and tried to appease somebody else esides themselves and it cost them.' In fact, every Priest bum since 1977 went at least gold Stateside, but *Turbo* nd *Ram It Down* did little for their credibility. *Painkiller* both song and album – represented an astonishing naissance, and Scott Travis's thunderous drumming chly merited *Kerrang!*'s verdict: 'The hammer hits the vil with even more earth-shattering might.'

THE SAW IS THE LAW
Sodom

BY Tom Angelripper, Chris Witchhunter, Michael Hoffman | PRODUCED BY Harris Johns | FROM *Better Off Dead* (Steamhammer, 1990)

After crashing charts in their homeland with 1989's *Agent Orange*, Sodom should have sailed into the new decade. Instead, they lost a guitarist to Kreator and cut an album that mostly turned its back on thrash and death in favour of traditional headbanging; it even included a cover of Thin Lizzy's 'Cold Sweat' (*see* 1983). But amid the disappointment was a gloriously singalong ode to the Leatherfaces of this world. No clever metaphors à la W.A.S.P.'s 'Chainsaw Charlie' here, as an extra-revving remix – the 'Splatting Version' – attests.

CHERRY PIE
Warrant

BY Jani Lane, Steven Chamberlin, Jerry Dixon, Joey Allen, Erik Turner | PRODUCED BY Beau Hill | FROM *Cherry Pie* (Columbia, 1990)

Hair metal's death knell was sounded precisely one year before 'Smells Like Teen Spirit', when 'Cherry Pie' was issued as a single. There was nowhere the genre could go after an anthem so insanely brainless, by a band so incompetent that Poison's CC DeVille had to be enlisted to provide a solo (hence singer Jani Lane's 'trained professional' aside after the guitar break), and with a video that made the Scorpions look like Morrissey. 'It wasn't the first hit song to offend people,' Lane observed to *BAM*, 'and it won't be the last. That's life, y'know.'

NO MORE TEARS
Ozzy Osbourne

BY Ozzy Osbourne, Zakk Wylde, Randy Castillo, Mike Inez, John Purdell | PRODUCED BY Duane Baron, John Purdell | FROM *No More Tears* (Epic, 1991)

'A gift from God,' said Ozzy of the Beatles-tinged ode to a serial killer that is the most remarkable song of his post-Randy Rhoads career. 'We were just messing around in rehearsals,' Zakk Wylde told songfacts.com. 'Mike [Inez] started jamming that on the bass, then Randy [Castillo] started playing drums, and then John [Purdell] started doing that keyboard bit.' Thanks to this track, the hit 'Mama, I'm Coming Home' and the Grammy-winning 'I Don't Want to Change the World', *No More Tears* became Ozzy's best seller since *Blizzard of Ozz*.

GIVE IT AWAY
Red Hot Chili Peppers

BY Anthony Kiedis, Flea, John Frusciante, Chad Smith | PRODUCED BY Rick Rubin | FROM *Blood Sugar Sex Magik* (Warner Bros., 1991)

'This idea of "give it away" was tornadoing in my head,' Anthony Keidis wrote in his autobiography *Scar Tissue*. 'When Flea started hitting that bassline, that tornado just came out of my mouth.' Inspiration came from an ex-girlfriend, German singer Nina Hagen (whose 1982 album *Nunsexmonkrock* was an obvious titular influence on *Blood Sugar Sex Magik*). Going through her closet, Kiedis 'came upon a valuable exotic jacket'. 'Take it – you can have it,' Hagen told him. 'It's always important to give things away: it creates good energy.'

JESUS BUILT MY HOTROD
Ministry

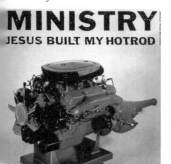

BY Al Jourgensen, Bill Rieflin, Michael Balch, Gibby Haynes, Paul Barker | PRODUCED BY Al Jourgensen, Paul Barker | FROM *Psalm 69: The Way to Succeed and the Way to Suck Eggs* (Sire, 1992)

Never give Ministry money. 'We, of course, shot it all up our arms and put it up our noses,' Al Jourgensen admitted to songfacts.com. 'For $750,000 I had one song done. It was ridiculous. And not only that, I didn't have vocals on it.' Enter Gibby Haynes. 'I pieced together these recordings of this drunk man howling over this guitar loop,' Jourgensen marvelled to the *Guardian*, 'and called it "Jesus Built My Hotrod". [Warner] actually told me I would never work in this industry again, but released it. And it sold more than the latest singles by Prince and Madonna.'

ONLY SHALLOW
My Bloody Valentine

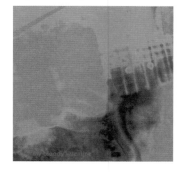

BY Kevin Shields, Bilinda Butcher | PRODUCED BY Kevin Shields | FROM *Loveless* (Creation, 1991)

'Production-wise,' Trent Reznor told *Hot Press* of *Loveless*, 'it was a massive step forward for guitar music. What I really like about My Bloody Valentine is their diversity. They can do balls-to-the-wall rock… but there's also this serene, otherworldly quality.' Nothing illustrates that better than 'Only Shallow', which pitches Bilinda Butcher's fairy-light vocals against a brutal backing. 'That opening snare drum figure – it's so anthemic,' Living Colour's Vernon Reid marvelled to *Classic Rock*. 'All the elements that make this record great are right there.'

PRIMAL SCREAM
Mötley Crüe

BY Tommy Lee, Nikki Sixx, Mick Mars, Vince Neil | PRODUCED BY Bob Rock | FROM *Decade of Decadence '81-'91* (Elektra, 1991)

'I really like the song "Primal Scream",' Nikki Sixx said to concertshots.com. 'That song has a special meaning for me, a special feeling. I don't know what it is.' Amping up the heavy from *Dr. Feelgood*, the track features Mick Mars's favourite of his own solos. 'It's very bluesy and it's a lot of fun for me to play,' he told *Guitar World*. 'The solo just screams the blues. I put a lot of different guitar players' styles in it; everyone from Jimmy Page to Johnny Winter to Michael Bloomfield. I took all of those influences and used them to create that solo.'

SLAVE TO THE GRIND
Skid Row

🇺🇸 🇨🇦

BY Sebastian Bach, Rachel Bolan, Dave 'The Snake' Sabo, Rob Affuso, Scotti Hill | PRODUCED BY Michael Wagener | FROM *Slave to the Grind* (Atlantic, 1991)

'We had our whole life to write the first one,' Rachel Bolan told *Billboard*'s Craig Rosen. 'For the second album, we really had to put our noses to the grindstone.' The band demoed the whole album and emerged mightier than ever. 'The song "Slave to the Grind" is from that session,' producer Michael Wagener told the *Decibel Geek* podcast. 'It was recorded and mixed in an hour; and that's what you're hearing on the record... Everything is live... Every band at the time would say, "Oh, our next album is way heavier," but we did it.'

I AM ONE
The Smashing Pumpkins

🇺🇸

BY Billy Corgan, James Iha | PRODUCED BY Butch Vig, Billy Corgan | FROM *Gish* (Caroline, 1991)

'A statement of spiritual unity, based on the gnosis of the holy trinity,' Billy Corgan wrote. 'Lyrically stripped from an article I'd read on Bishop Desmond Tutu.' The *Gish* cut – a heavier, better version of the Pumpkins' 1990 debut single – served notice that the band could riff with the best of 'em (check out the same album's 'Siva' and 'Tristessa'). 'I distinctly remember listening to Black Sabbath when I was nine and putting my head inside the speakers...' Corgan explained to *Melody Maker*. 'The vibrations from the bass would rumble your hair follicles!'

'NOT A LOT OF BANDS WOULD HAVE GOTTEN HEAVIER ON THEIR SECOND ALBUM'
SEBASTIAN BACH

COMA
Guns N' Roses

'I'M BASICALLY WATCHING THEM KILL THEMSELVES.
NOT SO MUCH AXL, BUT SLASH AND DUFF. MAN,
THESE GUYS WERE ON MY TOP TEN LIST OF
GUYS THAT MIGHT DIE THIS WEEK'

IZZY STRADLIN

BY Slash, Axl Rose, Izzy Stradlin, Duff McKagan PRODUCED BY Mike Clink, Guns N' Roses | FROM *Use Your Illusion I* (Geffen, 1991)

wrote some really cool shit when I was high,' Slash told *Q* in 1991. 'There's a song called "Coma" – a long song, really heavy – and I wrote that loaded.' The track was spawned in a Hollywood Hills drug den rented by Slash and Izzy Stradlin (who, with Duff McKagan, is credited as a writer by SCAP). 'It's fuckin' fifteen minutes long,' Izzy noted to Nick Kent during the *Illusion* tour. 'And I still don't know it, man. have to take a special chord chart out on stage with me whenever we play it. There's like fifty chords at the end of it nd I just can't follow them.'

Acknowledging to MTV that the song was Slash's 'baby', Axl explained his lyrics: 'I just grabbed this bottle of pills in an argument and gulped them down. I ended up in a hospital, but I liked that I wasn't in the fight anymore. My first real thoughts were, "You haven't toured enough; the record's going to be forgotten; you have work to do; get out of this," and I woke myself out of it.'

'The thing that's really interesting was the vamp-out...' Slash recalled to *The Guitar Magazine*. 'This circular rotating chord progression that never ended: the same chord progression every time, but it just kept changing key. That was my mathematical musical discovery.'

The song was a setlist shoo-in when GN'R reunited in 2016. 'I knew it would make Slash happy, I knew it would make the fans happy,' said Axl, initially hampered by a broken foot, 'and, since I was sitting in the chair, I knew I wouldn't have to run around so much.'

I WANT YOU (SHE'S SO HEAVY)
Coroner

BY John Lennon, Paul McCartney | PRODUCED BY Tom Morris | FROM *Mental Vortex* (Noise International, 1991)

Outgrowing your thrash roots is one thing. Taking on The Beatles? Pretty ballsy. But Coroner did it in style, climaxing their third and greatest album with a cover of *Abbey Road*'s doomiest cut. It's faithful to the original – note the abrupt end – but with Kent Smith's keyboards a marked improvement on George Harrison's Moog noodling. Of the song itself, John Lennon told *Rolling Stone*, 'When you're drowning, you don't say, "I would be incredibly pleased if someone would have the foresight to notice me drowning and come and help me." You just *scream*.'

BRING THE NOISE
Anthrax featuring Chuck D

BY Chuck D, Hank Shocklee, Eric Sadler, Charlie Benante, Joey Belladonna, Scott Ian, Frank Bello, Dan Spitz | PRODUCED BY Anthrax, Mark Dodson | FROM *Attack of the Killer B's* (Island/Megaforce, 1991)

'I told Charlie [Benante], "I wrote this riff based around [Public Enemy's] 'Bring the Noise'"...' Scott Ian recalled to *Louder Than Hell*. 'Within twenty minutes we had recorded it and we were like, "Wow, this is so fucking heavy."' Anthrax even toured with Public Enemy. 'They had never gotten groupies before...' Ian noted. 'Flavor Flav was out of his fucking mind for that. He couldn't get on our bus fast enough.' That tour, Benante noted to noisey.vice.com, 'predated things like Lollapalooza. I don't think anybody gives it the credit it deserves.'

TRIBAL DANCE
Armored Saint

BY Dave Prichard, Joey Vera, John Bush, Gonzo Sandoval | PRODUCED BY Dave Jerden | FROM *Symbol of Salvation* (Metal Blade, 1991)

Dropped by Chrysalis and knocked by guitarist Dave Prichard's leukaemia, Armored Saint hit back with their greatest album. Its funky highlight was fuelled by percussion from, they recalled, 'a spiritual guy... the rhythm itself was something that, tribally, means something about the power of manhood.' The song's lyric attacked North America's war on drugs, specifically cocaine. 'Everyone was saying, "The Colombian people are bringing this drug into our country,"' frontman John Bush scoffed. 'Well, we are *demanding* the drug into the country.'

BREED
Nirvana

BY Kurt Cobain, Krist Novoselic, Dave Grohl | PRODUCED BY Butch Vig, Nirvana | FROM *Nevermind* (DGC, 1991)

'I thought, and still think, that Nirvana has more balls than heavy metal,' Alcest's Neige noted to *Metal Hammer*. 'I don't care about Kurt Cobain and I don't listen to the lyrics; for me, the genius of Nirvana is their ability to compose extremely well-written songs that are also super-simple.' *Nevermind* ramped up the heavy, especially on 'Territorial Pissings', 'Smells Like Teen Spirit' and, most crushing of all, 'Breed'. Its lyrics, said Cobain, were aimed at Middle America: 'Marrying at age eighteen, getting pregnant, stuck with a baby – and not wanting it.'

INNUENDO
Queen

BY John Deacon, Brian May, Freddie Mercury, Roger Taylor PRODUCED BY Queen, David Richards | FROM *Innuendo* (Parlophone, 1991)

'Innuendo" was one of those things which could either be big – or nothing,' Brian May fretted to *Vox*. 'We had the same feelings about "Bohemian Rhapsody"… A lot of people say, "It's too long, it's too involved, and we don't want to play it on the radio."' But the 'Kashmir'-esque epic entered the UK chart at number one. 'I was fucking blown away,' said Yes's Steve Howe – who contributed 'crazy Spanish guitar flying around over the top' – to *Prog*. (And check out the *Innuendo* album's 'The Hitman' for Queen's final over-the-top rock monster.)

JESUS CHRIST POSE
Soundgarden

BY Chris Cornell, Matt Cameron, Ben Shepherd, Kim Thayil | PRODUCED BY Terry Date, Soundgarden | FROM *Badmotorfinger* (A&M, 1991)

'A criticism of fashion magazines,' Chris Cornell assured *Melody Maker* of his band's most manic cut. In fact, it was a dig at messianic rockers such as Axl Rose, with whom they toured that year. Spawned by bassist Ben Shepherd, the song was brought to life by Kim Thayil. 'It was hard to discern exactly what the notes and the rhythm were from what Ben was playing, because it was very loud, blurry and quick,' the guitarist told writer Greg Prato. 'While I was trying to figure out that groove, I came up with that weird "pterodactyl on crack" guitar line.'

SAD BUT TRUE
Metallica

BY James Hetfield, Lars Ulrich | PRODUCED BY Bob Rock, James Hetfield, Lars Ulrich | FROM *Metallica* (Elektra, 1991)

'They played me the demo and I told them I thought it was the "Kashmir" of the nineties…' Bob Rock recalled to musicradar.com. 'I told them that on Mötley Crüe's *Dr. Feelgood* [see 1989] – which I produced and Metallica loved – the band had tuned down to D. Metallica then tuned down to D, and that's when the riff really became huge.' The song itself, James Hetfield said, 'is about anyone who has struggled in their life, and got through it – with the help of friends, with the help of family, with the help of music.'

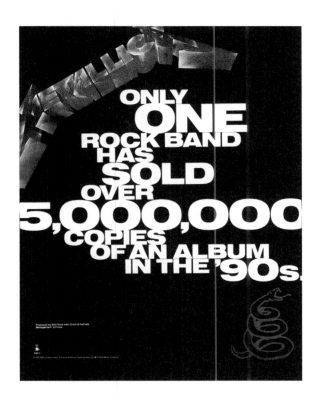

ONLY **ONE** ROCK BAND HAS **SOLD** OVER **5,000,000** COPIES OF AN ALBUM IN THE '90s.

LOCOMOTIVE (COMPLICITY)
Guns N' Roses

BY Slash, Axl Rose, Duff McKagan, Izzy Stradlin | PRODUCED BY Mike Clink, Guns N' Roses | FROM *Use Your Illusion II* (Geffen, 1991)

'I fuckin' hate Slash!' Axl complained to manager Doug Goldstein while GN'R wrote the *Use Your Illusion* albums. 'Have you heard the song "Locomotive" yet? How the fuck am I supposed to write lyrics to this shit?' So demanding is the nine-minute pounder – conjured by Slash from the same sparks that fuelled 'Coma' – that they rarely perform it live, but it remains a fan favourite. 'They dug down a little deeper into rock's roots,' Joe Perry noted to *Rolling Stone*. 'I heard a lot of Aerosmith in them, which meant I also heard a lot of bands that came before us.'

BODY COUNT
Ice-T

BY Ice-T, Ernie C | PRODUCED BY Ice-T | FROM *O.G. Original Gangster* (Sire, 1991)

'We went to school together,' Ice-T told *Musician* of Body Count's origins. 'When I'd make my albums they'd come into the studio. And then one night we had some downtime and I'm playing Slayer, "Angel of Death" [*see* 1986], and thought, "We got a band right here."' The result a cut that birthed the band of the same name, based on 'the attack of Slayer, the impending doom of Sabbath, the drive of Motörhead, and groove-oriented... what I call consumable hardcore music; a record that, once you hear it, you can sing it... that power hook'.

WHY GO
Pearl Jam

BY Eddie Vedder, Jeff Ament | PRODUCED BY Pearl Jam, Rick Parasher | FROM *Ten* (Epic, 1991)

'"Why Go" was written about a specific girl in Chicago,' Eddie Vedder told KLOL. 'Her mom caught her smoking pot or something. She was about thirteen years old and she was just fine. Her mom thought she had some troubles when I think it was really maybe the parents that were having troubles – and, the next thing you know, this young girl was in a hospital... for like two years.' Lyrics apart, *Ten*'s most direct rocker is notable for, as Mike McCready told *Guitar School*, Jeff Ament's 'thunderous' twelve-string bass: 'It sounded like a piano in your face.'

WALKING CORPSE
Brutal Truth

BY Kevin Sharp, Brent McCarty, Dan Lilker, Scott Lewis | PRODUCED BY Colin Richardson | FROM *Extreme Conditions Demand Extreme Responses* (Earache, 1992)

'Wack-ass grindcore,' observed bassist Dan Lilker of the band he formed after thundering through Anthrax, Stormtroopers of Death and Nuclear Assault. But there was nothing wack about Brutal Truth (unless you objected to them looting Napalm Death's sound and style; down to the logo, the three-second 'Collateral Damage' and production by Napalm/Carcass/Bolt Thrower man Colin Richardson). Their awesome debut has *actual songs* (check out 'Birth of Ignorance') but hits a crazed peak with the demonically screaming 'Walking Corpse'.

KILLING IN THE NAME
Rage Against the Machine

BY Zack de la Rocha, Tom Morello, Tim Commerford, Brad Wilk | PRODUCED BY Rage Against the Machine, Garth 'GGGarth' Richardson FROM *Rage Against the Machine* (Epic, 1992)

'We might have opened the door,' Scott Ian of Anthrax conceded to *Louder Than Hell*, 'but they drove the fucking truck through it.' 'We were melding hard rock, punk and hip-hop,' Tom Morello told *Rolling Stone*. And amid an album awash in classics was an anthem anchored by a killer groove. 'If they just want to headbang along in the car on the way home from work, that's inevitable,' Morello conceded to *Q*. 'We hope that we can put the resource of our fanbase to more productive use. Some of them will really get it. They will put ideas into action.'

SYMPHONY OF DESTRUCTION
Megadeth

BY Dave Mustaine | PRODUCED BY Max Norman, Dave Mustaine | FROM *Countdown to Extinction* (Capitol, 1992)

'As close to a "hit" as we got,' Marty Friedman noted. 'The original version of this song was much longer but we edited a lot.' Even edited, 'Symphony' is a highlight of *Countdown to Extinction* and, latterly, the band's shows, thanks to the Argentina-born 'Aguante Megadeth!' chant. 'On *Countdown...*' Dave Ellefson noted, 'our mindset was, "We are capable of so much more than just playing what our audience expects out of us. So let's give them a lot more than what they expect." That attitude helped us to produce songs like "Symphony of Destruction".'

GREEN MACHINE
Kyuss

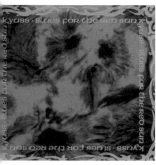

BY Brant Bjork | PRODUCED BY Chris Goss, Kyuss | FROM *Blues for the Red Sun* (Dali, 1992)

'I don't want to say I don't like Sabbath, but it's just not my bag,' protested then Kyuss guitarist Josh Homme. 'If you were into punk and you listened to Sabbath, someone's gonna beat your ass.' 'I don't see any Sabbath influence,' agreed drummer Brant Bjork. 'It's more of a coincidental thing.' So if you think 'Green Machine' sounds like 'Neon Nights' (*see* 1980), think again. 'It's one I always put in my setlist, no matter what band I'm playing in,' singer John Garcia told loudersound.com. 'A very intense, very heavy, very emotional song.'

WISH
Nine Inch Nails

BY Trent Reznor | PRODUCED BY Flood, Trent Reznor | FROM *Broken* (Interscope, 1992)

'One ultra-fast chunk of death,' Trent Reznor told *Guitar World* of *Broken*, which bequeathed the Grammy-winning 'Wish' to setlists for the next quarter-century. 'He literally goes, "I'd like to thank my live band for influencing me into this direction" – and that was the only credit I got,' rued then NIN guitarist Richard Patrick to songfacts.com. 'I was in his ear the whole time saying, "Mean. You're pissed. You're angry. That's what people want."' 'And what's my reward for all that?' Reznor moaned to *Alternative Press*. 'A heavy metal Grammy!'

UNHOLY
Kiss

BY Gene Simmons, Vinnie Vincent | PRODUCED BY Bob Ezrin | FROM *Revenge* (Mercury, 1992)

'Kiss had become a pop band,' manager Larry Mazer complained to *Kiss Alive Forever*. 'The prince of darkness was not in the mix... Gene Simmons was a sideman... He was managing Liza Minnelli, he had Simmons Records, he was making these terrible movies.' To claw back credibility, Kiss issued the grinding 'Unholy' as the first salvo from *Revenge*, complete with a voguishly grungy video. 'I just loved the word "unholy",' recalled Simmons. 'Vinnie [Vincent, former Kiss guitarist] stuck in some of the lyrics. He twisted the song inside out.'

SHITLIST
L7

BY Donita Sparks | PRODUCED BY Butch Vig, L7 | FROM *Bricks Are Heavy* (Slash, 1992)

'We have a very long shitlist...' Donita Sparks told *NME*. 'It's not a personal thing; it's just human rights violators are on that list. Like Operation Rescue, who block off clinics so women can't get in to have abortions.' The song earned a new lease of life on 1994's *Natural Born Killers* film soundtrack, after being relegated to the b-side of the chart-busting 'Pretend We're Dead'. 'Shitlist', Sparks mused to *Classic Rock*, 'could also have been a hit, if it didn't have the word "shit" in it. But had we left out that word, it would have been half the song it turned out to be.'

ZZLOBBER
Faith No More

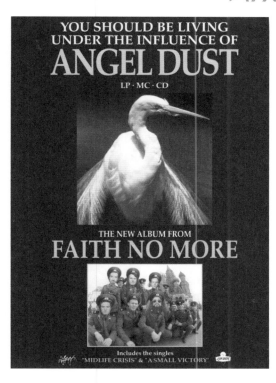

YOU SHOULD BE LIVING
UNDER THE INFLUENCE OF
ANGEL DUST
LP · MC · CD

THE NEW ALBUM FROM
FAITH NO MORE

Includes the singles
"MIDLIFE CRISIS" & "A SMALL VICTORY"

BY Mike Bordin, Roddy Bottum, Bill Gould, Jim Martin, Mike Patton | PRODUCED BY Matt Wallace, Faith No More | FROM *Angel Dust* (Slash, 1992)

ou know what jizz is?' Bill Gould asked *Hot Metal*. 'And ou know what the verb "to lob" is? Well, put them together. s written about some porno star, but I don't remember s name. I'm not the porno expert in the group. Who is? obably [Mike] Patton.' Inspiration aside, the stabbing zzlobber' might be the most spectacularly horrible song this book. '*Angel Dust* wasn't as commercially viable as *e Real Thing*,' Serj Tankian noted to *Spin*, 'but I think it's obably their best album. It's got stuff on it that isn't typical anything else they've ever done.'

FUCKING HOSTILE
Pantera

BY Dimebag Darrell, Phil Anselmo, Vinnie Paul, Rex Brown | PRODUCED BY Terry Date, Vinnie Paul | FROM *Vulgar Display of Power* (Atco, 1992)

'There's a lot of things that make [Phil Anselmo] angry, but he's not necessarily writing anger in a negative fashion,' Vinnie Paul assured *The Georgia Straight*. 'It's also an anger that turns positive.' *Riiight*. Kerry King, famously a fan of positive songs, told loudwire.com: 'Anytime Pantera came through town, I would go onstage and play "Fucking Hostile" with them. That was always a blast. On *Vulgar Display*, the band was really becoming what they were meant to be... It's like they said, "This is us. This is what we're gonna sound like till we're done."'

REMEDY
The Black Crowes

BY Chris Robinson, Rich Robinson | PRODUCED BY George Drakoulias, The Black Crowes | FROM *The Southern Harmony and Musical Companion* (Def American, 1992)

'"Remedy" is a song that essentially is about freedom,' Chris Robinson assured songfacts.com. 'We were into the whole idea that the "war on drugs" was just silly. It was this asinine concept to me and millions of other people. So that song, to me, is about freedom, plain and simple – just put in a rock 'n' roll framework.' Make that funk 'n' roll, as the splendidly Stonesy 'Remedy' also owes a small debt to Parliament's 'Night of the Thumpasorus Peoples'. 'My rhythm and stuff,' Robinson admitted to al.com, 'comes more from listening to Parliament/Funkadelic.'

HUSH
Tool

BY Maynard James Keenan, Adam Jones, Paul D'Amour, Danny Carey | PRODUCED BY Sylvia Massy, Steve Hansgen, Tool | FROM *Opiate* (Zoo, 1992)

'No one would take us seriously unless we pushed the more heavy metal ideas,' Adam Jones told *Louder Than Hell*. 'That explains *Opiate*. We got typecast as a metal band right off the bat.' At the time, Tool had most in common with Rage Against the Machine (on whose debut Maynard James Keenan sang because, he said, 'They couldn't find a bigger rock star to do it'). 'Hush' was a slyer take on Rage's agenda, complete with a satirical video. However, as Danny Carey noted to *MuchMusic*, 'We got our anticensorship video censored.'

ROOSTER
Alice in Chains

BY Jerry Cantrell | PRODUCED BY Dave Jerden, Alice in Chains FROM *Dirt* (Columbia, 1992)

'This incredible, beautiful song' (Lars Ulrich, *Rolling Stone*) was, wrote Jerry Cantrell, 'the start of the healing process between my dad and I from all the damage that Vietnam caused. This was all my perceptions of his experiences out there... He said it was a weird experience, a sad experience, and he hoped that nobody else ever had to go through it.' To musicradar.com, Corey Taylor praised the 'poetic and darkly real' lyrics. 'Cantrell did the harmonies with Layne [Staley],' Kerry King observed to loudwire.com, 'and they were haunting.'

KATHAARIAN LIFE CODE
Darkthrone

BY Fenriz, Nocturno Culto | PRODUCED BY Darkthrone | FROM *A Blaze in the Northern Sky* (Peaceville, 1992)

A Blaze in the Northern Sky's sleeve describes its makers as 'unholy black metal'. They had only just evolved from not-bad death metal, entranced by hiss-laden tapes of their forefathers. 'We were worshipping Bathory and Hellhammer, combined with Motörhead and Black Sabbath,' mouthpiece Fenriz admitted to *Louder Than Hell*. 'In early '91, we decided to start rocking out the black metal vibes.' But so unvibey was their metal (dedicated to murdered Mayhem guitarist Euronymous) that a new genre – necro – had to be invented to describe them.

ᑐUDSPEAKER
katenigs

BY Phildo Owen, Billy Jackson | PRODUCED BY Al Jourgensen | FROM *Stupid People Shouldn't Breed* (Megaforce, 1992)

ᑐmmanded by Al Jourgensen to create a support act ᵣ Ministry, Texas DJ Phildo Owen 'assembled a cast of ndesirables'. Having spawned Skatenigs, Owen was llisted into Jourgensen's Revolting Cocks stable for the ᴑD-fuelled *Beers, Steers and Queers* campaign. His own nd were signed to Jello Biafra's Alternative Tentacles ᵦel and, uncredited, Jourgensen produced their debut ᵦum. All of this wouldn't be worth a hill of beans were it ᵗ for 'Loudspeaker' – a Faith No More-esque monster ᵗt will make your life better and, yes, louder.

ᑐNEY BUⒸKET
Melvins

BY Buzz Osborne | PRODUCED BY Melvins | FROM *Houdini* (Atlantic, 1993)

ᵈon't know what the hell he's singing,' Mastodon's Bill ᵉlliher admitted to noisey.vice.com of the Melvins. 'But I ake up my own words about what's going on in the lyrics ᵈd it paints this picture in my mind.' The lyrics of this one ake no sense – for what it's worth, 'Honey Bucket' is a ᵣrtable toilet – but that's of no consequence. The song's ᵉtallica-esque snarling helped its parent album undercut ᵤzz Osborne's cynical prediction to *Melody Maker*. 'Why ᵈ we name it *Houdini*? Because it's magically going to ᵉ in the bargain bins within a week.'

SHE GOT ME (WHEN SHE GOT HER DRESS ON)
Masters of Reality

BY Chris Goss | PRODUCED BY Chris Goss, Ginger Baker, John 'Googe' Endieveri | FROM *Sunrise on the Sufferbus* (Chrysalis, 1992)

There's not much bluesy stuff in this book because there's not much bluesy stuff that doesn't make me flee into the arms of Bathory. But throw a rock at the slim Masters of Reality discography and you'll find splendid songs aplenty, from their Rubin-produced debut to the second album – with Ginger Baker on drums! – from which this irresistible bitch sprang into America's top ten. Truly, main man Chris Goss deserves all the kudos afforded to his pals in QotSA, Kyuss et al. (And for more astounding Ginger Baker stuff that isn't Cream, check out PiL's *Album*.)

PRISON SEX
Tool

BY Danny Carey, Paul D'Amour, Adam Jones, Maynard James Keenan | PRODUCED BY Sylvia Massy, Tool | FROM *Undertow* (Zoo, 1993)

'This song is about recognizing, identifying, the cycle of abuse...' announced Maynard James Keenan (presumably in case the unsettling 'Prison Sex' video hadn't made that clear). 'That's the first step of the process: realization; identifying. The next step is to work through it.' Tool's label had the brilliant idea of promoting 'Prison Sex' with child-sized shirts, as Adam Jones recalled to *Revolver*. 'Maynard goes, "Do you know what that song's about? It's about getting fucked in the ass as a little kid." They never sent the shirts out.'

FEAR OF THE DARK (LIVE)
Iron Maiden

BY Steve Harris | PRODUCED BY Steve Harris | FROM *A Real Live One* (EMI, 1993)

'We knew right away that it was going to be a standout live track…' Dave Murray declared to *Classic Rock*. 'The pacing of the song and the way it changes – it really sums up what Maiden is all about. The way the fans sing it… it really has become an anthem.' 'Steve [Harris], who wrote it, is really afraid of the dark,' Bruce Dickinson explained to *Hard Force*. 'It's the story of a man who walks in a park at night and, as it's getting darker, he sees all sorts of worrying things. He becomes totally paranoid 'cause his imagination is working overtime.'

MIDNIGHT MOUNTAIN
Cathedral

BY Garry Jennings, Lee Dorrian | PRODUCED BY David Bianco | FROM *The Ethereal Mirror* (Earache, 1993)

'It was a very difficult second album,' singer Lee Dorrian grumbled to *Terrorizer* of *The Ethereal Mirror*. 'I didn't feel comfortable with the way the band had changed… Now, on reflection, I think that it's a fantastic record. Certainly one of our best.' Dorrian's right – and amid sprightly takes on their stoner-psych Sabbath stomp is the thunderously funky 'Midnight Mountain'. The song eats the rock-disco likes of 'I Was Made for Lovin' You' and 'Another Brick in the Wall' for breakfast, then spits out the pieces. It's doom Jim, but not as we know it…

WHO WAS IN MY ROOM LAST NIGHT?
Butthole Surfers

BY Gibby Haynes, Paul Leary, King Coffey, Jeffrey Pinkus | PRODUCED BY John Paul Jones | FROM *Independent Worm Saloon* (Capitol, 1993)

'I was brought in to produce the Butthole Surfers,' John Paul Jones recalled to *Uncut*. 'I guess it was to give it a heavy rock vibe, but it didn't work like that. They were actually incredibly hard-working in the studio, but I do recall running up a phenomenal bar bill at the San Rafael studio.' Jones liked a tipple, frontman Gibby Haynes maintained to caughtinthecrossfire.com, 'but we were loaded too… We basically spent a fortune to hang out with some guy from Led Zeppelin.' But they got a good album with one great hit out of it.

REFUSE/RESIST
Sepultura

BY Max Cavalera, Igor Cavalera, Andreas Kisser, Paolo Jr. | PRODUCED BY Andy Wallace, Sepultura | FROM *Chaos A.D.* (Roadrunner, 1993)

'One of the coolest and heaviest intro/outros in all of heavy music,' Cancer Bats' Scott Middleton enthused to musicfeeds.com.au. The clattering percussion, mixing samba and metal, was the invention of drummer Igor Cavalera, whose brother Max explained the track to songfacts.com: 'The lyric was actually inspired by when I was in a subway in New York… There was a Black Panther in front of me… In his leather jacket, there was this whole speech [with] all this crazy Black Panther shit. And the very last part of this jacket [said], "Refuse and resist."'

SHAKE MY TREE
Coverdale · Page

🇬🇧
BY Jimmy Page, David Coverdale | PRODUCED BY David Coverdale, Jimmy Page, Mike Fraser | FROM *Coverdale · Page* (Geffen, 1993)

'We presented each other with a couple of ideas that we'd both presented to former associates and didn't get a bite,' David Coverdale recalled to *Classic Rock*. 'JP's was the rock-arse riff to "Shake My Tree". Soon as I heard that, I said, "I'll have that, thank you very much."' The result opened an album that was an entertaining addition to both parties' legacies. 'I would submit it's the best work I've done since the days of Zeppelin,' Page assured *Q*. 'We brought the best out of one another.' Added Coverdale: 'He brought the chest-beater out in me.'

HEART-SHAPED BOX
Nirvana

🇺🇸
BY Kurt Cobain | PRODUCED BY Steve Albini | FROM *In Utero* (DGC, 1993)

'You do know the song is about my vagina right?' Courtney Love tweeted to Lana Del Rey when she covered 'Heart-Shaped Box'. 'On top of which some of the lyrics about my vagina i contributed. So umm next time you sing it, think about my vagina will you?' Trolling popstars aside, Courtney did inspire the song, with a gift of a heart-shaped box. Kurt Cobain ensured the result was mixed to within an inch of its life, including excising an effects-laden solo. 'It was like, "Yeah. Shame about that solo,"' Krist Novoselic told *Alternative Press*.

STICK IT OUT
Rush

🇨🇦
BY Geddy Lee, Alex Lifeson, Neil Peart | PRODUCED BY Peter Collins, Rush | FROM *Counterparts* (Anthem, 1993)

After a decade of dicking about, Rush rocked once again on *Counterparts*. 'We had gone back to working with Peter Collins, who produced [1987's] *Hold Your Fire*,' Alex Lifeson explained to *Guitar World*. 'We used a much more direct approach to recording, moving back towards the essence of what Rush was about as a three-piece.' The result was the band's most relentlessly pummelling album. 'Lyrically and musically, it verges on parody,' Neil Peart admitted of the quasi-grungey 'Stick It Out'. 'That was one I think we just had fun with.'

CHERUB ROCK
The Smashing Pumpkins

🇺🇸
BY Billy Corgan | PRODUCED BY Butch Vig, Billy Corgan | FROM *Siamese Dream* (Hut/Virgin, 1993)

'I wrote "Cherub Rock" in half an hour,' Billy Corgan told *Creem*. 'I heard it one day while I was driving up the road and it was one of the last songs I wrote before we did the album. The thing is, there's parts of me that wonder what would have happened if I'd spent four hours writing it, and not done something else. How much better a song would it have been?' Not much, probably: 'Cherub Rock' is beautifully brutal. 'My weird masterplan hasn't changed at all,' Corgan told *Select*. 'I want to be the heavest, meanest, rockingest... you know, *all* those things.'

HEARTWORK
Carcass

BY Bill Steer, Michael Arnott, Jeff Walker | PRODUCED BY Colin Richardson | FROM *Heartwork* (Earache, 1993)

Playing clubs night after night, Carcass founder Bill Steer divined that 'spiky, weird, atonal shit' wouldn't necessarily reach the back of the room – hence the streamlined sounds of *Heartwork*. 'If you've been listening to AC/DC or Thin Lizzy,' he told noisey.vice.com, 'you're very aware of the power of having a strong musical motif.' The band's influence on guitarist Michael Arnott's next venture, Arch Enemy, is clear. 'I worked as a journalist... just so I could interview Carcass,' Arch Enemy vocalist Angela Gossow admitted. 'I loved them more than anything.'

ROOM FOR ONE MORE
Anthrax

BY Charlie Benante, Scott Ian, John Bush, Frank Bello, Dan Spit. PRODUCED BY Dave Jerden, Anthrax | FRO *Sound of White Noise* (Elektra, 1993)

'I got into metal in the nineties,' Cancer Bats' Scott Middleton explained to musicfeeds.com.au, 'and John Bush's amazing vocal hooks and their modern metal riffs on *Sound of White Noise* were what got me into this band. And, man, I love this song!' Of *White Noise*'s singles, 'Room for One More' – 'Inspired by karma,' said Bush – sounds most like classic Anthrax. 'Gene Simmons was a big fan,' producer Dave Jerden noted. 'I heard the album that Kiss wound up making [*Carnival of Souls*], and it sounded like the Anthrax record.'

ANIMAL
Pearl Jam

BY Eddie Vedder, Jeff Ament, Stone Gossard, Mike McCready, Dave Abbruzzese | PRODUCED BY Brendan O'Brien, Pearl Jam | FROM *Vs.* (Epic, 1993)

The short, sharp, snarling 'Animal' gave Pearl Jam's second album its working title, *Five Against One*. Their debut, *Ten*, had gone quadruple platinum by the time they began work on what became *Vs.* Consequently, as Stone Gossard explained to music.avclub.com, '[Eddie Vedder] was now this guy that everybody recognized on the street... So there was some unspoken tension among the five of us in terms of both loving each other and loving being in a band and being very thankful for it – and, at the same time, struggling with each other.'

INCOMPLETE
Bad Religion

BY Brett Gurewitz | PRODUCED BY Andy Wallace, Bad Religion | FROM *Stranger than Fiction* (Atlantic, 1994)

SABOTAGE
Beastie Boys

BY Mike D, Ad Rock, MCA | PRODUCED BY Beastie Boys, Mario Caldato Jr. | FROM *Ill Communication* (Grand Royal, 1994)

Pop-punk conquered the globe in 1994 and Bad Religion who helped invent it – deservedly scooped their biggest seller with their major label debut. 'Infected' and '21st Century (Digital Boy)' were *Stranger than Fiction*'s hits, but its gem is 'Incomplete', with a guitar solo and backing vocals by Wayne Kramer of the MC5 (*see* 1969). Kramer ally issued his first solo album, *The Hard Stuff*, on Epitaph, the label founded by Bad Religion's Brett Gurewitz. 'He asked, "Is it punk?"' Kramer recalled to *Swill* fanzine. 'I said, "Yeah." Then he said, "If it's punk, I'll put it out."'

'[MCA] came in one day with this idea…' Ad Rock recalled to *Rolling Stone*, 'where the fuzz bass keeps playing, and we would all do these hits and stops to bring suspense and drama.' But, as producer Mario Caldato Jr. admitted to soundonsound.com, 'The guys were saying, "It sounds too rock. We don't really want to go down that route."' The track remained an instrumental until two weeks before *Ill Communication* wrapped, when Ad Rock added vocals. 'It just had so much more energy…' Caldato enthused. 'When we'd play it to people, they'd freak out.'

BEASTIE BOYS
SABOTAGE   GET IT TOGETHER
THE DOUBLE A-SIDE SINGLE
27 JUNE

GET IT ON
LIM ED 10" INCLUDES 'GET IT TOGETHER' BUCK WILD REMIX AND UNRELEASED 'RESOLUTION TIME'
LIM ED 7" GREEN VINYL INCLUDES UNRELEASED 'DOPE LITTLE SONG'
CD INCLUDES 'GET IT TOGETHER' BEASTIE BOYS REMIX AND UNRELEASED 'RESOLUTION TIME'
CASSETTE INCLUDES UNRELEASED 'DOPE LITTLE SONG'
LIVE UK DATES • LONDON ASTORIA 22 JUNE • GLASTONBURY 24 JUNE
MARKETED BY PARLOPHONE

DET SOM EN GANG VAR
Burzum

🇳🇴

BY Count Grishnackh | PRODUCED BY Count Grishnackh, Eirik 'Pytten' Hundvin | FROM *Hvis Lyset Tar Oss* (Misanthropy Records, 1994)

Unleashed one month before Varg 'Count Grishnackh' Vikernes was jailed for murder, *Hvis Lyset Tar Oss* is the best of his solo project Burzum's discography: vicious yet haunting. Staggeringly spacious production – by black metal standards – helps make 'Det Som En Gang War' ('What once was') a contender for the genre's greatest song. At a quarter of a century's remove, the context of its release – Vikernes was about to stand trial for the killing of Mayhem guitarist Euronymous – is, rightly or wrongly, easier to overlook. This is a work of black art.

I'M BROKEN
Pantera

🇺🇸

BY Phil Anselmo, Dimebag Darrell, Vinnie Paul, Rex Brow PRODUCED BY Terry Date, Vinnie Paul | FROM *Far Beyond Driven* (Atco, 1994)

'Metallica's last record was amazing,' Vinnie Paul noted tc *Billboard*'s Craig Rosen, 'but it's not nearly as hard as this album.' Of 'I'm Broken' – to which Marilyn Manson's banc would listen before they took the stage on the *Mechanic. Animals* and *Holy Wood* tours – Tom Morello raved to revolvermag.com: 'I remember wishing I had written that. And on the *Far Beyond Driven* tour, as Billy Corgan told musicradar.com, the chief Pumpkin 'stood like a geeky fa backstage and declared, "Boys, you are now the greates metal band in the world!"'

INTERSTATE LOVE SONG
Stone Temple Pilots

🇺🇸

BY Robert DeLeo, Scott Weiland, Dean DeLeo, Eric Kretz | PRODUCED BY Brendan O'Brien | FROM *Purple* (Atlantic, 1994)

'She'd ask how I was doing,' Scott Weiland noted of his wife Janina's enquiring about his drug use and its influence on his band's much loved song. 'I'd lie; say I was doing fine.' Narcotic inspiration aside, 'Interstate Love Song' was Stone Temple Pilots' greatest hit. 'It was born in the back of a truck driving around the country,' Robert DeLeo told thestreet.com. 'I wanted to write something that would encompass everything – great power chords, great stringy chords – and tie it all together. [This song] accomplished that.'

MARCH OF THE PIGS
Nine Inch Nails

🇺🇸

BY Trent Reznor | PRODUCED BY Trent Reznor | FROM *The Downward Spiral* (Nothing, 1994)

'When we attained a certain level of success,' grumbled Trent Reznor, 'it was surprising to see the legion of peopl [who] can't wait to see you fail; hoping that you'll fuck up ripping you off... You go from being the darling to, "Well, we accidentally started selling some records." So they have to turn their backs on us.' Resentment fuelled *The Downward Spiral*'s fastest cut. 'There's no live drums,' Reznor told *Spin*, '[but] it didn't sound like a machine. No way someone could play that like that. It further added a kind of mind-fuck to it.'

SPIN THE BLACK CIRCLE
Pearl Jam

BY Stone Gossard, Eddie Vedder, Mike McCready, Jeff Ament, Dave Abbruzzese | PRODUCED BY Brendan O'Brien, Pearl Jam | FROM *Vitalogy* (Epic, 1994)

'was listening to demos Stone [Gossard] had given me with the pitch on the wrong setting,' remembered Eddie Vedder. 'It was really slow... I pulled Stone off to the side and said, "I think I've stumbled onto something. There's a killer song here if you'd play it this fast."' An ode to vinyl promptly evolved into Pearl Jam's punkiest hit. 'A tear-your-head-off uptempo number,' Gossard recalled to music.avclub.com. 'It's one of those songs where [Vedder] celebrates how much he loves music and what it does for him. That's always a nice place to go.'

MILQUETOAST
Helmet

BY Page Hamilton | PRODUCED BY Butch Vig | FROM *Betty* (Interscope, 1994)

Despite misgivings about boarding the post-Nirvana bandwagon, Helmet frontman Page Hamilton agreed to team up with producer Butch Vig for the *Crow* soundtrack's abrasive 'Milktoast'. For the track's rebirth on *Betty*, Hamilton told *Rolling Stone*, 'Butch gave me the idea to have no guitars on the first verse... Then he added that Pink Floyd, AM-radio effect to my voice. That all changed the feel of the song, because originally it was in-your-face right from the beginning – which is kind of our thing. Helmet's not really known for dynamics.'

CAKE AND SODOMY
Marilyn Manson

BY Marilyn Manson, Daisy Berkowitz, Gidget Gein | PRODUCED BY Trent Reznor, Marilyn Manson | FROM *Portrait of an American Family* (Nothing, 1994)

'They will show anything,' Manson told *The Miami Herald* of New York's public TV channels. 'The 976 number ads are real explicit there. On the next channel I see some guy talking about God and he's asking for money. It's almost like one god is pornography and the other god is Jesus.' Inspired by that TV, 'Cake and Sodomy' crowned Manson the God of Fuck' and, he wrote, 'was more than just a good song. As an anthem for the hypocritical America slobbering on the tit of Christianity, it was a blueprint for our future message.'

DAVIDIAN
Machine Head

BY Robb Flynn, Logan Mader, Adam Duce, Chris Kontos | PRODUCED BY Colin Richardson | FROM *Burn My Eyes* (Roadrunner, 1994)

'The heaviness of Pantera, the epic flair of Metallica, the thrash of Slayer and the bounce of Sepultura,' Chimaira's Mark Hunter marvelled to noisecreep.com. 'They were like the perfect hybrid of all of the great metal sounds.' Machine Head's flawless debut began with one of their most memorable cuts. 'Every time they play this live, the crowd explodes into the toughest pit,' Scott Middleton of Cancer Bats frothed to musicradar.com. 'The heaviness of the chugging is multiplied by Robb Flynn yelling "Slow!" as the tempo decreases. *Crushing!*'

DOGMAN
King's X

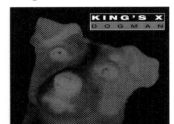

BY Doug Pinnick, Ty Tabor, Jerry Gaskill | PRODUCED BY Brendan O'Brien | FROM *Dogman* (Atlantic, 1994)

'Ty [Tabor, guitarist] said he set out to write the baddest riff that he had ever written,' frontman Doug Pinnick told songfacts.com of *Dogman*'s title track. 'He felt like he did it, and I agree.' Tabor described it to MuchMusic as 'an abstract painting of our feelings... whether it was anger or whatever', but Pinnick clarified: 'We were having all these big-time managers fly in from LA to meet with us, and it was just really overwhelming. And Ty wrote that song during that period. It's all about hand-shaking, glasses shaking, and the whole deal.'

LIAR
Rollins Band

BY Henry Rollins, Chris Haskett, Melvin Gibbs, Sim Cain | PRODUCED BY Theo Van Rock | FROM *Weight* (Imago, 1994)

'There was a moment when I was very fab,' Henry Rollins recalled to bullz-eye.com, 'when "Liar" was a big video on MTV.' An unlikely hit was created by Anton Corbijn's striking clip, showcasing its smooth verses and red-faced hook. 'Five minutes to write it, one lifetime to live it down,' Rollins groaned. 'We literally wrote it as we were tuning up for the first day of band practice with our new bass player. We would play it at CBGBs while we were warming up to make the album [and] the crowd would laugh. And the guy who ran Imago Records said, 'That's a single!''

WASTING AWAY
Nailbomb

BY Alex Newport, Max Cavalera | PRODUCED BY Alex Newport, Max Cavalera | FROM *Point Blank* (Roadrunner, 1994)

'We were listening to a lot of Ministry, Black Flag and Big Black,' Max Cavalera reminisced to *Metal Hammer*. 'Me and Alex [Newport] from [noise rockers] Fudge Tunnel got really inspired.' The beautifully explosive result blended Cavalera's metal with Newport's industrial leanings and sampling. 'The intro for "Wasting Away" is a mixture of Sonic Youth, Motörhead...' Cavalera confessed to Metal Wani. 'It changes so much when you put it into a sampler... It was two guys that really didn't give a shit; just wanted to make heavy music with a fuck-you attitude.'

EVERYTHING ZEN
Bush

BY Gavin Rossdale | PRODUCED BY Clive Langer, Adam Winstanley, Bush | FROM *Sixteen Stone* (Trauma, 1994)

'English bands were arrogant without anything to really back it up,' guitarist Nigel Pulsford related to *Rolling Stone* of Bush's origins in the Britpop era. 'We played [our songs] to the record companies and they were interested, but in the musical climate they weren't sure what to do with us.' America, however, hailed the band as a new Nirvana: 'Everything Zen' ignited a run of hits and platinum albums. It was even endorsed by trip-hop supremo Tricky. 'He was going mad about that line... "There's no sex in your violence,"' Rossdale boasted to *Kerrang!* 'He loved it.'

ET ME DROWN
Soundgarden

BY Chris Cornell | PRODUCED BY Michael Beinhorn, Soundgarden | FROM *Superunknown* (A&M, 1994)

didn't want to say this,' Chris Cornell confessed to *RIP*, because Nirvana put out that *In Utero* album, with the fetus all over it, but ["Let Me Drown"] was originally about crawling back to the womb to die... Salmon always do that. They go back to where they were born, then they die. I think it would be cool if humans could do that too.' im Thayil assured *Melody Maker* that *Superunknown* – which this opens – was 'about life, not death... maybe not affirming it, but rejoicing. Like the Druids: "Life is good, but death's gonna be even better!"'

SHOOTS AND LADDERS
Korn

BY Fieldy, Jonathan Davis, J. 'Munky' Shaffer, David Silveria, Brian 'Head' Welch | PRODUCED BY Ross Robinson | FROM *Korn* (Immortal/Epic, 1994)

Creepy if you're a fan, ridiculous if you're not, 'Shoots and Ladders' confirmed (as did the rest of their debut album) that Korn weren't interested in metal orthodoxy. There were nursery rhymes, nods to Cypress Hill and the most striking bagpipes since AC/DC's 'It's a Long Way to the Top' (*see* 1975). 'I learned stand-up bass, bagpipes and all kinds of other instruments,' Jonathan Davis explained to izotope.com. 'My dad had a music store, so I just picked up whatever instrument I could and got trained from the teachers there... It was pretty cool.'

DITTOHEAD
Slayer

BY Kerry King | PRODUCED BY Slayer, Toby Wright, Rick Rubin | FROM *Divine Intervention* (American, 1994)

The punkiest song I'd ever heard,' Kerry King told writer Arsenio Orteza of *Divine Intervention*'s unhinged highlight. 'The pissed-off lyrics were inspired by all the crazy things I'd seen on TV for the past couple of years at that time: all the blowout trials and lack of responsibility...' I thought, "Well, it sounds like a radicalized version of what [conservative talk show host] Rush Limbaugh does on TV everyday."' 'Most Dittoheads don't listen to Slayer,' suggested Orteza. ('Dittoheads' are Limbaugh fans.) That's probably true,' admitted King.

SLAYER
DIVINE INTERVENTION

Available on CD, Cassette and Vinyl

WELCOME TO PARADISE
Green Day

BY Billie Joe Armstrong, Mike Dirnt, Tré Cool | PRODUCED BY Rob Cavallo, Green Day | FROM *Dookie* (Reprise, 1994)

'We just play simple shit,' Tré Cool admitted to *Kerrang!* 'You could pick up a guitar and play a Green Day song without worrying too much about technique.' Air guitarists seized upon *Dookie*, especially its resurrection (from 1991's *Kerplunk*) of 'Welcome to Paradise', in which even the breakdown seethes with tension. 'It's about West Oakland, living in a warehouse,' Billie Joe Armstrong explained. 'Bums and junkies and thugs and gang members and stuff [lived] in that area. It's no place you want to walk around at night. But it's a neat warehouse.'

RECKONING DAY
Megadeth

BY Dave Mustaine, Marty Friedman, Dave Ellefson, Nick Menza | PRODUCED BY Max Norman, Dave Mustaine | FROM *Youthanasia* (Capitol, 1994)

From the GN'R-ish 'Train of Consequences' to the icily elegant 'A Tout Le Monde', *Youthanasia* saw Megadeth slip the shackles of thrash. But they didn't abandon their roots altogether: the rumbling 'Reckoning Day' – its title inspired by the 1993 film *Tombstone* – is as thunderous a testament to drummer Nick Menza as 'Wake Up Dead' (*see* 1986) is to Gar Samuelson. 'I liked the unorthodox structure of this one,' guitarist Marty Friedman noted. 'It wasn't your typical "verse, bridge, chorus times two, solo" structure that we had done so much of.'

SELF ESTEEM
The Offspring

BY Dexter Holland | PRODUCED BY Thom Wilson | FROM *Smash* (Epitaph, 1994)

'1994 was our crazy year,' Dexter Holland marvelled to *Kerrang!* 'Before *Smash* came out, we played a hometown show and there were maybe a hundred people there. At the end of the year, we were playing the Cobo arena in Detroit, where Kiss recorded *Alive!*... It just blew our minds.' Among the hits that made *Smash* the biggest independent album ever was the cheerily dopey 'Self Esteem'. 'I never knew so many people would relate to that,' Holland admitted to *Spin*. 'It's just kind of a turnaround. The girls are real cocky, and the guys are real passive.'

MISUNDERSTOOD
Mötley Crüe

BY John Corabi, Tommy Lee, Mick Mars, Nikki Sixx | PRODUCED BY Bob Rock | FROM *Mötley Crüe* (Elektra, 1994)

'We couldn't wait for Mötley fans to hear what we'd done,' John Corabi recalled of his sole album as the band's singer. 'We thought we had really made an intelligent Mötley Crüe record.' Amid its Aerosmith-meets-Pantera-style groovers and thrashers was the epic 'Misunderstood', begun at Corabi's first rehearsal and finished with backing vocals by Glenn Hughes. 'One fucking take!' Corabi goggled to sleazeroxx.com. 'I'm like, "Holy shit, how? Are you fucking kidding me?" I could not believe that he had done this off the cuff.'

NEGASONIC TEENAGE WARHEAD
Monster Magnet

BY Dave Wyndorf | PRODUCED BY Dave Wyndorf | FROM *S.F.W.* (A&M, 1994)

Amid Soundgarden, Marilyn Manson, Radiohead and Hole, the Hawkwind-esque 'Negasonic Teenage Warhead' stood out on the soundtrack for the rotten *S.F.W.* Then, reworked for Monster Magnet's own *Dopes to Infinity* in 1995, it became a hit. And *then*, as Dave Wyndorf marvelled to collideartandculture.com, comic writer Grant Morrison named an X-Men recruit after the song. The mutant hero, he noted, 'disappeared after about ten issues', but was resurrected for the *Deadpool* film. 'The character that will never die! It's unbelievable.'

HEY MAN NICE SHOT
Filter

BY Richard Patrick | PRODUCED BY Brian Liesegang, Richard Patrick | FROM *Short Bus* (Reprise, 1995)

The highlight of Richard Patrick's time in Nine Inch Nails, he explained to *Louder Than Hell*, 'was when I sat down by myself and wrote "Hey Man Nice Shot". Because I knew I would soon be out of the insanity and the pure emotional hardship of being in that band.' He did, however, offer it to Trent Reznor for *The Downward Spiral*. 'He said, "Yeah, fits really good." And that's huge for him... because he's so competitive.' However, as Patrick told clevescene.com, 'I thought if I don't take advantage of "Hey Man Nice Shot", I would be locked in NIN forever.'

DEMANUFACTURE
Fear Factory

BY Burton C. Bell, Dino Cazares, Raymond Herrera, Christian Olde Wolbers | PRODUCED BY Colin Richardson | FROM *Demanufacture* (Roadrunner, 1995)

'Fear Factory are awesome,' Kirk Hammett enthused to *Kerrang!* '*Demanufacture* got my blood going.' The title, guitarist Dino Cazares explained to songfacts.com, 'means to take apart or to break down, and that's basically how we saw LA... gang violence, police brutality, [the] Rodney King riots [and] massive fires.' The album was a game-changer for the band. 'We experienced parts of the world where we were like The Beatles, and we literally had to run away from girls,' Cazares laughed to myglobalmind.com. 'We were much younger and thinner and faster.'

STONE THE CROW
Down

BY Phil Anselmo, Pepper Keenan | PRODUCED BY Down, Matt Thomas | FROM *NOLA* (EastWest, 1995)

Despite the fanbases of Phil Anselmo and Corrosion of Conformity's Pepper Keenan, 'Stone the Crow' was only a minor hit. 'If one jackass would have taken a chance and put it on the radio, it would have taken off,' Keenan grumbled to riverfronttimes.com. 'We play this song and kids know every damn word. It's like playing "Freebird".' But, as Anselmo laughed to artistdirect.com, 'There are parts... where I'm not even saying anything. In time, those incomprehensible yellings become words and people can sing what they think I'm saying.'

SELLING JESUS
Skunk Anansie

🇬🇧

BY Skin, Len Arran | PRODUCED BY Sylvia Massy | FROM *Paranoid & Sunburnt* (One Little Indian, 1995)

'This was written when I was backpacking in California,' singer Skin explained to *Melody Maker*. 'The state was giving out $2,000 vouchers to new religions and, as a consequence, there were lots of weird cults springing up. They were just taking the money and using it to teach the kids a load of shit. ["Selling Jesus" is] not antireligious. It's more about the way people instil religious beliefs.' The snarling song – Skunk Anansie's debut – entranced director Kathryn Bigelow, who added it and the band to her film of the same year, *Strange Days*.

BULLET WITH BUTTERFLY WINGS
The Smashing Pumpkins

🇺🇸

BY Billy Corgan | PRODUCED BY Flood, Alan Moulder, Billy Corgan | FROM *Mellon Collie and the Infinite Sadness* (Virgin, 1995)

'The original riff from this song came to me during one of the *Siamese Dream* recording sessions...' Billy Corgan told *Guitar World*. 'I have a tape of us from 1993, endlessly playing the "world is a vampire" part over and over. But it wasn't until a year and a half later that I finished the song, writing the "rat in a cage" part on an acoustic guitar at the BBC studios.' The song replaced the equally brutal 'Jellybelly' as *Mellon Collie*'s first single; a decision made, Corgan quipped, when Virgin conducted a 'survey of Kmart shoppers between thirty and forty'.

I'LL STICK AROUND
Foo Fighters

🇺🇸

BY Dave Grohl | PRODUCED BY Barrett Jones, Foo Fighters | FROM *Foo Fighters* (Roswell, 1995)

The Foo Fighters' debut album has brutal moments ('Weenie Beenie', 'Wattershed') and classics in the making ('This Is a Call', 'Big Me', 'Alone+Easy Target'). But the war was won on its hammering second track. At the time, Dave Grohl would only admit – as he did to *Melody Maker* – 'that the personal experiences of the last four or five years' had informed the songs. However, as he eventually conceded to biographer Paul Brannigan, 'I don't think it's any secret that "I'll Stick Around" is about Courtney... Just read the fucking words!'

HEAD CREEPS
Alice in Chains

🇺🇸

BY Layne Staley | PRODUCED BY Toby Wright, Alice in Chains | FROM *Alice in Chains* (Columbia, 1995)

'Layne [Staley] came up with that,' Jerry Cantrell noted of the highlight of the singer's final album. 'It's a good fucking riff that turned out more brutal than I expected. I added that real stupid metal guitar to it to make it heavier.' The lurching monster's lyrics are oblique, but there's no mistaking their hounded bitterness. Possibly unwillingly to acknowledge that the band had conjured another album about heroin, Cantrell wrote in the *Music Box* collection's liner notes: 'It sounds like head creeps. Whatever that conjures up in your head, that's it.'

RAMMSTEIN
Rammstein

BY Till Lindemann, Richard Z. Kruspe, Paul H. Landers, Oliver Riedel, Christoph Schneider, Christian Lorenz | PRODUCED BY Jacob Hellner, Carl-Michael Herlöfsson | FROM *Herzeleid* (Motor Music, 1995)

...eventy people died in an air show disaster at Germany's ...amstein airbase in 1988. Never ones to shy away from ...tention-snaring controversy, the band who rose from ...e ashes of Orgasm Death Gimmick immortalised the ...vent in a churning yet strangely seductive song. 'They'd ...ay, "Ramstein, Ramstein!" singer Till Lindemann told ...MTV. 'So it came into our head and it stayed there. We just ...hanged the spelling slightly... It also became somewhat of ... provocation. By just repeating it, it became like a symbol ...or us; an anthem.'

ENGINE NO.9
Deftones

BY Stef Carpenter, Chi Cheng, Abe Cunningham, Chino Moreno | PRODUCED BY Terry Date, Deftones | FROM *Adrenaline* (Maverick, 1995)

'Engine Engine #9' was a hit for country singer Roger Miller in 1965. 'I was really into old classic music, like from the fifties and shit like that,' Stef Carpenter explained to Entertainment Ave. Thirty years later, Deftones looted the title for their debut album's most metal moment, although its inspiration was probably Black Sheep's sampling of Miller's song in their rap jam 'The Choice Is Yours (Revisited)'. The hip-hop connection was cemented when the band took to appending it in concert with Ice Cube's Korn-approved 'Wicked'.

CUCKOO FOR CACA
Faith No More

BY Mike Patton, Bill Gould, Roddy Bottum, Mike Bordin | PRODUCED BY Andy Wallace, Faith No More | FROM *King for a Day...Fool for a Lifetime* (Slash, 1995)

...don't use toilets,' Mike Patton boasted in 1992. 'I just ...on't. It's not a wild rock 'n' roll thing, it's a hobby: shit ...rrorism.' The singer's ever more lurid scatalogical tales ...ventually spawned what *Q* magazine hailed as 'the ...rrifyingly self-disgusted' 'Cuckoo for Caca' on Faith ...o More's fifth album. By that time, however, Patton had ...earned not to commit more coprophiliac confessions to ...ournalists' tape recorders. 'It's just... shit,' he grudgingly ...llowed to *NME* of the song's theme. 'Shit is... shitty people, ...arbage, everything.'

MORE HUMAN THAN HUMAN
White Zombie

BY Rob Zombie, Sean Yseult, Jay Yuenger | PRODUCED BY Terry Date, White Zombie | FROM *Astro-Creep: 2000 (Songs of Love, Destruction and Other Synthetic Delusions of the Electric Head)* (Geffen, 1995)

Awash with *Blade Runner* quotations ('I want more life, fucker,' 'More human than human, that's our motto'), White Zombie's biggest hit also owed a debt to Wiseblood's 'Stop Trying to Tie Me'. Quizzed on the similarity, Jim Thirlwell – half of Wiseblood, and producer of the demo that earned White Zombie a deal with Geffen – said, 'I know, I know...' But there was no denying the song's pounding power. 'It was like a John Bonham groove,' drummer John Tempesta told musicradar.com. 'Rob [Zombie] was like, "Keep playing that!"'

JESU DØD
Burzum

BY Varg Vikernes | PRODUCED BY Varg Vikernes | FROM *Filosofem* (Misanthropy, 1996)

'The greatest Norwegian black metal band...' Primordial singer A.A. Nemtheanga declared to loudersound.com of Varg Vikernes' solo project. 'Those first four albums are absolutely incredible. What Varg represents now [*see* 1994] is of no interest to me. If you don't listen to the first four Burzum albums then I think you're missing out.' You're also, probably, a great deal more cheerful – but if you want an eight-minute, horribly produced, monotonously riffed and yet singularly brilliant meditation on the crucifixion of Christ, look no further.

THE BEAUTIFUL PEOPLE
Marilyn Manson

BY Marilyn Manson, Twiggy Ramirez | PRODUCED BY Trent Reznor, Dave Ogilvie, Marilyn Manson | FROM *Antichrist Superstar* (Nothing/ Interscope, 1996)

'I remember recording it on my four-track with Twiggy [Ramirez] and my drummer Ginger [Fish] in a hotel room...' Marilyn Manson reflected to *Kerrang!* of his most durable hit. 'Playing the drum beat on the floor and then having m[y] drummer duplicate that on the drum machine... If I played you that four-track recording, it would sound identical.' As Ramirez recalled to artisannews.com, 'We were all on fire... and really good at what we were doing.' 'Maybe I'll end up in Las Vegas...' Manson mused to *Liquid*, 'singing easy listening versions of "The Beautiful People".'

TODAY IS A GOOD DAY TO DIE
Manowar

BY Joey DeMaio | PRODUCED BY Manowar FROM *Louder Than Hell* (Geffen, 1996)

'They're hilarious,' Robert Plant cackled to *Classic Rock*. 'Those little swords!' But this instrumental justifies Manowar's existence. Soaring orchestration and searing guitar bring to life 'Today Is a Good Day to Die' – a phrase attributed to Sioux chief Low Dog. Manowar dedicated it to 'All the muthafuckin' losers in the world who have tried to put us and our fans down. As the Indians fought and died for their way of life, so shall we. Great Spirit, we only wish to live long enough to piss on the graves of our enemies.' Watch out, Mr Plant...

BLEEDING ME
Metallica

BY James Hetfield, Lars Ulrich, Kirk Hammett | PRODUCED BY Bob Rock, James Hetfield, Lars Ulrich | FROM *Load* (Elektra, 1996)

'Have you lost inspiration?' producer Bob Rock asked during *Load*. James Hetfield's reply: 'There's plenty of hat[e] left in me.' Some of that was self-loathing; hailed by Flea in *Rolling Stone* as Metallica's 'infinite well of sadness – a hell of a lot of pain and anger'. That spurted forth on the lacerating 'Bleeding Me'. 'We loved playing it,' Hetfield noted to *Kerrang!* 'But the reaction was like, "Bleuurgh!", so we stopped... Then people would start coming up and saying, How come you're not playing "Bleeding Me"?, and[d] we'd say, Cos you didn't get it!'

GOOD GOD
orn

BY Fieldy, Jonathan Davis, J. 'Munky' Shaffer, David Silveria, Brian 'Head' Welch | PRODUCED BY Ross Robinson | FROM *Life Is Peachy* (Immortal, 1996)

's about a guy I knew in school who I thought was my end, but who fucked me,' Jonathan Davis noted of *Life Peachy*'s standout. 'He came into my life with nothing, ung out at my house, lived off me, and made me do shit I dn't really wanna do. I was into new romantic music and e was a mod, and he'd tell me if I didn't dress like a mod e wouldn't be my friend... Whenever I had plans to go a date with a chick he'd sabotage it, because he didn't ave a date or nothing. He was a gutless fucking nothing.' etty origins... but what a fabulous result.

QOODS
antera

BY Dimebag Darrell, Vinnie Paul, Phil Anselmo, Rex Brown | PRODUCED BY Terry Date, Vinnie Paul | FROM *The Great Southern Trendkill* (EastWest, 1996)

he *Great Southern Trendkill*, Vinnie Paul admitted to volvermag.com, is 'the most abrasive and darkest record antera's made'. Nonetheless, it boasts the band's most eautiful song, with a guitar solo regarded as Dimebag's est. It evolved out of what he described to *Guitar World* as long-assed, singalong-type lead section', from a lengthy strumental in Pantera's club-show era. 'It's a blazing solo ith a really cool rhythm section underneath it,' Rex Brown ld songfacts.com. 'I'm really proud of the bass line. I think at was Dime's favourite solo.'

THROUGH SILVER IN BLOOD
Neurosis

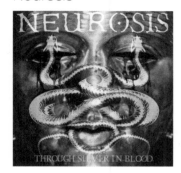

BY Dave Edwardson, Steve Von Till | PRODUCED BY Neurosis, Billy Anderson | FROM *Through Silver in Blood* (Relapse, 1996)

'Neurosis heavily influenced us,' Mastodon's Bill Kelliher confessed to noisey.vice.com. The title cut of *Through Silver in Blood* is a fine introduction to the post-metallers' claustrophobic blend of Toolesque prog, Sabbath-style sludge and Deftonesy anguish. And the title itself? 'A very spiritual statement to us,' bassist Dave Edwardson told chroniclesofchaos.com, 'dealing with humanity's place in the cosmos and... alchemy and psychedelics.' But the average metaller, he conceded, 'might think it means stab someone with a silver knife.'

(GOTTA GET SOME ACTION) NOW!
The Hellacopters

BY Nicke Andersson, Andreas Svensson, Kenny Håkansson, Robert Eriksson | PRODUCED BY Tomas Skogsberg | FROM *Supershitty to the Max* (White Jazz, 1996)

'How serious is The Hellacopters?' asked an interviewer in 1996. A fair question: Nicke Andersson drummed for death metallers Entombed and Andreas Svensson founded sleaze rockers Backyard Babies, yet now they called themselves Nicke Hellacopter and Dregen, and played Motörhead-fuelled garage rock. 'Deadly,' Svensson replied. 'I wouldn't call it "serious", though,' Andersson added, 'cos it sounds boring. It's from my heart.' Neither serious nor boring, '(Gotta Get Some Action) Now' sums them up in three explosive minutes.

VIETNOW
Rage Against the Machine

BY Zack de la Rocha, Tom Morello, Brad Wilk, Tim Commerfor[d] PRODUCED BY Brendan O'Brien, Rage Against the Machine | FROM *Evil Empire* (Epic, 1996)

Bludgeoning from beginning to end, *Evil Empire* fleetingl[y] flirts with a quirkier take on Rage's rock-rap formula. The funky 'Vietnow' is more impish than imposing – it even quotes The Sugarhill Gang's 'Rapper's Delight'. 'The grea[t] positive development…' Tom Morello enthused to *Guitar World*, 'is that it's now okay for people who like hip-hop to also like Soundgarden.' And while Zack's attack on right-wing radio hits targets that include Oliver North and Rodney King's assailant Stacey Koon, it's the 'fuck it, turn off!' refrain that will stay in your head all day.

NANCY BOY
Placebo

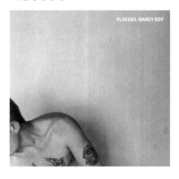

BY Brian Molko, Stefan Olsdal, Robert Schultzberg | PRODUCED BY Brad Wood | FROM *Placebo* (Hut, 1996)

'I'm still not even sure what that song is about,' Brian Molko confessed to noisey.vice.com of Placebo's first hit. 'It seems to be about pansexual hedonism.' 'Nancy Boy' was, as David Bowie remarked, 'a terrific song for a bunch of chaps to sing… they'll probably be huge.' But its success was by no means set in stone. 'We were in an indie club in Scotland…' Molko shuddered. 'The place was packed when they put "Nancy Boy" on and it cleared the dancefloor. I turned around to Stefan [Olsdal, bassist] and said, "I think we're fucked!"'

STINKFIST
Tool

BY Danny Carey, Adam Jones, Maynar[d] James Keenan, Paul D'Amour | PRODUCED BY Tool, David Bottrill FROM *Ænima* (Zoo Entertainment, 1996)

'The main riff here is so goddamn groovy!' Katatonia's Anders Nyström enthused to *Total Guitar*. 'What a prime example of how you can create something so striking with just two/three notes in the right pattern.' Tool, Alex Lifeson agreed to *Guitar World*, are 'intensely dynamic, ye[t] heavy, even when what they're playing is light'. And they even won over Fred Durst: 'Probably the best band on the planet,' he told MTV. 'There's something wrong with thos[e] guys. They're *too* good. They know something that the rest of the world doesn't know.'

ＲＯＯＴＳ ＢＬＯＯＤＹ ＲＯＯＴＳ
Sepultura

BY Max Cavalera, Igor Cavalera, Andreas Kisser, Paulo Jr.| PRODUCED BY Ross Robinson, Sepultura | FROM *Roots* (Roadrunner, 1996)

...ou wonder why we sound the way we do?' Max Cavalera ...ked *Kerrang!* 'We are born in scum, we live in filth and we ...e in dirt.'

In their first decade, Sepultura evolved from poorly ...oduced wannabes to grooving, thrashing, front runners. ...nd in 1996, they slowed, yet sacrificed not an iota of ...eaviness, on their sixth album, their masterpiece and their ...est seller: *Roots*. 'Produced by Ross Robinson, mixed ...y [Slayer associate] Andy Wallace, it's incredible,' Dave ...rohl marvelled to *Q*.

'IT'S A FUCKING METAL TRACK WITH A CARNIVAL PASSING THROUGH THE MIDDLE OF IT'
DAVE GROHL

Drawing on the tribal rhythms and issues of their homeland, it spawned an anthem in the grinding 'Roots Bloody Roots' – its title, obviously, influenced by Black Sabbath's 'Sabbath Bloody Sabbath' (*see* 1973).

'It's about believe in yourself; about be proud of your heritage, proud of where you come from,' Cavalera informed songfacts.com. 'I learned the value of simplicity; that sometimes, when you have less, there's actually more than if you have a bunch of stuff... *Roots* is full of simple riffs and simple songs that are very powerful.'

A staple for Sepultura, Soulfly and the Cavalera Conspiracy, the song has lived up to its video's opening quotation, from Nigerian writer Chinua Achebe: 'Suffering should be creative; should give birth to something good and lovely.'

ＢＲＥＡＴＨＥ
Prodigy

BY Liam Howlett, Keith Flint, Maxim Reality | PRODUCED BY Liam Howlett | FROM *The Fat of the Land* (XL, 1997)

...have to write angry music,' Liam Howlett told *Kerrang!* ...ot like Rage Against the Machine – not politically angry ...but just a reaction to the energy... that comes from angry, ...rd sounds.' To the astonishment of elder metalheads, ...*errang!* readers voted 'Breathe' single of the year. 'I'd ...e to see anyone challenge us,' commented Keith Flint, ...nd say we're not a loud band.' They went on to headline ...etal festivals. 'I'll get down to anything by the Prodigy,' ...nkin Park's Joe Hahn informed *Shortlist*. 'Let's go with ...reathe". It's so good for any club occasion.'

ＷＥＥＤＳ
Life of Agony

BY Alan Robert, Keith Caputo, Joey Z., Dan Richardson, Sal Abruscato | PRODUCED BY Phil Nicolo, Life of Agony | FROM *Soul Searching Sun* (Roadrunner, 1997)

'We played with metal bands, pop bands... even David Bowie,' bassist and lyricist Alan Robert reflected to uberrock.co.uk in 2017. 'We've played with Foo Fighters, Metallica and Tool... with Wu-Tang... So we kind of fit everywhere and nowhere.' Two decades before, Life of Agony had fit into the mainstream, having streamlined their hardcore sound for the radio-friendly 'Weeds', but that didn't stop the band falling apart. Happily, reunited with singer Keith – now Mina – Caputo, the band have restored the song to a singalong live staple.

DAMMIT
Blink-182

BY Mark Hoppus, Tom DeLonge, Scott Raynor | PRODUCED BY Mark Trombino | FROM *Dude Ranch* (MCA, 1997)

Two albums in, Blink-182 hit on the formula that would turn them into million-sellers. Like most of *Dude Ranch*, 'Dammit' was a sub-three-minute pop-punker. But unlike most of *Dude Ranch*, it stuck in your head after it finished. Remixed, censored and appended with '(Growing Up)', it became their first hit. The track was memorable for the band, too: 'When I sing "Dammit", a song written more than fifteen years ago,' Mark Hoppus told Reddit in 2012, 'I remember the exact day I wrote it; what I was going through; what it meant to me.'

LOCO
Coal Chamber

BY Dez Fafara, Miguel 'Meegs' Rascon, Rayna Foss, Mike 'Bug' Cox | PRODUCED BY Jay Gordon, Jay Baumgardner | FROM *Coal Chamber* (Roadrunner, 1997)

'People think I'm a little nuts, but really I'm crazy for music' frontman Dez Fafara revealed to songfacts.com of Coal Chamber's best-loved song. 'I was living in Los Angeles, trying to come out of that environment after it was totally devastated by hair metal.' His band's first single, guitarist Miguel 'Meegs' Rascon told lollipopmagazine.com, 'gets really heavy. It's spooky and kinda eerie.' But how would they recreate the crazed cut's layers live? 'If you see Miguel tap-dancing on stage,' bassist Rayna Foss quipped, 'you'll know why.'

FUEL
Metallica

BY James Hetfield, Lars Ulrich, Kirk Hammett | PRODUCED BY Bob Rock, James Hetfield, Lars Ulrich | FROM *Reload* (Elektra, 1997)

'Fuel', Kirk Hammett told *Guitar World*, 'was one of the first tracks [during the *Load* sessions] that I actually played a guitar solo on…That was a real treat for me, because it really felt like I was going in a new direction.' Reminiscent of 'The Train Kept A-Rollin'' (*see* 1965), the track became a live staple. Yet asked how they chose which songs went on which album, James Hetfield cackled, '*Reload* has all of the crappy ones… There's a little more extremeness on this one, but there are some big-time, epic, heavy riffs, too. They're not pop singles.'

LIKE THIS WITH THE DEVIL
Entombed

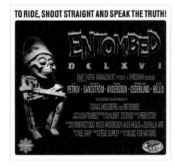

BY Nicke Andersson, Uffe Cederland, Alex Hellid, L.G. Petrov | PRODUCED BY Tomas Skogsberg, Entombed | FROM *DCLXVI: To Ride, Shoot Straight and Speak the Truth!* (Threeman Recordings, 1997)

'Entombed started to be a straight-up death 'n' roll band,' Cancer Bats' Scott Middleton raved to musicfeeds.com.au 'I was hooked! Amazing groove and riffs.' The acclaimed *DCLXVI: To Ride, Shoot Straight and Speak the Truth!* completed an evolution from the death metal of 1990's *Left Hand Path*. Along the way – via 1993's *Wolverine Blues* and Nicke Andersson's side-project the Hellacopters (*see* 1996) – Entombed embraced Motörhead-tinged punk. The result was an irresistible set on which roaring anthems tumbled one after another.

MY OWN SUMMER (SHOVE IT)
Deftones

BY Chino Moreno, Stef Carpenter, Chi Cheng, Abe Cunningham | PRODUCED BY Terry Date, Deftones | FROM *Around the Fur* (Maverick, 1997)

he Cure and Depeche Mode and bands like that were ...motionally heavy...' Chino Moreno opined to Dutch ...V. 'That moved me more than somebody screaming. ...o that's why I never really listened to heavy metal. So ...ith [*Around the Fur*], I figured I could make it equally as ...eavy... but without yelling.' And what inspired the sun-...ourning lines of the Deftones' first anthem? 'I'd be in the ...udio recording all night. I'd try to sleep during the day ...nd I couldn't because of all the light. I ended up putting ...nfoil over all the windows.'

MONKEY WRENCH
Foo Fighters

BY Dave Grohl, Nate Mendel, Pat Smear | PRODUCED BY Gil Norton | FROM *The Colour and the Shape* (Roswell, 1997)

'It was a riff that turned into another riff...' explained Dave Grohl, 'and ended up being a nice little power punk song.' The result: 'A song about realizing that you are the source of all of the problems in a relationship and you love the other person so much, you want to free them of the problem – which is actually yourself.' Its breathless second verse is formidable, as is Grohl's powerhouse drumming. On joining the Foos, Taylor Hawkins recalled to the *NME* that he thought, 'Oh my god, this song's going to kill me. It's really hard!'

...ETOX
...trapping Young Lad

BY Devin Townsend | PRODUCED BY Devin Townsend, Daniel Bergstrand | FROM *City* (Century Media, 1997)

...hat do you get if you cross one of metal's most inventive ...uitarists with one of its most astounding drummers? You ...et Devin Townsend and Gene Hoglan making an unholy ...cket. 'Strapping really needed a machine,' Hoglan told ...visibleoranges.com, 'a locomotive to just drive the ...ongs.' From what Townsend declared 'the real Strapping ...cord... the ultimate one', 'Detox' is like having your head ...peatedly sliced open. And its lyrics, he told *Instant* ...agazine, were 'therapeutic... *City* cleared me out of a lot ... stuff that I was going through'.

AFRAID
Mötley Crüe

BY Nikki Sixx | PRODUCED BY Scott Humphrey, Nikki Sixx, Tommy Lee | FROM *Generation Swine* (Elektra, 1997)

'Afraid' was inspired by Nikki Sixx's feelings for actress Donna D'Errico – who fled after seeing 'this ugly rock star in a robe coming out of a giant white-marble-filled house lit up by the rising sun. It looked like a scene from *Scarface*'. The song was one of an underrated album's more celebrated moments. 'I don't like computers and sampling,' Vince Neil grumbled to *Classic Rock* of *Generation Swine*'s industrial leanings. 'What's wrong with tape? But I was just getting back in the band, and there were a couple of good songs like "Afraid".'

ENGEL
Rammstein

BY Richard Z. Kruspe, Paul H. Landers, Till Lindemann, Christian 'Flake' Lorenz, Christoph 'Doom' Schneider | PRODUCED BY Jacob Hellner, Rammstein | FROM *Sehnsucht* (Motor Music, 1997)

Scorpions' 'Wind of Change' is hard rock's whistling peak – but, in an alternate universe, 'Engel' is on everyone's lips. It amped up the eeriness with vocals by Christiane Hebold of Bobo In White Wooden Houses (whose drummer Sascha Moser played with Richard Z. Kruspe in Rammstein's progenitors, Orgasm Death Gimmick). And as if a *From Dusk Till Dawn*-pastiching video wasn't enough, David Lynch – as *Revolver* noted – 'snuck in a small tribute [in his 2017 *Twin Peaks* reboot] by having his character Gordon Cole whistle the iconic refrain'.

GRADUATE
Third Eye Blind

BY Stephan Jenkins, Kevin Cadogan, Arion Salazar | PRODUCED BY Stephan Jenkins, Eric Valentine | FROM *Third Eye Blind* (Elektra, 1997)

'I'm still standing in front of some suit at a record company asking permission,' Stephan Jenkins griped to *Billboard*. 'I felt like some kind of lap-dancer, some student again, like I was still in high school... What it's really saying is, "I'm not really asking if I can graduate. I'm not asking for your permission. I'm beyond your permission. I'm beyond your control."' 'Graduate' was one of five hits that made Third Eye Blind's debut a smash. And, as Jenkins noted to songfacts.com, 'The audience, they ignite off of it. I'm a vampire. They fill me up with fresh blood.'

YE ENTRANCEMPERIUM
Emperor

BY Ihsahn, Samoth, Euronymous | PRODUCED BY Ihsahn, Pytten, Samoth | FROM *Anthems to the Welkin at Dusk* (Candlelight, 1997)

'Emperor really changed the dynamic...' Trivium's Matt Heafy noted to musicradar.com. '[*Anthems...*] opened up with clean guitar and there's this classical singing; it has chaotic moments and beautiful moments all in one. Emperor makes such interesting black metal with these big dramatic moments.' A prime example was 'Ye Entrancemperium', kickstarted by a Mayhem cut, hence the credit for that band's deceased Euronymous. The album, Rob Halford shivered to *Rolling Stone*, is 'sonic blasphemy from the dark side'.

BREED TO BREATHE
Napalm Death

BY Shane Embury | PRODUCED BY Colin Richardson | FROM *Inside the Torn Apart* (Earache, 1997)

'This album was a strange one...' bassist and writer Shane Embury reflected to decibelmagazine.com. 'What we did on this record [was] to add guitar lines to make the riffs weirder... Regardless of whether people agree or not, this stuff was exciting to us. Soundgarden was a band I'd love for years, especially how they had subtle guitar lines in the background to their riffs, so we tried to incorporate that into our normal riffing style.' Hardcore fans griped, but the groovetastic 'Breed to Breathe' is a stupendous opener that Cornell & Co would be proud of.

GREAT BIG WHITE WORLD
Marilyn Manson

🇺🇸

BY Marilyn Manson, Madonna Wayne Gacy, Twiggy Ramirez, Zim Zum | PRODUCED BY Michael Beinhorn, Marilyn Manson, Sean Beavan | FROM *Mechanical Animals* (Nothing, 1998)

'We weren't afraid to be bombastic...' Marilyn Manson declared to *Juice* of *Mechanical Animals*' songs, 'and to make them with elaborate arrangements.' The album's beautiful opener set the tone. 'Manson created a fictitious spaceman character for the record called Omega, who'd fallen down to earth, which was obviously very similar to Ziggy Stardust,' Creeper's Will Gould noted to loudersound.com. Manson confessed to *Kerrang!*: 'I have great admiration for David Bowie. This record reflects the music that meant a lot to me as a kid.'

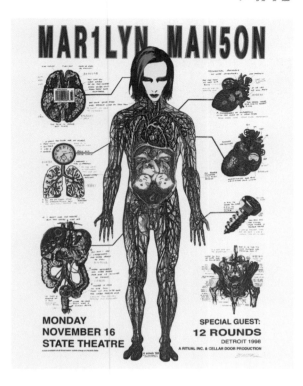

CELEBRITY SKIN
Hole

🇺🇸 🇨🇦

BY Courtney Love, Eric Erlandson, Billy Corgan | PRODUCED BY Michael Beinhorn | FROM *Celebrity Skin* (DGC, 1998)

'No self-respecting female,' declared Courtney Love, would have written the opening riff of Hole's biggest song: 'It's so cheesy.' Step forward *grand fromage* Billy Corgan. 'They can be mad about it if they want,' he bragged to Howard Stern, 'but it's still my riff.' 'He didn't play on the record,' guitarist Eric Erlandson clarified to *The Georgia Straight*. 'He came in and helped us arrange a few songs... I just get a little bit pissy about it because the sound on the album is more me and [producer] Michael Beinhorn than Billy Corgan.'

I THINK I'M PARANOID
Garbage

BY Duke Erikson, Shirley Manson, Steve Marker, Butch Vig | PRODUCED BY Garbage FROM *Version 2.0* (Mushroom, 1998)

'I Think I'm Paranoid' summed up Shirley Manson's feelings during the making of *Version 2.0*. 'I was living by myself in a hotel and I had no one to really talk to,' she complained to *CMJ New Music Monthly*. 'I'd go to the studio and we'd work and I'd come back by myself... The whole record is, in a way, very introspective... trying to reassure myself while I'm going crazy.' Twenty years later, she reflected to the *Guardian*: 'I was not good... in a weird hotel; couldn't drive; had no money; was at the mercy of my bandmates who tired of driving me around.'

FREAK ON A LEASH
Korn

BY Jonathan Davis, James 'Munky' Shaffer, Fieldy, Brian 'Head' Welch, David Silveria | PRODUCED BY Korn, Steve Thompson, Toby Wright | FROM *Follow the Leader* (Immortal, 1998)

'Prior to this, I'd only heard Bush and other rock bands like that, but nothing freaky,' Devin 'Ghost' Sola of Motionless in White told loudersound.com. 'This opened me up to Slipknot, Mudvayne... heavier rock.' 'That's my song that rails out against the music industry,' Jonathan Davis declared. 'I'm a fuckin' prostitute. Like I'm this freak paraded around, but I got corporate America fuckin' making all the money while it's taking a part of me. It's like they stole something from me. They stole my innocence and I'm not calm any more. I worry constantly.'

BITTER PEACE
Slayer

BY Jeff Hanneman | PRODUCED BY Rick Rubin, Slayer | FROM *Diabolus in Musica* (American, 1998)

'Sometimes our albums turn out godlike,' Jeff Hanneman told *Metal Hammer*'s Joel McIver, 'and sometimes they turn out lame. Sometimes people just don't like what we do.' Some Slayer fans – and Kerry King – dismiss *Diabolus in Musica* for its nu-metal leanings. Yet the most blatantly nu cut, 'Stain of Mind', is a setlist staple, and the opening 'Bitter Peace' is a quintessential slice of brutality. 'I was thinking, "What do I want to hear on this record?"' writer Hanneman declared. 'If it sounds modern, it's because we're into modern music and that shows.'

THE SOAPMAKERS
Clutch

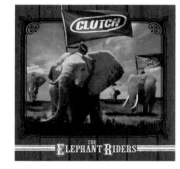

BY Neil Fallon, Tim Su Dan Maines, Jean-Pa Gaster | PRODUCED BY Jack Douglas | FROM *The Elephant Riders* (Columbia, 1997)

'This album still sounds as weird and awesome as it did when I bought it,' CKY's Jess Margera marvelled to *Metal Hammer*. 'A somewhat heavy band from Maryland, heavily influenced by Fugazi, Deep Purple and Bad Brains, went into Jimi Hendrix's studio and got John Lennon's producer. That is as strange as it gets, and the results are like nothing I have ever heard before.' But if a fifty-minute, airship-and-elephant-strewn retelling of the American Civil War sounds too much to take, check out this sub-three-minute, super-groovy motherfucker.

MERCYFUL FATE
Metallica

BY King Diamond, Hank Shermann | PRODUCED BY Bob Rock, James Hetfield, Lars Ulrich | FROM *Garage Inc.* (Elektra, 1998)

ate would play a great riff and never come back to it,' ames Hetfield grumbled to *Guitar World*. The solution: medley of the Danes' 'Satan's Fall', 'Curse of the haraohs', 'A Corpse Without Soul', 'Into the Coven' and vil' (*see* 1983). 'Their stuff was so incredibly heavy and rogressive,' Kirk Hammett noted. 'Fate had an incredibly uge influence on us.' 'They had long songs that were urneys through all different moods and dynamics,' Lars lrich explained to *Metal Hammer*. 'They were responsible or us lengthening our own songs.'

MOLINOS DE VIENTO
Mägo de Oz

BY Salvador Rogelio García, Francisco Javier Gómez De La Serna | PRODUCED BY Goyo Esteban | FROM *La leyenda de La Mancha* (Locomotive, 1998)

emember when Iron Maiden were possessed by the pirit of Jethro Tull and made the storytelling *Seventh Son f a Seventh Son*? Spanish nutters Mägo de Oz ('Wizard f Oz') surely do – they were, after all, originally called ansilvania, after the instrumental on Maiden's debut. or their third outing, Mägo conjured a concept album of eir own: *La leyenda de La Mancha*, based on the classic panish tale *Don Quixote*. Its windmills motif is the theme f their much loved 'Molinos de Viento' – a perky blend of edieval fiddle and, oh yes, Iron Maiden.

BAWITDABA
Kid Rock

BY Kid Rock, Uncle Kracker, Jason Krause, Busy Bee, Sylvia Robinson | PRODUCED BY Kid Rock, John Travis | FROM *Devil Without a Cause* (Atlantic, 1998)

'Tough to beat,' Kid Rock conceded to *Rolling Stone* of the cut that made *Devil Without a Cause* his breakthrough and biggest seller. 'I either do it when I come out or close to the end [of my set]. Put some fucking bitches shaking their ass, shoot some fire in the air, scream out your fucking name, people are pulling out their fucking hair.' The original version urged, 'Get in the pit and try to kill someone!' Rock changed 'kill' to 'love' and told *The Baltimore Sun* he was glad he'd done so. In a mosh pit, he noted, 'You fall down, someone helps you up.'

PRETTY FLY (FOR A WHITE GUY)
The Offspring

BY Dexter Holland | PRODUCED BY Dave Jerden | FROM *Americana* (Columbia, 1998)

'People in high school would go, "I know exactly who this guy's talking about,"' frontman Dexter Holland explained to *Spin*. His target? '[People who] are from, like, Omaha, Nebraska – regular, white-bread guys – but who act like they're from Compton. It's so fake.' The satire was heralded with a nod to the garbled German of Def Leppard's 'Rock of Ages'. Inevitably, the song was made a hit by, largely, the people whom it satirised. 'That's kind of the beauty,' said Holland. 'Making fun of people who don't know they're being made fun of.'

POWERTRIP
Monster Magnet

BY Dave Wyndorf | PRODUCED BY Dave Wyndorf, Matt Hyde | FROM *Powertrip* (A&M, 1998)

'When I was a kid, I went out and saw Kiss and the Ramones,' Dave Wyndorf reminisced. 'These guys rocked… They did it! And now I sit there and watch bands crying into their 7-Up, and it's just too much.' The antidote was Monster Magnet's most rocktastic album, from which the title cut was one of two anthems ('Space Lord' being the other). 'I wanted to make a full-on, devil-horn-in-the-air, fuck-everybody, I'm-gonna-burn-your-house-down record,' Wyndorf declared to *Spin*. 'It's time to put on a pair of leather pants and breathe fire.'

AGAINST
Sepultura

BY Andreas Kisser, Igor Cavalera | PRODUCED BY Howard Benson, Sepultura | FROM *Against* (Roadrunner, 1998)

'A very strong album, very passionate,' Igor Cavalera told chroniclesofchaos.com about Sepultura's first without his brother Max. 'It was very influenced by a lot of hardcore bands, which makes me very proud.' Nowhere is that punk influence more evident than on the title cut, while heavy-as-fuck Sepultura is represented by the monstrous 'Old Earth'. '*Against* is the most important album in our career,' Andreas Kisser reflected to metalunderground.com two decades later. 'Without *Against*, we wouldn't be able to continue as Sepultura.'

THE GHOST OF TOM JOAD
Rage Against the Machine

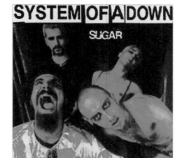

BY Bruce Springsteen | PRODUCED BY Brendan O'Brien | FROM *No Boundaries – A Benefit for the Kosovar Refugees* (Epic, 1998)

'One of Bruce [Springsteen]'s best songs,' Tom Morello remarked to *Rolling Stone* of 'The Ghost of Tom Joad'. 'It really cuts to the core of his social justice writing.' Originally a 'plaintive ballad' on Springsteen's 1995 album of the same name, the song became a monster in Rage Against the Machine's hands. A rough version graced a single packaged with a 1997 video, but the one to seek out is the extraordinary version that appeared on the *No Boundaries* benefit album (also featuring Korn and Sabbath) and later on Rage's *Renegades*.

DRAGULA
Rob Zombie

BY Rob Zombie, Scott Humphrey | PRODUCED BY Scott Humphrey, Rob Zombie | FROM *Hellbilly Deluxe* (Geffen, 1998)

'Aside from the fact that it's a super-badass song, it's the first song that we as a band covered,' Motionless in White's Chris Cerulli told loudersound.com. 'We recorded it and put it out on Hallowe'en years ago... People seemed to be really cool with what we did to it.' The 'Dragula' title came from a car in *The Munsters*; 'A classic show,' Rob Zombie told *Billboard*, 'with great comic characters.' He even rolled up to the 1998 MTV awards in the vehicle itself. Did he buy it? 'Ah, god, I don't have enough money. I'm no Herman Munster, baby.'

SUGAR
System of a Down

BY Serj Tankian, Daron Malakian, Shavo Odadjian, John Dolmayan | PRODUCED BY Rick Rubin, System of a Down | FROM *System of a Down* (American, 1998)

'There was no point of reference,' Rick Rubin told *Rolling Stone* of his Armenian-American charges. 'It was so unusual.' Case in point: System's first single (and regular set-closer). 'We never expected "Sugar" or "Spiders" to be embraced by MTV or to be on the radio,' drummer John Dolmayan told Shoutweb. 'We never expected *anything* to be on the radio. We thought we would be a very underground band. But, for some reason, the mainstream has kind of accepted it... It's pushing the boundaries of the mainstream, which is good.'

CHRISTEEN
Devin Townsend

🇨🇦 BY Devin Townsend, Ginger Wildheart | PRODUCED BY Devin Townsend | FROM *Infinity* (HevyDevy, 1998)

'Massive guitars, trombones, a choir, an orchestra and techno beats, two hundred tracks of vocals...' Devin Townsend told *Metal Hammer* of the first album issued under his own name. 'It's an organic chaos record.' *Infinity* hit a poppy peak with 'Christeen', co-written by Brit maverick Ginger – with whose band Townsend toured in 1994. 'They liked *action* and *activity* and *loud*,' he told Wildhearts biographer Gary Davidson. 'I don't like any of those... [Ginger is] a brilliant mind, but the level of activity that his person runs at makes me very tired.'

HIGHER
Creed

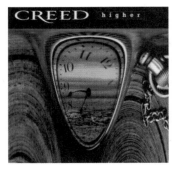

🇺🇸 BY Mark Tremonti, Scott Stapp | PRODUCED BY John Kurzweg | FROM *Human Clay* (Wind-Up, 1999)

'There was no such thing as a lukewarm Creed fan,' drummer Scott Phillips told *Classic Rock*. 'You either loved us or hated us.' Millions loved 'em: 'Higher' and *Human Clay* were chart-toppers. 'Kids who aren't allowed to listen to Marilyn Manson can listen to us,' guitarist Mark Tremonti assured cnn.com. 'There's nothing wrong with what we're saying.' However, as singer Scott Stapp admitted to songfacts.com, 'At the time I penned that song, my view of what heaven on earth meant was very narrow, very naïve and very wrapped up in ego and self-fulfillment.'

GIVEN TO FLY
Pearl Jam

🇺🇸 BY Mike McCready, Eddie Vedder | PRODUCED BY Brendan O'Brien, Pearl Jam | FROM *Yield* (Epic, 1998)

'One of those amazing coincidences,' cracked Robert Plant of this exultant classic's debt to 'Going to California'. 'Do you think that somebody sang it to them in the cradle?' 'That was definitely one of the songs I was listening to,' Mike McCready admitted to *Massive!* Of 'Given to Fly', Eddie Vedder told *The Philadelphia Inquirer*. 'The music almost gives you this feeling of flight. I really love singing the part at the end, which is about rising above anybody's comments about what you do... not condemning the whole world because of the actions of a few.'

FUJIYAMA ATTACK
Guitar Wolf

🇯🇵 BY Seiji, Toru, Billy | PRODUCED BY Guitar Wolf | FROM *Jet Generation* (Ki/oon, 1999)

'This is the loudest album ever recorded,' warn liner notes on Guitar Wolf's sixth outing. 'Playing at normal volume may cause irreparable damage to stereo equipment. Use at your own risk.' *Jet Generation* is the one to choose if you've yet to be Wolf-blooded, boasting as it does three of the trio's best-loved cuts: the title track, a cover of 'Summertime Blues' and 'Fujiyama Attack'. Think modern garage rock started with The Hives? Check out the gonzoid Ramonesing of Seiji [Guitarwolf], Billy [Basswolf] and Toru [Drumwolf], and think again.

STARFUCKERS, INC.
Nine Inch Nails

BY Trent Reznor, Charlie Clouser, Carly Simon | PRODUCED BY Trent Reznor, Alan Moulder | FROM *The Fragile* (Nothing, 1999)

't's about everybody that I thought was full of shit…' Trent Reznor told *NME*, asked if the 'Starfuckers' were Marilyn Manson and Courtney Love. 'There's bits of those guys n there… but it wasn't solely meant to be a "fuck you Manson" kind of song. It was also meant to be tongue-n-cheek and ridiculous.' By the time he and Manson kissed and made up for the song's release as a single and video – renamed 'Starsuckers, Inc.' – 'everybody' included Courtney, Fred Durst, Gene Simmons, Michael Stipe, and Reznor and Manson themselves.

STACKED ACTORS
Foo Fighters

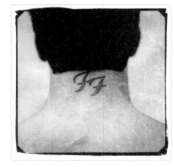

BY Dave Grohl, Taylor Hawkins, Nate Mendel PRODUCED BY Adam Kasper, Foo Fighters | FROM *There Is Nothing Left to Lose* (Roswell, 1999)

'I remember so clearly the first time that I heard it,' Mike Duce of Lower Than Atlantis noted to loudersound.com of 'Stacked Actors', 'because the riff is so heavy.' The music was matched by lyrical vitriol, whose targets are thought to include Courtney Love. 'There's a sentence or two probably dedicated to her,' Taylor Hawkins confided to *NME*. 'Dave would never fully admit it to you, but *I* know.' Courtney thought the same, and duly improvised a song for Grohl, entitled 'Kurt Hated You', on Howard Stern's radio show.

TESTIFY
Rage Against the Machine

BY Tim Commerford, Zack de la Rocha, Tom Morello, Brad Wilk | PRODUCED BY Brendan O'Brien, Rage Against the Machine | FROM *The Battle of Los Angeles* (Epic, 1999)

'From the very first rehearsals, the shit was just raw,' Tom Morello told *Spin* of Rage's final original album. 'It was thrilling to go into our little Hollywood rehearsal studio every day: the funk was deep, the rock was heavy… We could just close our eyes and picture sixty thousand people jumping up and down. Just going off.' Stick a pin in *The Battle of Los Angeles* and you'll hit an awesome anthem (including the storming singles 'Guerilla Radio' and 'Sleep Now in the Fire'), so why not start at the beginning, with the stadium-sized 'Testify'?

BEG FOR ME
Korn

BY Jonathan Davis James 'Munky' Shaffer, Fieldy, Brian 'Head' Welch, David Silveria | PRODUCED BY Brendan O'Brien | FROM *Issues* (Immortal, 1999)

'I was worried about losing my edge...' the newly sober Jonathan Davis fretted to *Melody Maker* during 1998's *Follow the Leader* tour. 'But there's so much shit from going through my anxiety attacks that this next album is going to be about that.' The ensuing *Issues* didn't stint on angst, and 'Beg for Me' summarised Davis' malaise. But his hand-wringing was mitigated by monstrous riffing. 'We wanted totally heavy, killer guitar riffs that were kinda weird, but really slamming,' Brian 'Head' Welch told writer Jon Wiederhorn. 'And they had to have a groove.'

BREAK STUFF
Limp Bizkit

BY Fred Durst, Wes Borland, Sam Rivers, John Otto, DJ Lethal, Brendan O'Brien | PRODUCED BY Terry Date, Limp Bizkit | FROM *Significant Other* (Flip, 1999)

'Break Stuff,' Fred Durst told *Blender*, 'was the one song that got us the most excited about what we were doing. Just taking one riff and attacking it with the bounce and the swing that we did was really powerful.' It was simple ('We're definitely a dumb rock band,' Wes Borland conceded to *Classic Rock*) but it was effective – although not everyone was won over. 'I couldn't understand why Limp Bizkit was big,' Kerry King complained to udiscovermusic.com. 'If this is the way that music's going, then fuck this, I hate it.'

FILLIP
Muse

BY Matt Bellamy | PRODUCED BY John Leckie | FROM *Showbiz* (Mushroom, 1999)

Before they became the new Queen, Muse were the new Radiohead, with Jeff Buckley on vocals. But at heart, they've always been rock-lovin' lads, as anyone who witnesses their riff-stuffed live show will attest. And amid the contrivances of their debut is this punchy winner. 'Not a fan favourite and somewhat forgotten,' mourns musewiki.org. However, it made 'regular appearances in most setlists... Upon the release of *Origin of Symmetry*, "Fillip" was performed far less than before, until November 2001 when it was performed for the last time.'

WHAT'S MY AGE AGAIN?
Blink-182

BY Mark Hoppus, Tom DeLonge, Travis Barker | PRODUCED BY Jerry Finn | FROM *Enema of the State* (MCA, 1999)

'We were really hitting our stride...' Mark Hoppus reflected to *Spin* of Blink's breakthrough. 'It was just the right cycle of music for us. People were over the boy-band, pop-princess, manufactured sensibility, and were excited for guitars and angst and energy and enthusiasm.' *Enema of the State* and its hits 'What's My Age Again?' (originally known as 'Peter Pan Complex'), 'All the Small Things' and 'Adam's Song' sold by the millions. 'I love the fact everybody thinks we're juvenile,' Tom DeLonge gloated to *Melody Maker*. 'We don't give a fuck.'

T THE HEART OF WINTER
mmortal

BY Abbath, Demonaz, Horgh | PRODUCED BY Peter Tägtgren | FROM *At the Heart of Winter* (Osmose, 1999)

'My mother is from the north of Norway,' Immortal lyricist arald 'Demonaz' Nævdal told *Kerrang!* 'The winters were really hard when we were visiting up there. I loved at. They were dark times, with only a couple of hours' unlight a day.' Hey presto: fans' favourite Immortal album. When the drums and the guitars and everything come ...' frontman Abbath noted to chroniclesofchaos.com of s elegant title cut, 'we go into the depths of the north... he beauty turns into a brutal realm of demons... I love to ompare the beauty and the evil and brutality.'

SURFACING
Slipknot

BY Shawn Crahan, Chris Fehn, Paul Gray, Craig Jones, Joey Jordison, Corey Taylor, Mick Thomson, Sid Wilson | PRODUCED BY Ross Robinson | FROM *Slipknot* (Roadrunner, 1999)

'Mick [Thomson] was messing around...' Corey Taylor recalled to *Kerrang!* of Slipknot's defining anthem. 'He started playing the now famous, crazy guitar line. We were like, "That's cool as shit"... It was unhinged.' Joey Jordison conjured the nihilistic yet defiant chorus. 'That's our whole thing...' the drummer declared to *NME*. 'When we play that song live, it's sickness.' 'Every day I am reminded of how much fucking filth there is in the world,' Shawn Crahan complained. 'I chose life [and] I'm going to make the best of it. But I hate every minute of it.'

RIVE
men

BY Casey Chaos | PRODUCED BY Ross Robinson | FROM *Amen* (Roadrunner, 1999)

am not famous,' Amen frontman Casey Chaos told bc.co.uk. 'I am nothing... I am just like everybody else. Ve are all flesh and blood.' Ironically, Chaos was a star rough and through: a dynamic stage presence and an stonishing writer. And his first two major albums (after e indie debut *Slave*) should be mandatory listening for nyone who thought AFI were the punks to follow.

CK KILLER
Amen

BY Casey Chaos | PRODUCED BY Ross Robinson | FROM *We Have Come for Your Parents* (Virgin, 2000)

'It's never been about commercialism,' Casey Chaos declared to *Metal Hammer*. 'It's been about following your heart, destroying it at every single opportunity you have.' Lo and behold, Amen's second outing inexplicably failed to make them one of metal's biggest bands. 'I love those first two albums,' Corey Taylor rued to noisey.vice.com. 'They're unbelievably amazing.'

'I WAS CONVINCED AMEN WAS GOING TO BE SO MUCH BIGGER THAN US'
COREY TAYLOR

ELITE
Deftones

BY Chino Moreno, Stephen Carpenter, Chi Cheng, Abe Cunningham | PRODUCED BY Terry Date, Deftones | FROM *White Pony* (Maverick, 2000)

'This is laughing at everybody trying to become what they already are,' explained Chino Moreno. 'If you want to be one of the elite, you are. I'm the asshole in the song, pretty much talking shit about everybody else. You're supposed to feel stupid after listening to it.' *White Pony*'s heaviest cut won the band their only Grammy. 'The name of the riff in "Elite", when we first wrote it, [was] "Cum On Your Face",' Moreno revealed to thequietus.com. 'On all the masters, it's still got the acronym on there: "COYF." So it's funny that we won a Grammy for [that].'

BLACK OBLIVION
Tony Iommi featuring Billy Corgan

BY Tony Iommi, Billy Corgan | PRODUCED BY Bob Marlette | FROM *Iommi* (Divine, 2000)

Serj Tankian, Phil Anselmo, Peter Steele and even Ozzy fronted tracks on Tony Iommi's first solo album. But none captured the spirit of Sabbath more expertly than Billy Corgan. 'Black Oblivion' – demoed as 'Firewall' – is eight minutes of riffmongering excellence (featuring the Great Pumpkin on bass). 'When we went into the studio with Billy Corgan, we didn't have anything written,' Iommi told *Guitar World*. 'I started to record some riffs. Before we knew it, we had this song with all these different changes in it... That was really inspiring.'

ONE STEP CLOSER
Linkin Park

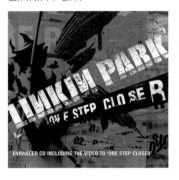

BY Mike Shinoda, Chester Bennington, Brad Delson, Joe Hahn, Rob Bourdon | PRODUCED BY Don Gilmore | FROM *Hybrid Theory* (Warner Bros., 2000)

'The biggest chuckle I get from it is the range of reviews,' Brad Delson told *Kerrang!* 'The most brilliant record ever, [or] the Backstreet Boys with hot pink polish on our nine-inch nails.' To a new generation trying to annoy its parents, Linkin Park *were* brilliant. ('*Hybrid Theory* still sounds amazing to me,' declared Bring Me the Horizon's Oli Sykes to *Metal Hammer* sixteen years later.) Their secret weapon, Chester Bennington, was showcased on 'One Step Closer': 'It's just me, man,' he told *Kerrang!* 'I can pretty much switch my scream off and on.'

HAND OF DOOM
Slayer

BY Tony Iommi, Ozzy Osbourne, Geezer Butler, Bill Ward | PRODUCED BY Slayer, Greg Gordon | FROM *Nativity In Black II: A Tribute to Black Sabbath* (Divine, 2000)

'I wanted to do "Hand of Doom" for a number of years,' Kerry King declared. 'Then the opportunity came to be on *N.I.B. II* [the follow-up to the 1994 tribute album *Nativity in Black*] and the timing was perfect, especially after just finishing two months on [1999's] Ozzfest, watching the originators crush nightly.' 'Hand of Doom' – originally on *Paranoid* – provides a welcome opportunity to hear Tom Araya's singing (rather than screaming) and his bass (not, for once, buried beneath the buzz of King and Jeff Hanneman's guitars).

ROLLIN' (AIR RAID VEHICLE)
Limp Bizkit

 BY Fred Durst, Wes Borland, Sam Rivers, John Otto, DJ Lethal, Swizz Beatz | PRODUCED BY Terry Date, Limp Bizkit | FROM *Chocolate Starfish and the Hot Dog Flavored Water* (Flip, 2000)

'"Rollin'" was a collaborative effort with this rap beat-maker called Swizz Beatz,' Wes Borland explained to songfacts.com. 'We like to have a variety of music on Limp Bizkit records... more traditional hip-hop and then more traditional rock or metal.' The song topped the UK chart, sealing Bizkit's rep as the band we loved to hate. 'We just started to poke fun at what people thought we were and embrace that,' Fred Durst protested to *Metal Hammer*. 'That's why we made the "Rollin'" video... How the hell did people not realize we weren't being serious?'

THE WICKER MAN
Iron Maiden

BY Adrian Smith, Steve Harris, Bruce Dickinson | PRODUCED BY Kevin Shirley, Steve Harris | FROM *Brave New World* (EMI, 2000)

I'm thinking about the buzz I used to get when I was a kid [at] rock festivals,' Bruce Dickinson said of his Maiden comeback single. 'You really felt you belonged to something bigger than yourself on that one day. You also felt... that you could change something.' 'The Wicker Man' – named after a 1973 film – was their first US hit since 'Can I Play with Madness?' (*see* 1988). Even Blaze Bayley was impressed: 'Every big, lovely, powerful, Maiden thing I love packed into a glorious, four-minute thirty-seven-second package,' he told *Classic Rock*.

FEEL GOOD HIT OF THE SUMMER
Queens of the Stone Age

BY Josh Homme, Nick Oliveri | PRODUCED BY Chris Goss, Josh Homme | FROM *Rated R* (Interscope, 2000)

'I'd heard rumour of them making this record,' Duff McKagan explained to thequietus.com, 'and the rumour behind it was they were getting all these people – like, "Rob Halford's on the record, what the fuck?" That record came out and it was such a brave turn.' 'Feel Good Hit of the Summer' – with, indeed, backing vocals by the Metal God – put QotSA on the map, thanks to its immortal ode to nicotine, Valium, Vicodin, marijuana, ecstasy, alcohol and 'c-c-c-cocaine!' 'A rock 'n' roll cocktail,' Halford declared on seeing the lyrics. 'I know this one!'

THE FIGHT SONG
Marilyn Manson

BY Marilyn Manson, John 5 | PRODUCED BY Dave Sardy, Marilyn Manson | FROM *Holy Wood (In the Shadow of the Valley of Death)* (Nothing, 2000)

Manson's greatest album isn't best represented by 'The Fight Song'. *Holy Wood* is sophisticated and thoughtful; 'The Fight Song' is a dumb rip-off of Blur's 'Song 2'. But if it doesn't make you bang your head or dance, there's something wrong with you. 'I tried to create something that's heavy,' he told *Classic Rock*, 'and yet has some irony and intelligence.' Its video pitches jocks against goths: a Columbine reference? 'People will put into it what they want if it helps them sell newspapers,' he shrugged to MTV. 'Flak is my job.'

STUPIFY
Disturbed

BY David Draiman, Da Donegan, Fuzz, Mike Wengren | PRODUCED BY Johnny K, Disturbed | FROM *The Sickness* (Giant, 200(

'My inner child has been warped, in a sense, by life experience – marred by life experience,' David Draiman explained of the inspiration for 'Stupify'. 'It looks to the world, and sees a world that's dark and frightening and mysterious.' The crushing, snarling song was Disturbed's first single but, as Draiman explained to loudwire.com, wa hardly an out-of-the-gate smash: "'Stupify" was actually a hard sell at radio... Giant Records, at the time, they worked it. They pushed it to where it got enough awareness that i did start to chart decently.'

ONLY FOR THE WEAK
In Flames

BY Anders Friden, Björn Gelotte, Jesper Strömblad | PRODUCED BY Fredrik Nordström, In Flames | FROM *Clayman* (Nuclear Blast, 2000)

'In Flames took all of these things that you never thought about combining,' Trivium's Matt Heafy enthused to musicradar.com of the band who, alongside At the Gates, spearheaded Swedish melodic death in the noughties. 'It's traditional Swedish folk music, death metal and New Wave of British Heavy Metal.' The result, noted As I Lay Dying's Nick Hipa, '[was] kind of like a more modern version of Maiden. They write great songs, great riffs, and they've got such solid vibrato. [Guitarists] Björn [Gelotte] and Jesper [Strömblad] are amazing players.'

BREED
Snake River Conspiracy

BY Jason Slater, Eric Valentine, Denny Porter, Jerry Goldsmit PRODUCED BY Jason Slater, David Kahne, Eric Valentine | FROM *Sonic Jihad* (Reprise, 2000)

'The thing that sucks about all other bands with girls is that all their songs are about some guy breaking up with them or some weak chick shit...' grumbled Snake River Conspiracy main man Jason Slater to *Kerrang!* 'I grew up listening to Maiden, Priest, Exodus and Slayer, so I can't really relate to that.' Enter tomboy Tobey Torres, who fronted ex-Third Eye Blind man Slater's cocktail of industrial pop, eighties covers and film soundtrack samples. 'I've been called the evil Gwen Stefani,' Torres cackled. 'But I'm just trying to be myself.'

LAST RESORT
Papa Roach

BY Jacoby Shaddix, Jerry Horton, Tobin Esperance, Dave Buckner | PRODUCED BY Jay Baumgardner | FROM *Infest* (DreamWorks, 2000)

'We were listening to a lot of Wu-Tang Clan...' bassist Tobin Esperance recalled to songfacts.com of the origins of Papa Roach's biggest hit, 'a lot of Fugees and a lot of East Coast hip-hop. And we were sampling classical music.' Listeners struggled to hear hip-hop, let alone classical music, but did hear Iron Maiden's *Killers* cut 'Genghis Khan'. 'I didn't become a Maiden fan until 2004...' frontman Jacoby Shaddix protested to *Metal Hammer*, 'and then I listened to it back and was like, "Well, of *course* it sounds like a fucking Maiden riff!"'

JUDITH
A Perfect Circle

BY Billy Howerdel, Maynard James Keenan | PRODUCED BY Billy Howerdel | FROM *Mer de Noms* (Virgin, 2000)

Tool set the bar high, but Maynard James Keenan's other band soared effortlessly with their first scathing classic, named after the singer's mother. 'She was paralysed, very early on, from an aneurysm,' he explained. 'It just strengthened her [Southern Baptist] faith, which is fine, because she really didn't have anything else but her faith. But the people around her, marching in like ghouls to tell her how strong in her faith she is, and then going home and talking behind her back... it was just amazing, the hypocrisy that went on.'

DISCIPLE
Slayer

BY Kerry King, Jeff Hanneman | PRODUCED BY Matt Hyde | FROM *God Hates Us All* (American, 2001)

'WHEN YOU'RE BORN, YOU'RE ONE OF GOD'S CHILDREN – AND AS YOU GROW AND SEE THE WORLD AS IT REALLY IS... IT'S NOT ALL ROSES'
KERRY KING

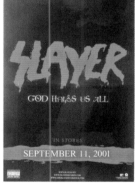

'This is my it-doesn't-get-any-heavier-than-this record,' Billy Corgan marvelled to musicradar.com of *God Hates Us All*. 'I thought Slayer could never top *Reign in Blood*. I was wrong. Dead wrong.'

'I played the songs for Pantera,' Kerry King told Ink19's David Lee Beowulf, 'and they were like, "Man, *God Hates Us All* would be a great shirt!" And I was like, "That would be a great title for the record!" It's the first chorus of the first real song on the album ["Disciple"], so it fell together.'

The brutal-even-for-Slayer album was unleashed on 11 September 2001. (The almost as hideously appropriate *Iowa* came out the week before.) Fittingly, 'Disciple' was, as Dethklok's Brendon Small observed to musicradar.com, 'another song about the refusal of God.'

Yet the spiritually-inclined Tom Araya had no issue singing it. 'I'm not gonna sit there and say something sucks 'cause it's not something I believe,' he assured crackmagazine.net. "The thought process goes like this: it has to be fuckin' awesome, or it doesn't make the cut. If it's not fuckin' awesome, then it's not Slayer."

JANE DOE
Converge

BY Kurt Ballou, Jacob Bannon, Nate Newton, Ben Koller | PRODUCED BY Kurt Ballou, Andy Hong | FROM *Jane Doe* (Equal Vision, 2001)

'"What the fuck is this?"' singer Jacob Bannon recalled to noisey.vice.com of the aghast reaction to Converge's game-changing and ferocious fourth album, *Jane Doe*. 'I remember all of us wanting to write a hardcore record the kids were going to hate,' bassist Nate Newton told music.avclub.com. Its themes, Bannon revealed to exclaim.ca, were 'loss, betrayal, the search for hope, and desperation. It's a very desperate record and, for me, a very tragic record from a really, really low point in my life. It's about coping with that, dealing with that.'

FEUER FREI!
Rammstein

BY Christoph 'Doom' Schneider, Doktor Christian Lorenz, Richard Z. Kruspe, Till Lindemann, Paul Landers, Oliver Riedel | PRODUCED BY Jacob Hellner, Rammstein | FROM *Mutter* (Motor Music, 2001)

'After playing on several festivals with them...' marvelled Megadeth's Dave Ellefson in 2001, 'there is nothing more metal than attaching a flamethrower to your face and spewing twelve-foot flames during the show with your bandmates!' Ellefson duly picked 'Feuer Frei!' – the final hit from *Mutter* – as his theme song of the year. It solidified Rammstein's pyrotechnic reputation – which they had initiated, Christoph Schneider recalled to the *Washington Post*, 'to break through the noise... We did it with fire. Now, in a way, we're the victims of it.'

HOW YOU REMIND ME
Nickelback

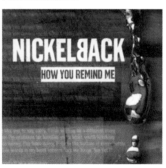

BY Chad Kroeger, Ryan Peake, Mike Kroeger, Ryan 'Vik' Vikedal | PRODUCED BY Rick Parashar, Nickelback | FROM *Silver Side Up* (EMI, 2001)

'Definitely Metallica,' Chad Kroeger told menshealth.com of his influences. 'But also Anthrax, Megadeth, Guns N' Roses. Anything in that genre... There's a lot of melody in a great metal song.' The bitter break-up anthem 'How You Remind Me' may not be metal, but it *is* great. And its success meant Chad Kroeger could ease the woes of his single life on the road. 'I had three band members who weren't interested in doing much, and I'm the singer of the band,' he bragged to *Playboy*. 'So I didn't exactly have to squabble with anybody.'

BLACKWATER PARK
Opeth

BY Mikael Åkerfeldt, Peter Lindgren | PRODUCED BY Opeth, Steven Wilson | FROM *Blackwater Park* (Music for Nations, 2001)

'A lot of fans [won't] listen to anything unless it is pure metal...' Opeth's Mikael Åkerfeldt mourned to *Metal Hammer*. 'If you are confined to one type of music, then you are missing out on so many worlds and colours. You are depriving yourself of some great experiences... If there is a message in *Blackwater Park*, then that's what it is.' The message was stunningly realised on the twelve-minute title track. 'You have parts that are beautiful and sad and super-emotive,' Mark Tremonti told musicradar.com. 'Then you have brutal parts bookending them.'

HE HERETIC ANTHEM
lipknot

BY Shawn Crahan, Chris Fehn, Paul Gray, Craig Jones, Joey Jordison, Jim Root, Corey Taylor, Mick Thomson, Sid Wilson | PRODUCED BY Ross Robinson, Slipknot | FROM *Iowa* (Roadrunner, 2001)

 came up with the chorus after I passed a house with the umber 555,' Joey Jordison recalled to *Kerrang!* 'I thought, you're 555 then I'm 666." I knew that should be the horus.' The result was a Slipknot classic (check out an xplosive version on 2002's *Pledge of Allegiance* album). hey seem like nice boys,' remarked Steve Harris – whose umber of the Beast' is an obvious antecedent – to *Q*. ve only heard a couple of tracks of theirs, so I can't really omment. But I guess, at the end of the day, I like my music th a bit more melody.'

PLUG IN BABY
Muse

BY Matt Bellamy | PRODUCED BY David Bottrill, Muse | FROM *Origin of Symmetry* (Mushroom, 2001)

'We got the name for the song from an Argos [shopping] catalogue,' Matt Bellamy told Absolute Radio DJ Dave Berry. 'It was like a baby monitor and it was called a "Plug In Baby"… We thought, "That's a great song name."' Written – according to Bellamy – 'above a sex shop', and apparently recorded under the influence of mushrooms, the song was exhumed from demos that predated Muse's debut *Showbiz*, and updated to fit *Origin of Symmetry*'s rockier feel. In 2010, *Total Guitar* readers voted it the greatest riff of the noughties.

CHISM
ool

BY Danny Carey, Maynard James Keenan, Adam Jones, Justin Chancellor | PRODUCED BY Tool, David Bottrill | FROM *Lateralus* (Volcano, 2001)

vant to thank Satan,' Danny Carey declared when chism' beat Black Sabbath, Slayer, Slipknot and System a Down to a 'Best Metal Performance' Grammy. The n crowned Tool's ascent, after *Lateralus* topped the US art. 'The twiddly "Schism" riff came from fooling around,' stin Chancellor told *Bass Player*. 'I just play as much possible, and I don't write stuff down. So when I get a od idea, I play it until I can't forget it.' That 'twiddly riff' mbined with Maynard James Keenan's oblique lyrics to eate progressive metal's greatest hit.

CHOP SUEY!
System of a Down

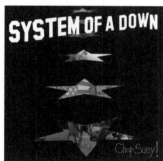

BY Serj Tankian, Daron Malakian, Shavo Odadjian, John Dolmayan | PRODUCED BY Rick Rubin, Daron Malakian, Serj Tankian FROM *Toxicity* (American, 2001)

'So melodic and schizophrenic,' marvelled Avenged Sevenfold's M. Shadows to *Rolling Stone*. 'Chop Suey!', Tom Morello noted to musicradar.com, 'combines the unique flavour of the band's Armenian heritage with absolutely brutal riffage' and was originally titled 'Self-Righteous Suicide'. Daron Malakian explained it to *NME*: 'The song is about how we are regarded differently depending on how we pass… Like, if I were now to die from drug abuse, they might say I deserved it because I abused dangerous drugs.'

JUST A DAY
Feeder

🇬🇧 BY Grant Nicholas | PRODUCED BY Grant Nicholas, Feeder | FROM *Just A Day EP* (Echo, 2001)

'It's very much a youthful song, so it was nice to see all these young people with their interpretation of it,' said frontman Grant Nicholas to cnet.com of the cut that – of all those in this book – has by far the greatest video. 'You had the girl who saw it as a quite dark, serious thing and you had kids goofing around and jumping on the bed. It was interesting for me as a writer to see how people interpret songs.' Bolstered by its brilliant visuals, 'Just A Day' gave Feeder their biggest hit, bar the same year's 'Buck Rogers'. It remains a fan favourite.

BLEED AMERICAN
Jimmy Eat World

🇺🇸 BY Jim Adkins, Rick Burch, Zach Lind, Tom Linton | PRODUCED BY Mark Trombino, Jimmy Eat World | FROM *Bleed American* (DreamWorks, 2001)

'The one bit of bad luck we had was with the title track,' bassist Rick Burch recalled to *Rock Sound* of the album that turned Jimmy Eat World into stars. 'It was getting a good reaction with radio – but, when 9/11 happened, it was thrown on the blacklist. No one would play it any more. It was incredibly frustrating to have this great song that was making waves, and then having to abandon it. It was like, "Okay, let's shift gears and move onto something else."' That 'something else' was the huge 'The Middle', but 'Bleed American' slays to this day.

THE ROCK SHOW
Blink-182

🇺🇸 BY Mark Hoppus, Tom DeLonge, Travis Barker | PRODUCED BY Jerry Finn | FROM *Take Off Your Pants and Jacket* (MCA, 2001)

'There used to be a club in San Diego called Soma,' Mark Hoppus wrote in the *Take Off Your Pants and Jacket* tour programme. 'It was covered with graffitti, it stunk, it was made of metal, the sound sucked, and the toilets were always overflowing... we loved it... Blink-182 began in this club. This song is about those days. Soma isn't around any more. The city hates it when kids have somewhere to go and hang out. Fuck them.' Like 'First Date' (*Jacket*'s other hit), 'The Rock Show' was one of the last yet best songs written for the album.

PARTY HARD
Andrew W.K.

🇺🇸 BY Andrew W.K. | PRODUCED BY Andrew W.K., Scott Humphrey | FROM *I Get Wet* (Mercury, 2001)

'Metal is perceived as a joke and has been for quite some time,' complained Disturbed's David Draiman to *Billboard*. 'Someone like Andrew W.K. doesn't do much to help that situation. He continues to perpetuate the myth that we're a bunch of idiotic, nonsensical thugs.' The man himself was unapologetic: 'I just tried to make the most absolutely exciting, invigorating thing that would make me want to dance.' He wasn't even rattled by suggestions that 'Party Hard' resembled Starship's 'We Built This City'. 'It's certainly a good song,' he told *Blender*.

AVENOUS
rch Enemy

BY Angela Gossow, Michael Arnott, Christopher Arnott | PRODUCED BY Fredrik Nordström, Michael Arnott | FROM *Wages of Sin* (Century Media, 2001)

…was an Arch Enemy fan because I'm still a huge Carcass …,' Angela Gossow told enslain.net of her tryout for …itarist Michael Arnott's post-Carcass band. 'It was the …ost similar thing of all of them to Carcass… but I was the …ly one who liked Arch Enemy… I knew all the metalheads … the scene, and no one was big on Arch Enemy. So, I …dn't have the feeling that, "This is going to be my future."' …ut her appointment made scene-leaders of the band that, …th singer Johan Liiva, had been also-rans. 'Ravenous' …earheaded their raging resurrection.

FAT LIP
Sum 41

BY Deryck Whibley, Dave Baksh, Steve Jocz, Greig Nori | PRODUCED BY Jerry Finn | FROM *All Killer No Filler* (Aquarius, 2001)

'Cocaine, ecstasy and strippers' are Deryck Whibley's memories of Sum 41's debut, he told bandwagon.asia. 'Lots of partying… Nineteen to twenty-year-old kids with too much record company money.' Still, they emerged with a snotty anthem that paid homage to their metal heritage. (The same album's 'Pain for Pleasure' is an obvious Maiden pastiche, and gave its name to their metal alter egos.) 'Absolutely amazing,' Whibley told DJ Matt Pinfield of the song's success. 'It was the coolest thing that we could ever have imagined.'

ODIES
rowning Pool

BY Dave Williams, Mike Luce, C.J. Pierce, Stevie Benton | PRODUCED BY Jay Baumgardner | FROM *Sinner* (Wind-up, 2001)

…ust kinda said, "Let the bodies hit the floor,"' singer Dave …illiams recalled to Ballbuster. 'The guys in the band go, …hat's cool"… then it just turned into this monster.' The …t became a moshpit anthem. 'It's about my perspective …hen I look out,' Williams instructed hiponline.com. 'Leave …ur bullshit at the door and get it all out. But you have … have respect for the others in the pit. If you push them …own, you have to pick them back up. I'm not going to get …ehind the violence thing. It *is* violent, but there is a certain …nount of respect and a code.'

COCHISE
Audioslave

BY Chris Cornell, Tom Morello, Tim Commerford, Brad Wilk | PRODUCED BY Rick Rubin | FROM *Audioslave* (Epic, 2002)

Apache warrior Cochise 'attacked everything in his path', Tom Morello informed MTV. 'This song kinda sounds like that.' 'It was probably the epitome of what people had guessed that band would sound like,' Chris Cornell told music.avclub.com. 'If you did the math on paper, with Rage Against the Machine and then me screaming over it, it's gonna be "Cochise".' The riff monster was immortalised in a pyrotechnic-packed video. Police and TV stations were inundated by calls from people who, Morello cackled, thought 'the city was under siege'.

BATTLE READY
Otep

🇺🇸

BY Otep Shamaya, Rob Patterson, Evil J, Moke | PRODUCED BY Terry Date | FROM *Sevas Tra* (Capitol, 2002)

'We hope to create something very dark, very dangerous, emotional, heavy as hell,' Otep Shamaya announced to unearthed.com in 2001, 'but also intelligent, therapeutic, and poetic. Something like the great tragedies of Greece, but with a contemporary skin – full of scars, full of beauty. Violent and ecstatic.' What she and her band conjured was an unoriginal but brilliant – and, thanks to producer Terry Date, pulverising – fusion of nu and death metal. Check out this gonzoid anthem, then do yourself a favour and listen to everything else Otep have done.

DEAD STAR
Muse

🇬🇧

BY Matt Bellamy | PRODUCED BY John Cornfield, Muse | FROM 'Dead Star/In Your World' (Mushroom, 2002)

The heaviest of Muse's early songs concerns, said Matt Bellamy, 'how everyone reacted to the eleventh September thing. We were in Boston at the time. We got stuck there, and that's when we recorded those songs. So in some ways, the lyrics are a little bit about the hysteria around that time and how people were really quick to point fingers at everyone else when they should have pointed fingers at themselves.' The savage single version is pretty good, but check out a thrilling live take on their *Hullabaloo Soundtrack* for the full monty.

ONE LITTLE VICTORY
Rush

🇨🇦

BY Geddy Lee, Alex Lifeson, Neil Peart | PRODUCED BY Rush, David Northfield | FROM *Vapor Trails* (Anthem, 2002)

A seven-second drum salvo is the heartwarming way Rush kick off 'One Little Victory', *Vapor Trails*' explosive opener. It marked their return after a four-year hiatus, prompted by the deaths of Neil Peart's daughter and wife. 'I'd been working on that tune and came up with that double-bass part,' Peart observed to *Modern Drummer*. 'It worked perfectly for the end of the song. But Geddy said, "That's a great part. You ought to open the song with it. That would just kill." Frankly, I wouldn't have done it that way. I don't think I would have been so assertive.'

CAN'T STOP
Red Hot Chili Peppers

🇺🇸

BY Anthony Keidis, Flea, John Frusciante, Chad Smith | PRODUCED BY Rick Rubin | FROM *By the Way* (Warner Bros., 2002)

'It was difficult... for Flea and mine's relationship,' John Frusciante confessed of *By the Way*. 'I didn't think we should have any funk on that album... At the time Flea wanted to do more funk, and I wasn't feeling it. I wanted to do a Chili Peppers album that didn't sound like the Chili Peppers.' However, the result was one of their finest effort – and, for Flea and funk fans, there was succour in the form of 'Can't Stop'. 'The real energy comes from the four of us,' Frusciante admitted to *Total Guitar*. 'That's number one over any of our individual efforts.'

TIMES LIKE THESE
Foo Fighters

BY Dave Grohl, Taylor Hawkins, Nate Mendel, Chris Shiflett | PRODUCED BY Nick Raskulinecz, Foo Fighters | FROM *One by One* (Roswell, 2002)

A mid-tempo number with a really weird chording that's kinda reminiscent of Mission of Burma or Television, or kind of a jangly, post-punk, New York, new wave theme,' Dave Grohl said of the song that brought the then fractious Foos back together. ('In two takes, we had "Times Like These",' Taylor Hawkins told *Rhythms*. 'It felt great.') In fact, its obvious antecedent is The Cult's classic 'She Sells Sanctuary' – but, as Grohl said, 'I think actually that this is the best song I've ever written. It's very emotive and passionate and universal.'

JUST BECAUSE
Jane's Addiction

BY Perry Farrell, Dave Navarro, Chris Chaney, Stephen Perkins, Bob Ezrin | PRODUCED BY Bob Ezrin, Brian Virtue FROM *Strays* (Capitol, 2003)

'It was punk rock,' Perry Farrell explained to the *Guardian* of Jane's Addiction's original incarnation. 'In those days, taking the usual steps to success, we had disdain for those kinds of [steps]. Now there's not much use in struggling against it because there's no place to go. There's not a real underground any more, so you might as well succeed on the overground.' The band led their charge to the overground with the hit 'Just Because' – as brilliant, bruising and piercing as anything they had conjured in their smacked-out days of yore.

BELIEVE IN A THING CALLED LOVE
The Darkness

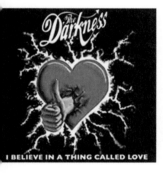

BY Justin Hawkins, Dan Hawkins, Frankie Poullain, Ed Graham | PRODUCED BY Pedro Ferreira | FROM *Permission to Land* (Must... Destroy!!, 2003)

'That cat has got his thing going on,' Perry Farrell noted to *Rolling Stone* of Darkness frontman Justin Hawkins. 'He loves to rock, the people love him and he puts it out there for the crowd. We love that. And he's silly.' Unquestionably silly but stupendously successful, The Darkness etched themselves into history with 'I Believe in a Thing Called Love' – first issued on a 2002 EP, then a smash from their debut album. 'It was a relief when [*Permission to Land*] finally went to number one...' Hawkins admitted to *Kerrang!* 'We kept Iron Maiden off the top spot.'

"The Darkness are the greatest rock 'n' roll band of the last twenty years" (KKKKK) – KERRANG!

The Darkness

PERMISSION TO LAND
THE DEBUT ALBUM

MONDAY 7th JULY 2003

PASCHENDALE
Iron Maiden

🇬🇧 BY Adrian Smith, Steve Harris | PRODUCED BY Kevin Shirley, Steve Harris | FROM *Dance of Death* (EMI, 2003)

'I could hear the different parts echoing the differing parts of a battle,' Adrian Smith said of this classic. 'A frantic part had to be about the conflict and another, more relaxed section would definitely represent the calm before the storm... "Paschendale" is classic proggy Maiden territory... But it's an area which I hadn't ever really attempted to write before. People usually associate me with our more commercial material, like "Wasted Years" or "Two Minutes to Midnight". But I thought I'd have a go at writing a Maiden epic. And five days later I was still there writing it!'

NEEDLED 24/7
Children of Bodom

🇫🇮 BY Alexi Laiho | PRODUCED BY Anssi 'Viiksi' Kippo | FROM *Hate Crew Deathroll* (Spinefarm, 2003)

'"Needled 24/7" is heavy as fuck and fast as shit,' frontman Alexi Laiho bragged to loudersound.com. 'And the main melody is so catchy that, whether you like it or not, it's going to stick with you.' Children of Bodom's fourth album broke them free of the underground, rising into the US chart. 'We were anxious to even get a shot to play in America,' Laiho told crypticrock.com. 'When we finally got that first tour opening up for Dimmu Borgir, we were so stoked... Word must have gotten out that we were a pretty good live band. The crowds were amazing.'

I DON'T WANNA BE ME
Type O Negative

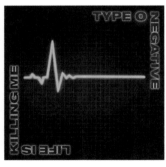

🇺🇸 BY Peter Steele | PRODUCED BY Josh Silver, Peter Steele | FROM *Life Is Killing Me* (Roadrunner, 2003)

'I can't expect somebody to wanna be with me and love me unless I love myself,' Peter Steele conceded to metalstorm.net. 'I am far from perfect and I wanna try to be as perfect as I can for the person that I wanna be with. [Until then] I am going to remain alone.' That feeling fuelled a song that was as addictive as it was commercially underwhelming. 'If *Sgt. Pepper* or *Highway to Hell* or *Stained Class* or *Paranoid* came out today,' Steele grumbled to ink19.com, 'it would not even chart, simply because people like this "rap 'n' roll" shit.'

MINERVA
Deftones

🇺🇸 BY Chino Moreno, Stephen Carpenter, Chi Cheng, Abe Cunningham, Frank Delgado | PRODUCED BY Terry Date, Deftones | FROM *Deftones* (Maverick, 2003)

'It was one of my favourite songs on the record,' Chino Moreno told *Spin*. 'Since *Adrenaline*, we'd been fighting an uphill battle with some of our old-school fans who just love us for the aggressive part of our band. As much as I like it too – I've had this conversation many times – I'm not always there. I'm not always mad. Life doesn't suck.' Not in the slightest bit radio-friendly, 'Minerva' was chosen as the lead single from *Deftones*, and remains – with the exception of *White Pony*'s 'Change (In the House of Flies)' – their most successful hit.

THE OUTSIDER
A Perfect Circle

BY Billy Howerdel, Maynard James Keenan | PRODUCED BY Billy Howerdel | FROM *Thirteenth Step* (Virgin, 2003)

'The Outsider' – as vicious as 'Judith' (*see* 2000) – is, Maynard James Keenan explained, 'the perspective of a person who doesn't understand at all what their friend is going through... They think that it's more like a sprained ankle; they can just kind of walk it off.' Its inspiration was Alice in Chains' Layne Staley. 'Being a friend to someone like Layne, it really does your head in,' Keenan told MTV. 'I don't understand [drug addiction], but I do want to help other people... who might hear and go, "You know what, I think I want to try to live."'

HYSTERIA
Muse

BY Matt Bellamy, Chris Wolstenholme, Dominic Howard | PRODUCED BY Rich Costey, Muse | FROM *Absolution* (Taste Media, 2003)

One of modern rock's best bass lines – 'hyperpowered, overdriven,' noted bassplayer.com – began as a lead part in soundchecks on the *Origin of Symmetry* tour. Inspired by the *Origin*-era b-side 'Futurism', 'Hysteria' evolved into Muse's most monster cut. 'A kinda fat bass line with a groovy straight beat,' Matt Bellamy remarked. Chris Wolstenholme explained: 'The bass is playing one melody, the guitar is playing another melody, and you can almost imagine violins and cellos... The bass is as much of a lead instrument as the guitar.'

BLOOD ON YOUR HANDS
Killing Joke

BY Jaz Coleman, Geordie Walker, Youth, Andy Gill | PRODUCED BY Andy Gill | FROM *Killing Joke* (Zuma Recordings, 2003)

'We liked a lot of high-energy music like AC/DC,' Jaz Coleman admitted to *Louder Than Hell*, 'and it was there that our tradition started.' That tradition – corrosive guitars and pounding proto-industrial beats – influenced Kate Bush and Kurt Cobain. Given the Nirvana connection (compare 'Come as You Are' to 'Eighties'), it made sense that Dave Grohl drummed on Killing Joke's self-titled 2003 album. The brilliant 'Death and Resurrection Show' is a fine showcase for The Grohl – but, if you've time for only one, proceed straight to this banger.

NUMB
Linkin Park

BY Mike Shinoda, Chester Bennington, Brad Delson, Joe Hahn, Rob Bourdon, Dave Farrell | PRODUCED BY Don Gilmore, Linkin Park | FROM *Meteora* (Warner Bros., 2003)

'Just one week before the band entered NRG Studios to begin recording, this song was conceived,' Linkin Park revealed in *Meteora*'s liner notes. 'Built around the intro hook, the song came together quickly and almost effortlessly.' For a last-minute addition, 'Numb' proved staggeringly successful and enduring. '[We] are just trying to make something that's good,' Mike Shinoda told the *Guardian*. 'We like what we're doing, but we're sure our intentions are exactly the same as all of those artists who are awful.'

PURE HATRED
Chimaira

BY Mark Hunter, Rob Arnold, Matt DeVries, Andrew Herrick, Jim LaMarca, Chris Spicuzz | PRODUCED BY Ben Schigel, Mark Hunter, Rob Arnold | FROM *The Impossibility of Reason* (Roadrunner, 2003)

'Chimaira should become its own brand,' frontman Mark Hunter declared to burnyourears.de. 'Emocore, metalcore, whatevercore – we don't want to go there. We just want to crush your city and play devastating heavy metal.' Lots of Chimaira songs fit those criteria, but none with such visceral economy as 'Pure Hatred'. 'It's not like we're reinventing the wheel or anything,' guitarist Rob Arnold conceded to metalrefuge.wordpress.com. 'We just put out own spin.' Check out 'Power Trip', too, for another reason to seek out *The Impossibility of Reason*.

99 PROBLEMS
Jay-Z

BY Jay-Z, Rick Rubin, Leslie West, Felix Pappalardi, John Ventura, Norman Landsberg, Billy Squier, Ice-T | PRODUCED BY Rick Rubin | FROM *The Black Album* (Roc-A-Fella, 2003)

The ingredients were simple. Billy Squier's barnstorming 'The Big Beat' (see 1980). Ice-T's 'I got ninety-nine problems but a bitch ain't one' (from *Home Invasion*'s '99 Problems'). Mountain's much-sampled 1969 song 'Long Red'. ('I always thought to myself, "Why don't they use heavy guitar in rap?"' Leslie West said to songfacts.com. 'Rick Rubin produced ["99 Problems"]... and I think it may have been his idea.') Well-worn as those ingredients were, Jay-Z and Rubin alchemised them into a headbanging, barrier-burying colossus.

HONOR THY FATHER
Dream Theater

BY Mike Portnoy, John Petrucci, John Myung, Jordan Rudess | PRODUCED BY John Petrucci, Mike Portnoy | FROM *Train of Thought* (Elektra, 2003)

'Do you just want to bang your frickin' head?' singer Jame LaBrie mused to *Classic Rock*. 'You might be able to do that here and there with some songs, but it's going to be a shock to the system when we start going into the more progressive and complicated areas.' 'Some songs' include 'The Mirror' (*Awake*) and 'The Glass Prison' (*Six Degrees of Inner Turbulence*) – which, like 'Honor Thy Father', originated with metalhead Mike Portnoy. 'I'm not very good at writing love songs,' the drummer confessed to Reddit, 'so I decided to write a hate song!'

PROGENIES OF THE GREAT APOCALYPSE
Dimmu Borgir

BY Silenoz, Galder, Shagrath, Mustis | PRODUCED BY Dimmu Borgir, Fredrik Nordström | FROM *Death Cult Armageddon* (Nuclear Blast, 2003)

Symphonic black metal got a new national anthem in 2003. Awash in orchestration from the Prague Philarmonic, also boasted vocals by 'The Son of Northern Darkness', Immortal frontman Abbath. 'We want this album to sound like the theme to the end of the world,' guitarist Silenoz assured metalstorm.net. 'There's definitely an underlying theme,' he expanded to chroniclesofchaos.com. 'I wrote the lyrics from the perspective that mankind is heading toward its own destruction and we can't blame anyone or anything but ourselves.'

SIC TRANSIT GLORIA... GLORY FADES
Brand New

BY Jesse Lacey, Vincent Accardi | PRODUCED BY Steven Haigler | FROM *Deja Entendu* (Triple Crown, 2003)

Emo won't detain us for long in this book, but every now and then those moping boys made a tune worth listening to. In 2003, Brand New alchemised their misery into *Deja Entendu*, with fan favourites 'The Quiet Things that No One Ever Knows', 'The Boy Who Blocked His Own Shot', 'Okay I Believe You, But My Tommy Gun Don't' and, most rockishly, 'Sic Transit Gloria... Glory Fades'. It might have been about date rape; it might have a metaphor for Brand New being swallowed by the industry. Either way, it was a bright spot in a grey morass.

MEIN TEIL
Rammstein

BY Christoph "Doom" Schneider, Christian Lorenz, Paul Landers, Till Lindemann, Oliver Riedel, Richard Z. Kruspe-Bernstein | PRODUCED BY Jacob Hellner, Rammstein | FROM *Reise, Reise* (Universal, 2004)

'We thought it to be so unbelievable that one man fries the penis of the other in a pan and then they will eat it together,' Till Lindemann boggled to *Playboy*. It was more believable that a group named after an airshow disaster would have a hit about a real-life case of cannibalism. And its music was as jawdropping as its lyric, forsaking electronic sublety for massive fucking beats. Nonetheless, it earned a Grammy nomination – and, as Lindemann shrugged, 'The Pet Shop Boys [who remixed it] seemed to have liked the song.'

JESUS OF SUBURBIA
Green Day

BY Billie Joe Armstrong, Mike Dirnt, Tré Cool | PRODUCED BY Rob Cavallo, Green Day | FROM *American Idiot* (Reprise, 2004)

'Lyrically, it's everything about my past,' Billie Joe Armstrong noted of *American Idiot*'s most beloved song, 'but... written on the outside as well. That song is like purging everything.' Part of the fun was identifying the musical inspirations for the multipart epic: David Bowie's 'Moonage Daydream' ('Jesus of Surburbia'), Black Sabbath's 'Children of the Grave' ('I Don't Care'), and Mott the Hoople's 'All the Young Dudes', Mötley Crüe's 'On with the Show' *and* Bryan Adams' 'Summer of '69' ('City of the Damned').

METALINGUS
Alter Bridge

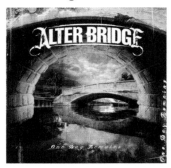

BY Mark Tremonti, Myles Kennedy, Brian Marshall, Scott Phillips | PRODUCED BY Ben Grosse, Alter Bridge | FROM *One Day Remains* (Wind-Up, 2004)

'"Metalingus" came from us jamming...' Mark Tremonti recalled to *Metal Hammer*. 'The record label owner came to hear us play and, when he asked what the name of the song we just played was, [we] explained it was just a filler title. He said, "No, you've got to name that song Metalingus; it's a great name!"... It's got a real rock 'n' roll vibe to it and it's still one of my favourite songs.' Never a single, 'Metalingus' nonetheless became an Alter Bridge anthem. 'All four of us are extremely grateful for getting that kind of response,' Myles Kennedy declared.

NOW YOU'VE GOT SOMETHING TO DIE FOR
Lamb of God

BY Randy Blythe, Mark Morton, Willie Adler, John Campbell, Chris Adler | PRODUCED BY Machine, Lamb of God | FROM *Ashes of the Wake* (Epic, 2004)

'The [Iraq] war was on pretty much everyone's mind,' frontman Randy Blythe told writer Jon Wiederhorn. 'Politicians were saying one thing, but it didn't take a lot to see that what was really going on was something else entirely... All these soldiers were being led into a situation they didn't sign up for.' Cynicism and disillusionment with US foreign policy suffused *Ashes of the Wake*, Lamb of God's major label debut and biggest seller, peaking on the blisteringly bitter yet thrillingly pummelling 'Now You've Got Something to Die For'.

SOME KIND OF MONSTER (EDIT)
Metallica

BY James Hetfield, Lars Ulrich, Kirk Hammett, Bob Rock | PRODUCED BY Bob Rock, Metallica | FROM *Some Kind of Monster* (Elektra, 2004)

Two people told Bob Rock how much they liked *St. Anger*, Jimmy Page and Jack White. 'If two people in the world like the record,' the producer told musicradar.com, 'and it's those two people, I'm fine with it.' The rest of the world was baffled by the album's clanging production and unwieldy epics. '*St. Anger* was a bold, fuck-you kind of record,' Lars Ulrich admitted to *Kerrang!* 'It seemed to really confuse people.' However, slashed in half and remixed for a 2004 EP, the song that gave the film-of-the-making its name proved a, well, monster.

NYMPHETAMINE FIX
Cradle of Filth

🇬🇧

BY Dani Filth, Paul Allender, Martin Powell, Dave Pybus, Adrian Erlandsson | PRODUCED BY Rob Caggiano, Cradle of Filth | FROM *Nymphetamine* (Roadrunner, 2004)

'Nymphetamine is like a marriage between sex and drugs,' Dani Filth explained to metalrage.com. 'An addiction. An addiction to women, an addiction to one particular woman in question... You'll get the impression from how we're singing – when Liv [Kristine, singer-songwriter] is singing the main hook, then I'll sing... – there's a struggle between this guy's sanity and this woman, whom he can't hate, but loves.' If a love song wasn't unlikely enough for these tongue-in-cheek former death metallers, 'Nymphetamine Fix' earned a Grammy nomination.

PROPHECY
Soulfly

🇧🇷 🇺🇸

BY Max Cavalera | PRODUCED BY Max Cavalera | FROM *Prophecy* (Roadrunner, 2004)

'They asked me if I would contribute some bass,' Dave Ellefson told darkside.ru about Soulfly's fourth album. 'I considered it an honour and said, "Absolutely!" Of course, it's something very different than what I've ever done or do, which I like. I like to be able to push myself to come up with some new ideas and new playing.' The *Prophecy* album and its grinding title cut – complete with guitarist Marc Rizzo's 'whammy pedal squeal sounds' – proved that, twenty years after Sepultura's formation, Max Cavalera's muse was as mighty as ever.

DUALITY
Slipknot

🇺🇸

BY Shawn Crahan, Chris Fehn, Paul Gray, Craig Jones, Joey Jordison, Jim Root, Corey Taylor, Mick Thomson, Sid Wilson | PRODUCED BY Rick Rubin | FROM *Vol. 3: (The Subliminal Verses)* (Roadrunner, 2004)

'I WAS TRYING TO FIGURE OUT THE STRUGGLE WITHIN MYSELF – THE DUALITY OF THE SOUL. THIS WAS MY WAY OF FIGURING OUT HOW ONE'S GOOD HALF LIVES WITH THE BAD HALF'
COREY TAYLOR

'I wrote the music to this one while I was watching TV,' Joey Jordison reflected to *Kerrang!*'s Tom Bryant. 'I thought it was a throwaway. Then, when [Jordison's band] Murderdolls and [Corey Taylor's band] Stone Sour were touring together in the UK, Corey came up with a melody for it backstage at [London's] Brixton Academy. I knew right then that it was a hit.'

Taylor delivered a soaring vocal. "He's always been a melodic singer," Jim Root noted to radiometal.com. "He's gifted enough to do it all." Yet, as the frontman grumbled to *Revolver*'s Jon Wiederhorn, "I'm not happy with the vocals on that record. I didn't get a lot of say in anything. There were a lot of takes that I thought were much better than the ones they used... The songs are great. My performances could have been so much better."

Vol. 3's first single, "Duality" was initially a sensation because of its house-trashing video, but has since become a singalong staple. 'It's been played to death,' Taylor admitted to noisey.vice.com. 'But that song, man, when we play it live, people still lose their shit.'

BLOOD AND THUNDER
Mastodon

BY Troy Sanders, Brent Hinds, Bill Kelliher, Brann Dailor | PRODUCED BY Matt Bayles, Mastodon | FROM *Leviathan* (Relapse, 2004)

Mastodon, Behemoth's Nergal told getreadytorock.com, 'keep our music fresh and interesting.' The band's second album put them on the (nautical) map. 'It was definitely the siren call that we were here to stay,' Brann Dailor told noisey.vice.com. '"Hearts Alive" was the big epic… But we could also write something that was heavy and straightforward like "Blood and Thunder".' Of the brutal thumper, Dethklok's Brendon Small raved to musicradar.com, 'I get that feeling that something is going to happen, and what's going to happen is something bad.'

GHOST LOVE SCORE
Nightwish

BY Tuomas Holopainen | PRODUCED BY Tuomas Holopainen, Tero Kinnunen | FROM *Once* (Spinefarm, 2004)

'I'm a big fan of old prog rock…' bassist Marco Hietala confessed to loudersound.com. 'This is a song that has a lot of different parts going on, and different atmospheres in different places… My biggest influence from the prog world would be Jethro Tull.' *Once*'s 'Romanticide' is heavier and 'Nemo' is better known, but 'Ghost Love Score' is *the* Nightwish classic. 'It's very much like a soundtrack to a movie,' main man Tuomas Holopainen told dprp.net. 'It's ten minutes long and the most ambitious piece of work that we have ever done.'

PRIDE
Damageplan

BY Vinnie Paul, Dimebag Darrell, Pat Lachman | PRODUCED BY Vinnie Paul, Dimebag Darrell, Sterling Winfield, Pat Lachman | FROM *New Found Power* (Elektra, 2004)

'With Pantera, at the end, it was a lot of "me, myself and I",' Vinnie Paul grumbled to musicomh.com. 'It didn't have that fuckin' bond; that fuckin' power that four people together can have. With Damageplan, we have that.' That fuckin' power came together most brilliantly on 'Pride', which married the Abbott brothers' legendary groove with an awesome Alice in Chains vibe. 'We have old-school roots but we are reborn,' Dimebag assured smnnews.com. 'We aren't new school, but we are fresh up-to-date… We just wanted people to know it's not Pantera.'

SLITHER
Velvet Revolver

BY Scott Weiland, Slash, Dave Kushner, Duff McKagan, Matt Sorum | PRODUCED BY Josh Abraham, Velvet Revolver | FROM *Contraband* (RCA, 2004)

remember Slash coming in with the riff,' Dave Kushner recalled to musicradar.com. 'Matt [Sorum] kept changing the tempo by 1bpm faster or 2bpm slower, to the point where everyone was frustrated with each other and fighting among ourselves because it didn't sound right. Is funny that it came out to be a favourite riff.' The track's classic status was crowned when it was added to Guns N' Roses' setlists in 2018, at Axl's behest. 'He really dug it,' Slash told revolvermag.com. 'It was a really cool and cathartic thing to go out and play that song.'

B.Y.O.B.
System of a Down

BY Daron Malakian, Serj Tankian | PRODUCED BY Rick Rubin, Daron Malakian FROM *Mezmerize* (American, 2005)

'I wanna make music that makes everyone shit their pants,' Serj Tankian assured *Kerrang!* As if 'Chop Suey' (*see* 2001) hadn't been nutty enough, System blasted back with an antiwar psycho-metal anthem that became the most improbable of their unlikely hits. 'It's got a really interesting arrangement...' Daron Malakian noted to *Metal Hammer*. 'Kind of a Motörhead drive to it in the beginning and then it turns into a Funkadelic chorus. I was just trying things. Some experiments work and some don't... and I'm really proud of the ones that did.'

WELCOME HOME
Coheed and Cambria

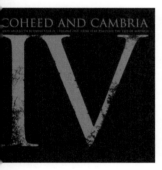

BY Claudio Sanchez, Travis Stever, Josh Eppard, Mic Todd | PRODUCED BY Michael Birnbaum, Chris Bittner, Coheed and Cambria | FROM *Good Apollo I'm Burning Star IV, Volume One...* (Columbia, 2005)

o nuts that it makes *2112* seem like the Ramones, Coheed and Cambria's album and comic book industry as fired the odd salvo into the mainstream. Best loved the strident 'Welcome Home', which is more to do with writer Claudio Sanchez than with the heroes of his *Amory Vars* odyssey. It was remixed by Slipknot's Clown (who amped up the classical elements) and found a receptive ome in the *Rock Band* game. 'That stuff's incredible – hat it does for a band,' guitarist Travis Stever marvelled to ongfacts.com. 'We made a lot of fans.'

SACRIFICE UNTO SEBEK
Nile

BY Karl Sanders | PRODUCED BY Neil Kernon | FROM *Annihilation of the Wicked* (Relapse, 2005)

'Sebek was the principal crocodile god in Ancient Egypt,' wrote frontman Karl Sanders. 'When the canals dried up, the crocodile wandered the fields at will, killing and eating whatever or whoever crossed its path. The Egyptians came to regard the crocodile as a personification of the powers of evil and death... The Nile crocodile is one of the very few animals... that actively hunts and preys upon humans.' So while *Annihilation of the Wicked* is like having a pyramid collapse on your head, 'Sacrifice Unto Sebek' is like being eaten by a death metal crocodile.

SUGAR, WE'RE GOIN DOWN
Fall Out Boy

BY Patrick Stump, Pete Wentz, Joe Trohman, Andy Hurley PRODUCED BY Neal Avron | FROM *From Under the Cork Tree* (Island, 2005)

'This was a fun one,' bassist Pete Wentz reminisced to loudersound.com. 'Patrick [Stump, singer] played that chorus as a throwaway when we were writing in the practice room, and I was like, "What was that part?" And he couldn't remember. Eventually he did, but it almost never happened.' The song became an inescapable – and eventually quadruple platinum – hit, and turned Fall Out Boy into pop-punk leaders. 'It was like being on the other side of the precipice,' Wentz recalled, 'and that was, like, terrifying and great.'

CRAZY BITCH
Buckcherry

BY Josh Todd, Keith Nelson | PRODUCED BY Keith Nelson, Mike Plotnikoff, Paul DeCar FROM *15* (Universal, 2005)

'It's just about a girl who's good in bed but a terrible girlfriend,' singer Josh Todd shrugged to songfacts.com. That undersells a cut so crass that its only rival in this book is 'Cherry Pie' (*see* 1990). But for a band whose first hit was the coke anthem 'Lit Up', it was ideal. 'It was never meant to be misogynistic,' guitarist Keith Nelson protested to *Classic Rock*. 'So many women love it and know all the lyrics... So anyone out there who still thinks we're sexist? Talk to the girls who go around calling themselves the Crazy Bitch. They understand, even if you don't.'

STRICKEN
Disturbed

BY David Draiman, Dan Donegan, Mike Wengren | PRODUCED BY Johnny K, Disturbed | FROM *Ten Thousand Fists* (Reprise, 2005)

'I don't even know that we necessarily belong within "metal" any more,' David Draiman mused to *Billboard*. 'Any metal that we identify ourselves with is old-school... Lamb of God, Atreyu, Shadows Fall and Killswitch Engage are very talented... But, to me, songs in general need to have powerful, compelling, engaging melodies.' 'Stricken' accomplished that in style, topped with a searing solo by Dan Donegan. 'We just became more focused on the riffs and syncopation,' he told ultimate-guitar.com. 'But [the band] have been encouraging me [to solo].'

ḄAT ƆOUNTRY
venged Sevenfold

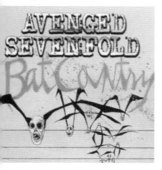

BY M. Shadows, Synyster Gates, Zacky Vengeance, The Rev | PRODUCED BY Mudrock, Avenged Sevenfold | FROM *City of Evil* (Warner Bros., 2005)

ll we were listening to was Sonata Arctica, a European ower metal band, and Blind Guardian and Queen,' . Shadows recalled to *Louder Than Hell*, 'where it's all uilt around pop melodies with lots of backup vocals.' ne resultant 'Bat Country' turned a cult act into heroes. here's a quote from one of the biggest psychopaths the world, Hunter S. Thompson, and the whole drug ference, [and] it's sitting on top of [MTV request show] RL,' Zacky Vengeance marvelled to revolvermag.com. he joke's on mainstream music at that point.'

I'M SO SIƆK
Flyleaf

BY Lacey Mosley, James Culpepper, Sameer Bhattacharya, Jared Hartmann, Pat Seals | PRODUCED BY Howard Benson | FROM *Flyleaf* (Octone, 2005)

'Sometimes the world can be a sick and messed-up place,' singer Lacey Mosley said of a song that helped Flyleaf's debut sell a million. 'Even though we grow up in those kinds of situations, it doesn't mean that, when we can make decisions for ourselves, we have to stay... We recognize what's sick and messed up around us, and then change things so that we can break the cycle.' Angst raged through *Flyleaf*, and nowhere was Mosley's disillusionment and disgust – but, ultimately, hope – more explicit than on its monstrous opener.

ḄEMESIS
rch Enemy

BY Angela Gossow, Michael Arnott, Christopher Arnott, Daniel Erlandsson | PRODUCED BY Rickard Bengtsson | FROM *Doomsday Machine* (Century Media, 2005)

he vocal coach surely didn't teach me screaming,' ngela Gossow protested to theaquarian.com of the oman who helped save her extraordinary voice. 'She as rather shocked, really, and doubted I would last very ng... I proved her wrong, and many others who saw me s a gimmick.' The singer's third album with Arch Enemy rthed a clutch of classics, including 'My Apocalypse' nd 'Taking Back My Soul'. But the most extraordinary and nduring was 'Nemesis', its 'one for all, all for one' refrain aking it a modern metal anthem.

THE ƆRAND ƆONJURATION
Opeth

BY Mikael Åkerfeldt, Per Wiberg | PRODUCED BY Opeth, Jens Bogren FROM *Ghost Reveries* (Roadrunner, 2005)

'We have an interest in the occult,' guitarist Peter Lindgren confessed to musicomh.com. 'It doesn't go further than it does with anybody else... but if people want to think we're evil, then that's cool.' 'The Grand Conjuration' certainly sounded pretty evil, with proggy flourishes more Tool than King Crimson. For the song's release as a single, Opeth hacked it from ten minutes and made a video. 'We thought that the first time that we would do a video, it would turn out great,' Lindgren exclaimed to themetalforge.com. 'Instead it looks like my cat sat on it!'

BEST OF YOU
Foo Fighters

BY Dave Grohl, Taylor Hawkins, Nate Mendel, Chris Shiflett | PRODUCED BY Nick Raskulinecz, Foo Fighters | FROM *In Your Honor* (Roswell, 2005)

'We demoed so many songs for *In Your Honor*, I'd kind of forgotten about "Best of You",' Dave Grohl confessed to *Kerrang!* 'It was our manager who came in and said, "What happened to that 'Best of You' song?" So we pulled it out.' It became one of the Foos' three double platinum US hits – alongside 'Everlong' and 'The Pretender' (*see* 2007) – and Prince sang it at the Super Bowl. 'Most people think it's a love song,' Grohl explained to *Kerrang!* 'But it's meant to be more universal, which I think is one of the reasons so many people sing along when we play it.'

A GUNSHOT TO THE HEAD...
Trivium

BY Matt Heafy, Corey Beaulieu, Travis Smith, Jason Suecof | PRODUCED BY Jason Suecof, Matt Heafy | FROM *Ascendancy* (Roadrunner, 2005)

'It's a sad and sickening thought that some people live in fear of their own families,' declared Matt Heafy. 'Spousal abuse, child abuse, neglect or sexual abuse – it's all tragic on a life-threatening scale. Monsters will create monsters through their own actions. This song reflects the outright anger that I have for these people.' But Trivium turned that anger into an anthem. And while purists rate *Ascendancy*'s 'Pull Harder on the Strings of Your Martyr' higher, the Maiden-via-Metallica vibe of 'A Gunshot to the Head of Trepidation' still sounds triumphant.

TEARS DON'T FALL
Bullet for My Valentine

BY Matt Tuck, Michael Paget, Jason James, Michael Thomas | PRODUCED BY Colin Richardson | FROM *The Poison* (Visible Noise, 2005)

'It was a bit of a moment for the band's career – even at that early stage – and a bit of a moment for the hard rock/metal genre,' Matt Tuck told downloadfestival.co.uk of the song that helped turn Welsh hopefuls Bullet into a transatlantic sensation. 'It's a song that's really connected and has passed the test of time. That song will never drop because of the importance of it. We know the significance... It's a song that means a lot to us as well as the fans who were there in the early days.' Trivium's Matt Heafy posted an acoustic cover of it in 2018.

HOT KISS
Juliette and the Licks

BY Juliette Lewis, Todd Morse | PRODUCED BY Dylan McLaren, Sid Riggs | FROM *Four on the Floor* (Hassle, 2006)

'Dave was just really supportive of us,' Juliette Lewis told *Rolling Stone* of the ubiquitous Mr Grohl, 'and I felt I could talk to him about anything. Then, later on, when we were looking for a new drummer, he said, "I'll do it!"... He has such power and is so dynamic. To be next to that kind of powerhouse of a player, I always joke it was like being next to Zeus.' Grohl indeed drums up a storm throughout the Licks' last album – check out the *Making Four on the Floor* videos. But the star is Lewis, who is as charismatic a rocker as she is a film star.

OCEAN PLANET
Gojira

BY Joe Duplantier, Christian Andreu, Jean-Michel Labadie, Mario Duplantier | PRODUCED BY Gojira | FROM *From Mars to Sirius* (Mon Slip, 2005)

'France,' frontman Joe Duplantier admitted to *Rolling Stone*, 'has no tradition of metal bands at all.' That changed with Gojira's breakthrough third album, which is as heavy as the whales that are its recurring motif. 'Ocean Planet' is the mind-blowing scene-setter. 'The opening riff is so massive and epic,' Cancer Bats' Scott Middleton frothed to musicradar.com. Of its ecological theme, Duplantier told metalunderground.com: 'We live on this planet and there's nothing we know about anything except this planet... So if we don't take care of it, we may be lost.'

EMERGENCY
Paramore

BY Hayley Williams, Josh Farro | PRODUCED BY Mike Green | FROM *All We Know Is Falling* (Fueled by Ramen, 2005)

'This song is about love,' Hayley Williams explained, 'and not love in a good way. People have started to abuse love... You can see it with the divorce rates. And you can tell in the way people are treated. I see it all around and want to change it.' 'Emergency' was one of the largely ignored singles from Paramore's debut album ('Pressure' eventually went gold in the US over a decade later); its commercial failure giving no hint that the band – initially outsold by Flyleaf – would help redefine metal for the twenty-first century.

KNIGHTS OF CYDONIA
Muse

BY Matt Bellamy | PRODUCED BY Rich Costey, Muse | FROM *Black Holes and Revelations* (Helium 3, 2005)

'Bands come along every now and again to neutralize the flamboyance of rock,' Matt Bellamy complained to *The Times*. 'The Ramones, Sex Pistols, Nirvana, even The White Stripes... What we're doing is kind of punk, if you like. To be flamboyant and excessive and over the top is more against the system than what most bands are doing.' Nowhere was that excessive flamboyance better captured than on the *Black Holes and Revelations* closer that is, wrote Paul Elliott in *Q*, 'the most heroic, ambitious and ridiculous song in Muse's armoury.'

COMING UNDONE
Korn

BY Jonathan Davis, James 'Munky' Shaffer, Fieldy, David Silveria, The Matrix (L. Christy, G. Edwards, S. Spock) | PRODUCED BY Jonathan Davis, The Matrix | FROM *See You on the Other Side* (Virgin, 2005)

'Coming Undone', Jonathan Davis told presstelegram.com, 'is when you've reached your point and you're like, "I can't take this any more," and you do something crazy.' So far, so Korn. But 'Coming Undone' – and much of *See You on the Other Side* – mitigated the usual lyrical misery with bouncy backing, courtesy of pop producers The Matrix (check out the irresistible 'Politics'). The fun of 'Coming Undone' was compounded by its debt to Queen's 'We Will Rock You' (*see* 1979), which Korn duly incorporated into performances of the song.

ROSES FOR THE DEAD
Funeral for a Friend

BY Matthew Davies-Kreye, Kris Coombs-Roberts, Darran Smith, Ryan Richards, Gareth Ellis-Davies | PRODUCE BY Terry Date, Funeral for a Friend | FROM *Hours* (Atlantic, 2005)

'A heavy song,' said frontman Matthew Davies to *Kerrang!* about 'Roses for the Dead', 'but not in the way metal is typically considered to be heavy. This is about the death of close friends; I saw my friends and family all grieving, but I didn't know how to react. I felt odd because I wasn't crying; I sat there and took it all in. I wanted to pay tribute to the memory of those people.' A heartbreaking video helped make 'Roses' the fans' favourite song, and its parent album *Hours* – home to three other hits – Funeral for a Friend's best loved.

ROSENROT
Rammstein

BY Christoph 'Doom' Schneider, Christian Lorenz, Paul Landers, Till Lindemann, Oliver Riedel, Richard Z. Kruspe | PRODUCED BY Jacob Hellner, Rammstein | FROM *Rosenrot* (Universal, 2005)

'They didn't like that song so much,' video director Zoran Bihać told *Metal Hammer*. 'They didn't know what to do with it as they thought it was a bit boring.' Rammstein's on-screen solution was to dress as self-flagellating priests, and the song became a fan favourite anyway. Inspired by Johann Wolfgang von Goethe's poem *Heidenröslein*, it had been recorded for 2004's *Reise, Reise* (*Rosenrot*, the album, was envisaged as *Reise, Reise Vol. 2*), but was held over because that album, brimming with potential hits, didn't need what was clearly another.

OILED FROGS
Alexisonfire

🇨🇦

BY George Pettit, Dallas Green, Wade MacNeil, Chris Steele, Jordan Hastings | **PRODUCED BY** Julius Butty, Alexisonfire | **FROM** *Crisis* (Distort Entertainment, 2006)

Ve definitely wrote the album to be bangers,' frontman eorge Pettit told noisey.vice.com of his band's third and est. 'There are a lot of big choruses that we knew would e soaring... When we started writing songs, it's like we 'ere planning what we'd do while we're playing live. Stuff e pulling out of a song and having the crowd sing the horus... A lot of it had to do with us getting better playing ve.' The fan pick is 'This Could Be Anywhere in the World', ut certified banger 'Boiled Frogs' is the best introduction o these post-hardcore heroes.

R.A.M.O.N.E.S.
Motörhead

🇬🇧 🇩🇰

BY Lemmy, Phil Campbell, Würzel, Phil 'Philthy Animal' Taylor | **PRODUCED BY** Cameron Webb | **FROM** *Kiss of Death* (Sanctuary, 2006)

'I love the fucking Ramones,' Lemmy explained to theartsdesk.com. There were, he said, parallels between the Ramones and Motörhead: 'Not much appreciation, looked upon as a joke for a long time.' Joey Ramone was delighted by the tribute: 'The ultimate honour. Like John Lennon writing a song for you.' Based on a riff by Phil Campbell, 'R.A.M.O.N.E.S.' debuted on Motörhead's *1916* (1991), but the greatest version is a re-recording on US and Canadian editions of *Kiss of Death*, with Mikkey Dee's crazed drumming upping the damage.

EDNECK
amb of God

🇺🇸

BY Randy Blythe, Mark Morton, Willie Adler, John Campbell, Chris Adler | **PRODUCED BY** Machine | **FROM** *Sacrament* (Epic, 2006)

was trying to incorporate some blues-influenced, outhern swagger into metal,' guitarist Mark Morton ecalled to *Total Guitar*. 'I was thinking about some of the lder music that I'm into, like Lynyrd Skynyrd and The llman Brothers... It makes me think of being a kid and reaking beer bottles in the park. It has that rowdy feel to that connects with people. I wish I could write twenty ore!' The Grammy-nominated anthem, Morton enthused o *Metal Hammer*, 'opened up a new section of audience or us. That was exciting to be a part of.'

THROUGH THE FIRE AND FLAMES
DragonForce

🇬🇧

BY ZP Theart, Herman Li, Sam Totman, Vadim Pruzhanov | **PRODUCED BY** Sam Totman, Herman Li, Vadim Pruzhanov | **FROM** *Inhuman Rampage* (Noise, 2006)

'We didn't think, "Oh, this is going to be some big, popular song,"' Sam Totman admitted to songfacts.com. 'We must have liked it the best on the album – that's why we put it first. But we didn't think, "Oh wow, we've got some amazing hit here"... I still don't think it's better than any of our other stuff.' Nonetheless, 'Through the Fire and the Flames' became DragonForce's signature song, not least because Totman and Herman Li's spectacularly speedy axemanship means it's considered the most challenging number in the *Guitar Hero* franchise.

DEFEATIST
Hatebreed

BY Jamey Jasta, Sean Martin, Frank Novinec, Chris Beattie, Matt Byrne | PRODUCED BY Chris 'Zeuss' Harris | FROM *Supremacy* (Roadrunner, 2006)

'We are what we are at this point,' Jamey Jasta observed to lambgoat.com of his hardcore band's fourth outing. 'If you hate us, you're definitely going to hate the new album. If you love us, I think you're going to love it. It kind of is what it is. We want to speed it up on some parts... We're definitely going in almost a more metal route.' But if *Supremacy* was essentially more of the same, its opening blast more than lived up to Jasta's promise of being 'pretty fast and in-your-face'. For fans of wrestling-style anthems, there's also 'Destroy Everything'.

MY CURSE
Killswitch Engage

BY Howard Jones, Adam Dutkiewicz, Joel Stroetzel, Mike D'Antonio, Justin Foley | PRODUCED BY Adam Dutkiewicz | FROM *As Daylight Dies* (Roadrunner, 2006)

'That's just about chicks,' Adam Dutkiewicz informed songfacts.com. 'A lot of [singer] Howard [Jones]'s songs are about girls. It's always a topic guys can relate to.' *As Daylight Dies* consolidated the breakthrough success of its predecessor *The End of Heartache*, and a lot of the credit goes to the extraordinary vocals of Jones (one of the few who could take on Dio's 'Holy Diver' and win). 'My Curse' brilliantly blended melody and metalcore, the first of which was amplified when Trivium's Matt Heafy posted an acoustic cover to YouTube in 2018.

MAKE THEM SUFFER
Cannibal Corpse

BY Pat O'Brien, Paul Mazurkiewicz | PRODUCED BY Erik Rutan | FROM *Kill* (Metal Blade, 2006)

'There's no dead babies hanging,' Corpsegrinder frowned to noisey.vice.com of *Kill*. 'There's no torture cover with a bunch of bodies hanging, there's no corpse sex... We like to think that the hoopla is about our music, and it's just people freaking out that we write great songs.' People had in fact freaked out about Cannibal Corpse since their 1990 debut, and rarely was that connected to the quality of their songs. But the likes of 'Necrosadistic Warning', 'Death Walking Terror' and 'Make Them Suffer' ensured *Kill* was *Now That's What I Call Cannibal Corpse*.

COME CLARITY
In Flames

⊞ BY Jesper Strömblad, Björn Gelotte, Anders Fridén | PRODUCED BY Pelle Henricsson, Eskil Lövström | FROM *Come Clarity* (Nuclear Blast, 2006)

or four minutes, In Flames abandoned the melodic death metal of which they are exemplars: *Come Clarity*'s brilliant, brooding title track is more akin to the booming ballads on Marilyn Manson's *Mechanical Animals* (*see* 1998). 'It's way easier if you want to gather the masses,' frontman Anders Fridén admitted to roughedge.com. Lyrically, it was as heavy as ever. 'I don't mind taking you through whatever problems you might have or struggle you're going through,' Fridén observed. 'I can't write about demons and dragons because I've never met any.'

THE LORD'S SEDITION
Deicide

▬ BY Glen Benton, Steve Asheim | PRODUCED BY Steve Asheim | FROM *The Stench of Redemption* (Earache, 2006)

Epic yet accessible, complex yet catchy, fast yet rhythmic, even a slower part or two...' drummer Steve Asheim vowed to metalstorm.net of Deicide's eighth album. Fans were thrilled by 'Homage for Satan', but the soaring 'The Lord's Sedition' – with echoes of Slayer's 'Seasons in the Abyss' – superbly showcased a band revitalised by guitarists Jack Owen (ex-Cannibal Corpse) and Ralph Santolla (ex-Death). They asked me whether I minded if they did some of their own stuff,' Asheim recalled to chroniclesofchaos.com. And they just went nuts!'

DIFFERENT WORLD
Iron Maiden

⊠ BY Adrian Smith, Steve Harris | PRODUCED BY Kevin Shirley, Steve Harris | FROM *A Matter of Life and Death* (EMI, 2006)

'We write a batch of songs and they come out as they come out,' Steve Harris assured theaquarian.com. 'It just turns out there are loads of epics on this album.' *A Matter of Life and Death* was awash with weighty songs, such as fan favourite 'For the Greater Good of God'. But its opener was Maiden's most brilliantly poppy song since 'Can I Play with Madness?' (*see* 1988), even opening with a bellow by Nicko McBrain. 'It's one of the little things he's always done,' Harris reported. 'Some of the lyrics are fairly serious, so we thought we'd leave it in for fun.'

OUR TRUTH
Lacuna Coil

BY Andrea Ferro, Chris Migliore, Marco 'Maus' Biazzi, Marco Coti Zelati, Cristiano 'Criz' Mozzati | PRODUCED BY Waldemar Sorychta, Lacuna Coil | FROM *Karmacode* (Century Media, 2006)

'Arabian parts, tribal parts, and the rhythmic sections...' Cristina Scabbia told Wishyouplease of Lacuna Coil's fourth album. 'At the same time there are a lot of American-y vibes... but still really passionate.' This cocktail blended brilliantly on 'Our Truth'. 'We are saying, "We are raising our truth" – which is actually the history [of] Lacuna Coil,' Scabbia explained. 'We started to propose a music which was not exactly the trend of the moment. Especially in Italy, there was this big boom of power metal and we were proposing a new goth rock metal.'

REBORN
Stone Sour

BY Corey Taylor, Jim Root, Josh Rand, Shawn Economaki | PRODUCED BY Nick Raskulinecz | FROM *Come What(ever) May* (Roadrunner, 2006)

'It's not goth rock, it's not fucking emo, it's not garage...' Corey Taylor promised revolvermag.com of Stone Sour's second album. 'It's good, heavy rock that's going to kick you in the face. Why would you want anything else?' *Come What(ever) May* shifted from catchy ('30/30-150') to sad ('Through Glass'), and hit maximum heaviosity on 'Reborn' – the cut that would sound most at home on a Slipknot album. It was a favourite of drummer Roy Mayorga – because, he told metalfan.ro, 'That was the first track I recorded and it was a first take.'

WELCOME TO THE BLACK PARADE
My Chemical Romance

BY Gerard Way, Ray Toro, Frank Iero, Mikey Way, Bob Bryar PRODUCED BY Rob Cavallo, My Chemical Romance | FROM *The Black Parade* (Reprise, 2006)

'When My Chemical Romance were making *The Black Parade*,' frontman Gerard Way revealed to *Rolling Stone*, 'we watched tons of documentary footage about *A Night at the Opera*, Queen's best album. We used Brian May amps and wrote songs with different movements. But we didn't try to make another "Bohemian Rhapsody". Whenever someone tries to do that, they fail.' In fact, My Chemical Romance's ambitious mini-epic 'Welcome to the Black Parade' became a chart-topping, era-defining classic that still sounds ace today.

the new album
THE BLACK PARADE
Featuring 'Welcome To The Black Parade'
www.mychemicalromance.com

CULT
Slayer

BY Kerry King, Dave Lombardo | PRODUCED BY Josh Abraham | FROM *Christ Illusion* (American, 2006)

'My thing,' Kerry King assured ultimate-guitar.com, 'is just rebelling against organized religion... I think it's a crutch for people that are too weak to get through life on their own. I'm the kind of guy that says, if I don't see it, then it doesn't work. And nobody can show me God.' The result was an album awash in stinging sentiment. But what made *Christ Illusion*, and 'Cult' in particular, spectacular was the back-in-the-saddle Dave Lombardo, hammering up a storm while Tom Araya (an avowed Christian) hollered his way through King's indignation.

THE PRETENDER
Foo Fighters

BY Dave Grohl, Taylor Hawkins, Nate Mendel, Chris Shiflett | PRODUCED BY Gil Norton | FROM *Echoes, Silence, Patience & Grace* (Roswell, 2007)

Everyone's been fucked over,' Dave Grohl observed to UK radio station XFM, towards the end of George W. Bush's administration. 'A lot of people feel fucked over right now and they're not getting what they were promised.' His annoyance fuelled what he hailed as 'a stomping Foo Fighters uptempo song, with a little bit of Chuck Berry'. A late addition to *Echoes, Silence, Patience & Grace*, it became one of their biggest-selling hits. Not bad for a song inspired by *Sesame Street*'s 'One of These Things (Is Not Like the Others)'.

FIRST BLOOD
Evile

🇬🇧

BY Matt Drake, Ol Drake, Ben Carter | PRODUCED BY Flemming Rasmussen FROM *Enter the Grave* (Earache, 2007)

So old-school that it should be produced by Flemming Rasmussen – oh, it is – and contain the phrase 'metal madness' – oh, it does – 'Thrasher' is Evile's signature song. But the brutal 'First Blood' is the cut on which the quartet alchemised gold from their influences – principally Exodus and Slayer, although a shout of 'Master!' tips a hat to Rasmussen's most famous charges. 'The only way my brain knows is what I've learned from when I was growing up,' guitarist Ol Drake told *Decibel*. 'It's bound to have some Metallica in it.'

MAD BUTCHER
Destruction

BY Schmier, Mike Sifringer, Tommy Sandmann | PRODUCED BY Destruction | FROM *Thrash Anthems* (AFM, 2007)

'These guys were ahead of their time,' Flotsam & Jetsam's Michael Gilbert noted to phoenixnewtimes.com. 'Speed metal? Death metal? Maybe both?' Originally, Destruction were part of a German thrash boom that also included Sodom and Kreator, and that entranced fans worldwide. 'We were all fans of Destruction,' Gene Hoglan confirmed to *Louder Than Hell*. 'Mad Butcher' was one of the early classics that the band rescued from their original, Venom-esque fidelity with the remakes collection *Thrash Anthems* – a handy primer for this primal force.

A FAREWELL TO ARMS
Machine Head

🇺🇸

BY Robb Flynn, Phil Demmel, Adam Duce | PRODUCED BY Robb Flynn | FROM *The Blackening* (Roadrunner, 2007)

The Blackening is so crazily great that it feels treacherous not to include more of it here (hello, 'Halo', 'Aesthetics of Hate' and 'Clenching the Fists of Dissent'), but it really does save the best for last. The unrelenting 'A Farewell to Arms' is the 'In My Time of Dying' (*see* 1975) of its era. 'I wasn't sure how people would react to those ten-minute songs,' Robb Flynn admitted to *Metal Hammer*. Also notable were the antiwar lyrics. 'We were all pissed off and angry about the war in Iraq...' Flynn explained, 'and about shit that was going on in society generally.'

LIVING IS A PROBLEM...
Biffy Clyro

BY Simon Neil | PRODUCED BY Garth Richardson, Biffy Clyro FROM *Puzzle* (14th Floor, 2007)

I lost my mum between [2004's] *Infinity Land* and [2007's] *Puzzle*, and I started to take the music very seriously,' Biffy main man Simon Neil explained to noisey.vice.com. 'I was away on tour when she died, and I thought that if this music is keeping me apart from her at that point... we're going to fully commit.' Opener 'Living Is a Problem Because Everything Dies' made that commitment clear: it introduced the band's more streamlined sound, yet its remarkable strings set Biffy apart from more conventional *Kerrang!* cover stars.

BLEED IT OUT
Linkin Park

BY Mike Shinoda, Chester Bennington, Rob Bourdon, Brad Delson, Dave Farrell, Joe Hahn | PRODUCED BY Rick Rubin, Mike Shinoda | FROM *Minutes to Midnight* (Warner Bros., 2007)

'One of the band's goals on this record was to enjoy it,' Linkin Park said of *Minutes to Midnight*. 'This track is one of the places that it is most evident.' In fact, much of the album is weapons-grade glum, making even the snarling 'Bleed It Out' sound poppy – or, as Mike Shinoda told *Kerrang!*, 'a bizarre death-party-rap hoedown.' As a single, its double platinum sales were hard won. Shinoda's words were endlessly rewritten until the band were satisfied: 'I was bringing in the lyrics, getting punched in the face and then going back to the drawing board.'

TO HOLMGARD AND BEYOND
Turisas

BY Mathias Nygård | PRODUCED BY Mathias Nygård, Janne Saksa | FROM *The Varangian Way* (Century Media, 2007)

Sometimes you get bands calling themselves "epic" and they just write overly long songs,' Turisas main man and 'Viking metal' standard bearer Mathias Nygård complained to metal-discovery.com. 'We as a band are epic in the music in itself. It's kind of storytelling in itself. Even if you don't read the lyrics or even know the track titles, you can follow the musical drama.' So if 'Viking metal' (i.e. Manowar without the screeched vocals) appeals, proceed directly to the Finnish warriors' second album and, in particular, 'To Holmgard and Beyond'.

MILK LIZARD
The Dillinger Escape Plan

BY Benjamin Weinman, Greg Puciato | PRODUCED BY Steve Evetts, Benjamin Weinman | FROM *Ire Works* (Relapse, 2007)

'Unashamed rock 'n' roll with unconventional time signatures and aggressively weird instrumentation' was loudwire.com's verdict on 'Milk Lizard'. That's a better description than the dreary 'math rock' label often attached to the New Jersey wrecking crew. 'It's so awesome when Dillinger completely switch it up,' Blood Youth's Kaya Tarsus enthused to *Metal Hammer*. 'I'm really into this style, just as much as the classic TDEP songs. When I was sixteen, the band I was in used to cover this song. I'm pretty sure we butchered it!'

COME TO LIFE
Alter Bridge

BY Mark Tremonti, Myles Kennedy, Scott Phillips, Brian Marshall PRODUCED BY Michael 'Elvis' Baskette | FROM *Blackbird* (Universal Republic, 2007)

Celebrated for the lighter-waving 'Rise Today', 'Watch Over You' and 'Blackbird', Alter Bridge's second album storms out of the gate with songs so heavy that they seem designed to scare lingering Creed fans. 'Ties That Bind' and 'Brand New Start' are fine, but it's 'Come to Life' that bludgeons best, scything and swirling like '95-era Alice in Chains. 'It's more aggressive,' Mark Tremonti observed of this new sound to guitarmessenger.com. 'We added Myles [Kennedy] on the guitar, so it's more layered… and just more interesting.'

AFTERLIFE
Avenged Sevenfold

BY The Rev, Synyster Gates, M. Shadows, Zacky Vengeance | PRODUCED BY Avenged Sevenfold | FROM *Avenged Sevenfold* (Warner Bros., 2007)

Drummer The Rev, recalled Zacky Vengeance, 'said, "I've got a song for you guys"… We just flipped out… Lyric-wise, it's really a cool concept because you can apply it to your own life and relationships and stuff… The actual storyline is about a person that finds himself in the afterlife and they realize they have too much stuff left on Earth to do… They have to escape from their afterlife, so they can go back and make amends with the people they love and care about.' As a fitting tribute to the deceased drummer, 'Afterlife' has become Ax7's best-loved song.

MISERY BUSINESS
Paramore

BY Hayley Williams, Josh Farro | PRODUCED BY David Bendeth | FROM *Riot!* (Fueled by Ramen, 2007)

'"Misery Business" is not a set of lyrics that I relate to as a twenty-six-year-old woman,' Hayley Williams wrote in 2015. 'It wasn't really meant to be this big philosophical statement about anything. It was quite literally a page in my diary about a singular moment I experienced as a high schooler.' Producer David Bendeth explained to *Billboard*: 'She wrote, "Once a whore, you're nothing more"… She said, "Okay, I'm going to sing it. I'm not going to like it, but I'm going to sing it."' The result was Paramore's first smash and, to this day, the fans' favourite song.

LETTING YOU
Nine Inch Nails

BY Trent Reznor | PRODUCED BY Trent Reznor, Atticus Ross, Alan Moulder | FROM *The Slip* (The Null Corporation, 2008)

Having once toiled for years on albums, the detoxed Trent Reznor became downright prolific in the mid-noughties. Hot on the heels of 2007's concept album *Year Zero* came 2008's *Ghosts I-IV* and *The Slip*. Initially issued as a free download, the latter ticked all the NIN boxes, from goth disco ('Discipline') to shit-freezing scariness ('The Four of Us Are Dying'). Its most glorious moment, however, was the seething 'Letting You', whose artwork (above) and government-skewering lyrics made clear its connection to *Year Zero*'s dystopian concept.

SAINTS OF LOS ANGELES
Mötley Crüe

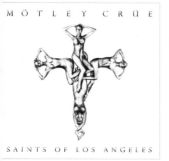

BY Nikki Sixx, James Michael, DJ Ashba, Marti Frederiksen | PRODUCED BY James Michael, Nikki Sixx, DJ Ashba | FROM *Saints of Los Angeles* (Mötley Records, 2008)

'Mötley Crüe started something in the eighties that's still with us today,' Vince Neil wrote in his autobiography in 2010. 'There was a certain sound that came up in rock 'n' roll at a certain time and a certain place, and we were at the forefront. We were *it*.' That legacy was celebrated in the Grammy-nominated title cut of their final studio album. 'You don't go, "Who's this? It kind of sounds like Mötley Crüe,"' Nikki Sixx told *Rolling Stone*. 'You go, "Fuck, new Mötley Crüe!"... It's not the band trying to make you like them. It's the band doing what they do.'

DECODE
Paramore

BY Hayley Williams, Josh Farro, Taylor York PRODUCED BY Rob Cavallo | FROM *Twilight (Original Motion Picture Soundtrack)* (Chop Shop, 2008)

Paramore sealed their status as angsty adolescent icons by contributing the yearning 'Decode' and 'I Caught Myself' to the soundtrack of an angsty vampire film franchise. '*Twilight* is the first series of books I've ever read,' Hayley Williams explained. 'Decode' itself, she said, concerns 'the love affair between the series' protagonists, Bella and Edward... the building tension, awkwardness, anger and confusion... Bella is the only mind Edward can't read, and I feel like that's a big part of the first book and one of the obstacles for them to overcome'.

CHELSEA SMILE
Bring Me the Horizon

BY Oli Sykes, Matt Kean, Lee Malia, Matt Nicholls, Curtis Ward | PRODUCED BY Fredrik Nordström, Henrik Udd | FROM *Suicide Season* (Visible Noise, 2008)

'We've always wanted to be a really heavy band,' Oli Sykes explained to exclaim.ca. 'But I think it's good when a band can be really heavy and still have catchy hooks and riffs.' *Suicide Season* was a huge step from BMtH's debut (*Count Your Blessings*, 2006) and no cut better signposted their evolution than the one *Metal Hammer* described as 'one of the nastiest songs to ever be called catchy'. Of its meaning, Sykes told coupdemainmagazine.com, 'You can't always tell when someone's keeping something inside and not really happy.'

KNIFEMAN
The Bronx

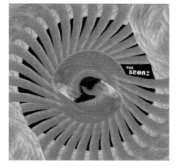

BY Matt Caughthran, Joby J Ford, Ken Horne, Brad Majors, Jorma Vik | PRODUCED BY Dave Schiffman | FROM *The Bronx* (White Drugs, 2008)

The opening salvo of The Bronx's third album, frontman Matt Caughthran told loudersound.com, is about 'disenchantment with what we thought the dream of being in a signed, touring band would be... being on the borderline of heaven and hell'. The California quintet had already given the finger to the industry by titling their first three albums *The Bronx*. Then they gave their fiery punk a Mexican-themed makeover, transformed into the uproarious Mariachi El Bronx – and, naturally, issued three albums named *Mariachi El Bronx*.

ROCK N ROLL TRAIN
AC/DC

BY Angus Young, Malcolm Young | PRODUCED BY Brendan O'Brien | FROM *Black Ice* (Columbia, 2008)

A brave interviewer once suggested to Angus Young that the album he was promoting sounded just like the previous one. As Gene Simmons recalled to thequietus.com, 'Angus said, "I don't agree. I think our new record sounds like *every* record we've ever made."' So it was with *Black Ice*, which doubled the sales of its predecessor (2000's *Stiff Upper Lip*) but wasn't necessarily twice as good. Still, it bequeathed an anthem in the defiantly unpunctuated form of 'Rock n Roll Train', the set opener throughout the blockbusting *Black Ice* tour.

SANCTUARY
Cavalera Conspiracy

BY Max Cavalera, Igor Cavalera, Marc Rizzo | PRODUCED BY Max Cavalera, Logan Mader | FROM *Inflikted* (Roadrunner, 2008)

Strained silence characterised a ten-year estrangement between brothers Max and Igor Cavalera. When they reunited, Max told loudersound.com, the first lyrics were those of the raging 'Sanctuary' – 'My own warped way of finding happiness in dark topics… We'd created this insane, killer song and accomplished something huge and awesome. This song is so metal!' If the reunion of the Sepultura siblings wasn't quite the earthshaker that fans expected, the likes of 'Sanctuary' and 'Black Ark' ensured that no one was too disappointed.

THE END OF THE LINE
Metallica

BY James Hetfield, Kirk Hammett, Lars Ulrich, Rob Trujillo | PRODUCED BY Rick Rubin | FROM *Death Magnetic* (Warner Bros., 2008)

'Metallica are fucking rad!' Flea declared to *Rolling Stone* in the aftermath of 2003's divisive *St. Anger*. 'The music is bitchin'… And they continue to rock on. Whatever gets thrown at them, they persevere and they get stronger.' Renewed strength flowed through *Death Magnetic* – and while there were more overtly thrashy standouts, the stealth bomber was the swaggering 'The End of the Line'. Based on the riff from an unreleased song played live in 2006, it's a gloriously damning verdict on the debauched lifestyle that James Hetfield ditched in 2002.

COMBUSTION
Meshuggah

BY Tomas Haake, Fredrick Thordendal, Jens Kidman, Mårten Hagström | PRODUCED BY Meshuggah | FROM *ObZen* (Nuclear Blast, 2008)

'*ObZen* is practically catchy, by Meshuggah standards,' marvelled blabbermouth.net of the extreme Swedes' sixth album. '"Combustion" is about as straight-ahead as these guys get.' This opening blast is a better introduction to one of metal's maddest acts than *ObZen*'s classic 'Bleed', although admirers of superhuman drumming should check that out too. 'Combustion' also inspired the most majestic verdict on voting website thetoptens.com: 'I do meth to this song then I usually go outside and yell at small children until they cry.'

TWILIGHT OF THE THUNDER GOD
Amon Amarth

BY Johan Hegg, Olavi Mikkonen, Johan Söderberg, Ted Lundström, Fredrik Andersson | PRODUCED BY Jens Bogren | FROM *Twilight of the Thunder God* (Metal Blade, 2008)

Amon Amarth, explained Metal Blade supremo Brian Slagel to loudersound.com, 'started out as an underground death metal act... They began to get more melodic and really kicked into gear. I recall hearing ['Twilight of the Thunder God'] for the first time, and absolutely loved it. I told the band it had to be the opening track on the album.' The result came as no surprise to *Metal Hammer*'s Dom Lawson: 'Songs about Thor are always brilliant, because Thor is the most metal of all gods (and superheroes) and has a massive fucking hammer.'

GEMATRIA (THE KILLING NAME)
Slipknot

BY Shawn Crahan, Chris Fehn, Paul Gray, Craig Jones, Joey Jordison, Jim Root, Corey Taylor, Mick Thomson, Sid Wilson | PRODUCED BY Dave Fortman, Slipknot | FROM *All Hope Is Gone* (Roadrunner, 2008)

'Probably our heaviest album by far,' bassist Paul Gray enthused to puregrainaudio.com. 'I love the song "All Hope Is Gone". I love the opening song, "Gematria".' The lurching latter – six minutes of riff upon ferocious riff – was named after a Greek-derived, Hebrew term. Explaining its sentiments to *Kerrang!*, Corey Taylor said: 'I love the people that still exercise their right to disagree and voice their discontent, but there are a lot of people who are disguising politics as religion, and dictating taste, and turning it into policy, and that hurts me.'

INSIDE THE FIRE
Disturbed

BY David Draiman, Dan Donegan, Mike Wengren | PRODUCED BY Dan Donegan, David Draiman, Mike Wengren | FROM *Indestructible* (Reprise, 2008)

The teenaged David Draiman, he told FaceCulture, 'had a girlfriend who took her own life – and it was a result of our break from each other.' Depressed in the aftermath, he said, 'I had this image of the devil talking to me, over the shoulder, telling me I should take my own life... so I could still be with her in the afterlife.' The theme was grim, but the song expertly blended guttural heaviness, deft melody and Rammstein-esque electronics. The result: Disturbed's biggest hit since 'Stricken' (*see* 2005) and a third consecutive number one album.

ALL I WANTED
Paramore

BY Hayley Williams, Taylor York | PRODUCED BY Rob Cavallo, Paramore | FROM *bran new eyes* (Fueled by Ramen, 2009)

'"All I Wanted" almost didn't make the record,' Hayley Williams admitted to *Alternative Press*. 'I can't remember why we didn't think it would work. We would've been pissed right now if it wasn't there.' Indeed: nestled after bangers like 'Brick After Boring Brick' is this elegiac epic, featuring extraordinary vocals. 'I never really pulled [the lyrics] from any specific incident,' Williams wrote. '[Boyfriend] Chad [Gilbert of New Found Glory] was going on tour for the first time in a while and I was bored with writing and being in Franklin. Just an "emo" kind of day.'

A LOOKING IN VIEW
Alice in Chains

BY Jerry Cantrell, William DuVall, Sean Kinney, Mike Inez | PRODUCED BY Nick Raskulinecz, Alice in Chains | FROM *Black Gives Way to Blue* (Virgin, 2009)

'That darkness is becoming positive,' Corey Taylor rhapsodised to musicradar.com of Alice in Chains' comeback. 'There are some lines on *Black Gives Way to Blue* that are phenomenal... "Looking In View" is probably my favourite... It is just a gorgeous song.' The album's only group composition, '[it] speaks to any number of things that keep you balled up inside,' said Jerry Cantrell. 'It's funny how hard we fight to hang on to a bone we can't pull through a hole in the fence, or how difficult it is to put down the bag of bricks and move on.'

RAMMLIED
Rammstein

BY Christoph 'Doom' Schneider, Doktor Christian Lorenz, Till Lindemann, Paul Landers, Richard Z. Kruspe, Oliver Riedel | PRODUCED BY Jacob Hellner, Rammstein | FROM *Liebe Ist Für Alle Da* (Pilgrim, 2009)

'The overriding theme,' Christoph 'Doom' Schneider declared to thrashhits.com of *Liebe Ist Für Alle Da*, 'is extreme forms of love.' That explains the singles 'Ich tu dir weh' ('I hurt you') and the notorious 'Pussy' (not to mention a box set with Rammstein dildos). But, as Richard Z. Kruspe noted, 'There are a couple of songs on this record that are to do with the band itself, about the return of Rammstein, and they have a different flavour.' Chief of these is the opening 'Rammlied' – a churning declaration of intent that's easily the equal of 'Rammstein' (*see* 1995).

WEIGHTLESS
All Time Low

BY Alex Gaskarth, Jack Barakat, Zack Merrick, Rian Dawson, Matt Squire | PRODUCED BY Matt Squire | FROM *Nothing Personal* (Hopeless, 2009)

'The whole mentality of the song is, like, you feel like you're stuck in this, like, negative space and you just want to get out,' Alex Gaskarth told MTV. 'Everybody's finishing up with school and everybody's getting, like, the exam beatdown.' The good thing about All Time Low's most popular song is it's, like, aware of its debt to every other pop-punk band. Witness the scene-skewering video, in which Fall Out Boy's Pete Wentz messages Blink-182's Mark Hoppus to say, 'ATL rips off FOB so bad,' only for Hoppus to reply, 'ATL and FOB rip off Blink-182.'

KINGS AND QUEENS
Thirty Seconds to Mars

BY Jared Leto | PRODUCED BY Flood, Steve Lillywhite, Thirty Seconds to Mars | FROM *This Is War* (Virgin, 2009)

Jared Leto began writing his crowning anthem at home in America. 'The other half,' he recalled to musicradar.com, 'was written in South Africa, which has proved to be a very lucky and magical place for the band... The minute I touched down, I finished the rest of it. I took that as a good omen.' 'Kings and Queens' brilliantly deployed the band's fans as a backing chorus and – thanks to producers Flood and Steve Lillywhite – shoved Tom DeLonge's Angels & Airwaves aside at the altar of U2. The result sounded like a stadium, even on the radio.

DARK HORSE
Converge

BY Jacob Bannon, Kurt Ballou, Nate Newton, Ben Koller | PRODUCED BY Kurt Ballou | FROM *Axe to Fall* (Epitaph, 2009)

After *Jane Doe* (see 2001), Converge toyed with actual songs, and *Axe to Fall* has some that you might even call metal (although not to their faces). The title track is one, the dizzying 'Dark Horse' another. 'An underdog or "dark horse" is a common theme throughout punk and hardcore,' Jacob Bannon explained to *Decibel*. '[We] carved out our own homes and built our own lives... This song is a tribute to the people in my life who have done – and continue to do – just that. It's also for those I've known who have died trying.'

WORLD PAINTED BLOOD
Slayer

BY Jeff Hanneman, Tom Araya, Kerry King | PRODUCED BY Greg Fidelman | FROM *World Painted Blood* (American, 2009)

'Every one of their albums has some killer tracks,' Arch Enemy's Angela Gossow assured music.avclub.com. 'If you don't like Slayer, there's something wrong with you.' Much of *World Painted Blood* sounded like Slayer paying homage to their own late eighties heyday, but the title cut provided a twist by adding a low-slung groove to its gallop. 'Even though we're all fun-loving guys,' Jeff Hanneman chuckled to musiquemag.com of the album's end-of-the-world theme, 'when it comes to Slayer, when we write stuff, it's all about hate.'

JUGGERNAUTS
Enter Shikari

🇬🇧

BY Rou Reynolds, Rory Clewlow, Chris Batten, Rob Rolfe | PRODUCED BY Andy Gray, Enter Shikari | FROM *Common Dreads* (Ambush Reality, 2009)

'It's not exactly our heaviest track,' singer Rou Reynolds admitted to loudersound.com of 'Juggernauts'. 'But it's certainly not a part of the pop world either, and it's got a really strange, progressive song structure. We were over the moon that the radio considered it playable.' Other songs from *Common Dreads* are heavier ('Solidarity') and some are better ('Fanfare for the Conscious Man'), but none sums up Enter Shikari better than 'Juggernauts'. Its synths and spoken words are more The Streets than Sabbath – but it is brilliantly brutal.

DIVINATIONS
Mastodon

🇺🇸

BY Brann Dailor, Brent Hinds, Bill Kelliher, Troy Sanders | PRODUCED BY Brendan O'Brien | FROM *Crack the Skye* (Reprise, 2009)

Czarist Russia. Astral travel. Out-of-body experiences. Stephen Hawking. *Crack the Skye* isn't short of ambition – nor epics, as fans of 'Oblivion' and 'The Czar' will attest. Mastodon's fourth album, Bill Kelliher assured premierguitar.com, 'is definitely an ode to traditional rock 'n' roll records like *The Wall* [*see* 1979] or *Zeppelin II* [*see* 1969].' But unless you're patient or stoned, skip to the hardest-hitting track, 'Divinations'. Psychedelic yet scything, it's as Sabbath circa 1970 as the same year's *Heaven & Hell* album is Sabbath circa 1980.

APOCALYPTIC HAVOC
Goatwhore

🇺🇸

BY Sammy Duet, Louis Benjamin Falgoust II, Zack Simmons | PRODUCED BY Erik Rutan | FROM *Carving Out the Eyes of God* (Metal Blade, 2009)

Appalled that All Time Low are in this book? Goatwhore are for you. Officially they're 'blackened death metal'. In fact they're traditional metal to the core and 'Apocalyptic Havoc' is Motörhead via Venom. The lyrics pack 'hell', 'hand of doom', 'death', 'madness', 'mayhem', 'torture', 'plague', 'decay', 'carnage', 'horror', 'nightmares', 'genocide', 'slaughter' and 'Satan' into three minutes. And, as if that isn't sufficiently Slayeresque, there's a gloriously gratuitous guitar solo. When Anvil sang 'Metal on Metal' (*see* 1982), this is what they meant.

BIBLE BLACK
Heaven & Hell

🇬🇧🇺🇸

BY Geezer Butler, Ronnie James Dio, Tony Iommi | PRODUCED BY Ronnie James Dio, Tony Iommi, Geezer Butler | FROM *The Devil You Know* (Roadrunner, 2009)

On Ronnie James Dio's passing, Sebastian Bach frothed to *Classic Rock*: 'His best album – the one I fucking love the most – was his most recent... *The Devil You Know*. "Bible Black" was his best fucking song ever.' Heaven & Hell were certainly a more satisfying sequel to the post-Ozzy incarnation of Black Sabbath than the Dio lineup's 1992 reunion for *Dehumanizer*. *Live from Radio City Music Hall* (2007) is a strong contender for the best live Sabbath album, *The Devil You Know* is vintage doom and gloom, and 'Bible Black' is bloody brilliant.

SHEMHAMFORASH
Behemoth

BY Nergal | PRODUCED BY Behemoth, Daniel Bergstrand, Sławomir and Wojciech Wiesławski, Colin Richardson | FROM *Evangelion* (Mystic Production, 2009)

'We are on a different planet doing our own thing,' frontman Nergal bragged to skartnak.com. '*Evangelion* is our biggest and strongest material to date. There's hardly anything that can interfere with its domination. This album is doomed for success.' Having lurked on the extremes for over a decade, Behemoth went worldwide with their thunderous ninth album. 'Shemhamforash' ('an epithet for a 216-letter name of God discovered by medieval kabbalists,' Nergal explained) is relentless, chiming, cinematic death metal par excellence.

KNOW YOUR ENEMY
Green Day

BY Billie Joe Armstrong, Mike Dirnt, Tré Cool | PRODUCED BY Butch Vig, Green Day | FROM *21st Century Breakdown* (Reprise, 2009)

'A rock 'n' roll battle cry,' said Tré Cool, who pounds out the commanding opening seconds of 'Know Your Enemy'. *21st Century Breakdown* may not have amounted to much more than a rerun of *American Idiot*, but – like its brilliant predecessor – the album was packed with fist-pumping, chant-along moments. '"Know Your Enemy" just seems to be one of the songs that's a broad, bold stroke,' Billie Joe Armstrong told bluntmag.com.au. 'It seemed like the obvious choice for the first single because it was, you know, a call-to-arms.'

THAT GOLDEN RULE
Biffy Clyro

BY Simon Neil | PRODUCED BY Garth Richardson, Biffy Clyro | FROM *Only Revolutions* (14th Floor, 2009)

Of the many fan favourites on *Only Revolutions*, heaviest is 'That Golden Rule', which became a live staple. 'Always fun,' frontman Simon Neil noted to laist.com, 'because we open with it.' Complementing its whip-fast feel are orchestral stabs that hark back to 'Living Is a Problem Because Everything Dies' (*see* 2007). These, bassist James Johnston gleefully recalled, 'initially managed to baffle sixteen of the best string players LA has to offer. It was really funny to watch a whole room of people melt down when they tried to work that one out.'

GHOST OF DAYS GONE BY
Alter Bridge

BY Mark Tremonti, Myles Kennedy | PRODUCED BY Michael 'Elvis' Baskette | FROM *AB III* (Roadrunner, 2010)

'It's really about longing for the past and coming to terms with the fact that time will go on,' Myles Kennedy explained to roadrunnerrecords.com. 'It's kind of, at the same time, a reminder of your mortality... The clock's ticking, and there's really nothing you can do to change it or stop it.' Alter Bridge hit their stride early, and by album number three they could do little wrong. But even by the standards they had established, 'Ghost of Days Gone By' is staggering, blending heaviness and heart in a way that may not be original but is indisputably immaculate.

BLODTØRST
Kvelertak

BY Erlend Hjelvik, Vidar Landa, Bjarte Lund Rolland, Maciek Ofstad, Marvin Nygaard, Kjetil Gjermundrød | PRODUCED BY Kurt Ballou | FROM *Kvelertak* (Indie Recordings, 2010)

Owl-crazed Norwegians weren't obvious candidates for success, but Kvelertak flew in the face of logic with their spectacular debut. The influence of producer Kurt Ballou, from Converge, was obvious, but the band's huge hooks made Kvelertak much more uplifting than their Massachusetts mentors. 'The vocals make us edgy,' guitarist Vidar Landa observed to read.tidal.com. 'But the music is guitar-driven, and the riffs are really hooky... We weren't afraid to reach out outside the hardcore fan base in our hometown, and to be catchy.'

WHEN THE WILD WIND BLOWS
Iron Maiden

BY Steve Harris | PRODUCED BY Kevin Shirley, Steve Harris | FROM *The Final Frontier* (EMI, 2010)

'It's a big song,' Dave Murray told *Billboard* of *The Final Frontier*'s epic closer. 'We learned it in sections, just because it was such a complex arrangement.' Fittingly, for one of Maiden's most proggy albums, the song was inspired by Raymond Briggs' book *When the Wind Blows* – the basis of a 1986 film scored by Pink Floyd's Roger Waters. '"When the Wild Wind Blows" was Steve playing and singing parts to us,' producer Kevin Shirley told musicradar.com. 'We didn't know where he was going, but he did, and it came together in the end.'

SNAKES FOR THE DIVINE
High on Fire

BY Matt Pike, Des Kensel, Jeff Matz | PRODUCED BY Greg Fidelman | FROM *Snakes for the Divine* (E1 Entertainment, 2010)

'I challenge you to listen to the first two minutes without banging your head or even feeling the involuntary movement of your hands forming fists and punching the air,' Michael Nelson wrote on stereogum.com. 'There's a reason the band usually reserve this song for the end of their live sets... if they played it any earlier, the venue would burn to the ground.' The song's title, main man Matt Pike explained to ultimate-guitar.com, 'is based on the premise that Adam and Eve weren't the first people on Earth, and Adam having a wife that was a Reptilian.'

YOU'VE SEEN THE BUTCHER
Deftones

BY Chino Moreno, Stephen Carpenter, Abe Cunningham, Frank Delgado, Sergio Vega | PRODUCED BY Nick Raskulinecz | FROM *Diamond Eyes* (Reprise, 2010)

'Aggressive overtones and lush openness,' Chino Moreno promised *Spin* of Deftones' first release without bassist Chi Cheng. *Diamond Eyes* indeed swung from beguiling ('Sextape') to brutal (most strikingly, 'CMND/CTRL' and 'Rocket Skates'). But the woozily brilliant 'You've Seen the Butcher' pulled the two aspects together to conjure quintessential Deftones. 'I don't think I've ever heard a metal band pull off something quite like it,' synthesist Frank Delgado marvelled to keyboardmag.com. 'It's heavy as fuck, but it's still sexy.'

T NEVER ENDS
Bring Me the Horizon

BY Oli Sykes, Lee Malia, Matt Kean, Matt Nicholls, Curtis Ward | PRODUCED BY Fredrik Nordström, Henrik Udd FROM *There Is a Hell Believe Me I've Seen It. There Is a Heaven Let's Keep It a Secret.* (Visible Noise, 2010)

don't think we want to completely change,' Oli Sykes old altpress.com in 2009. 'We want to keep our sound. We just want to push it more and make it better.' Mission accomplished: *There Is A Hell...* maintained the gung-ho of 008's *Suicide Season* (notably on the thrilling 'Anthem') ut added classical and electronic elements – most rilliantly on this anguished yet uplifting epitaph for Sykes' ruggy days. 'It's not about the actual heaven and hell,' uitarist Lee Malia told oxfordstudent.com. 'It's more... your wn personal heaven and hell.'

CARAVAN
Rush

🇨🇦 BY Geddy Lee, Alex Lifeson, Neil Peart | PRODUCED BY Nick Raskulinecz, Rush | FROM 'Caravan/BU2B' (Anthem, 2010)

'Caravan' and 'BU2B' were unleashed as a single two years before the storming concept album *Clockwork Angels* – then a 'work in progress'. The former, Geddy Lee explained to musicradar.com, '[is] basically about a young guy who's got big dreams, big desires, and a very romantic vision of what the world's supposed to bring him.' As usual, however, behind the conceptual flourishes and monster riffs was a glimpse into the imagination of Neil Peart. 'To paraphrase "Caravan",' the lyricist told *Classic Rock*, 'I couldn't stop thinking big.'

THE GUN SHOW
In This Moment

🇺🇸 BY Maria Brink, Chris Howorth, Jeff Fabb, Blake Bunzel, Kevin Churko | PRODUCED BY Kevin Churko | FROM *A Star-Crossed Wasteland* (Century Media, 2010)

'There are some people who just hate it,' guitarist Chris Howorth noted to thegauntlet.com of *A Star-Crossed Wasteland*'s deliriously heavy opener. 'They like more melodic stuff and don't understand why we would do something like that... We just wanted to come out with a really heavy metal track to show everybody that In This Moment is back in metal.' It hardly mattered that the rest of the album sounded like Evanescence meets Linkin Park; 'The Gun Show' – 'About self-respect,' said singer Maria Brink – is a screaming, staggering sensation.

I KNOW HOW TO DIE
Motörhead

🇬🇧 🇸🇪 BY Lemmy, Phil Campbell, Mikkey Dee | PRODUCED BY Cameron Webb | FROM *The Wörld Is Yours* (UDR, 2010)

Fun from start to finish, Motörhead's twentieth album hits a peak with 'I Know How to Die', a rollicking thrasher that would slot straight into *Ace of Spades*. The song 'stares into – or rather shouts at – the abyss of mortality', opined theartsdesk.com. 'I'm not scared of it,' Lemmy responded. 'It'll show up one day and say [makes beckoning gesture], and off you go. There's no control over it, is there? You could be under a bus tomorrow. There's no logic to it, no acceptance, nothing. It's just going to happen, so you might as well get used to it.'

YOUR BETRAYAL
Bullet for My Valentine

🇬🇧 BY Matt Tuck, Michael 'Padge' Paget, Jason 'Jay' James, Michael 'Moose' Thomas, Don Gilmore | PRODUCED BY Don Gilmore | FROM *Fever* (Jive, 2010)

'I try to keep my emotions locked in,' Matt Tuck assured *Kerrang!* 'My private life has always been kept very private.' Fortunately, Bullet's main man channelled his feelings into sensational songs, and third album *Fever* is packed with them. 'Your Betrayal' is a stupendous opener, its thunderous first eighty seconds giving way to an arena-worthy anthem. 'The album as a whole is solid,' Tuck told ultimate-guitar.com. 'An album like [Metallica's] "The Black Album" has that quality from track one to track whatever. Every single song is a potential hit.'

RITUAL
Ghost

BY A Ghoul Writer | PRODUCED BY Tobias 'Gene Walker' Forge | FROM *Opvs Eponymovs* (Rise Above, 2010)

'People might take offence,' Tobias Forge confessed to *Classic Rock*, 'if they knew we're more influenced by The Beach Boys than [New Wave of British Heavy Metal doom metal pioneers] Witchfinder General.' The bonkers Swedes' mix of melody and harmony in fact yielded a sound closer to Blue Öyster Cult – but, either way, it struck a spooky chord. 'Ritual' – 'The chirpiest song about human sacrifice I know,' wrote stereogum.com's Brandon Stosuy – set the satirically Satanic band on an implausible path to worldwide stardom.

ALL I WANT
A Day to Remember

BY Josh Woodard, Neil Westfall, Jeremy McKinnon, Alex Shelnutt, Kevin Skaff | PRODUCED BY Chad Gilbert, Andrew Wade, Jeremy McKinnon | FROM *What Separates Me from You* (Victory, 2010)

'It's still pop-punk,' singer Jeremy McKinnon told rocksound.tv of A Day to Remember's fourth album, 'but with a darker edge.' That description fit the muscular yet irresistibly catchy 'All I Want' to a tee. The single and *What Separates Me from You* went gold, and established a formula for the future. 'There aren't many bands who can go on tour with super-heavy bands like The Acacia Strain or Parkway Drive,' McKinnon noted to altpress.com, 'and then come off it and go straight on a New Found Glory tour and get the exact same response.'

MADE OF STONE
Evanescence

BY Amy Lee, Terry Balsamo, Troy McLawhorn, Tim McCord, Will Hunt, William B. Hunt | PRODUCED BY Nick Raskulinecz | FROM *Evanescence* (Wind-Up, 2011)

'I've always loved that one,' Amy Lee told nme.com. 'I think it has a really cool, dark, sexy quality... It's strong and defiant and badass.' The storming cut began as an electronic experiment by the singer. 'It only got better when the band started really being involved in it and writing that guitar part...' she enthused. 'It popped up in a big way when the guys got involved.' Evanescence's self-titled fourth album has several cuts that prove a powerful band lurks beneath the goth trappings; check out this and 'Disappear' for starters.

COMING DOWN
Five Finger Death Punch

BY Zoltan Bathory, Jason Hook, Ivan Moody, Kevin Churko, Jeremy Spencer | PRODUCED BY Kevin Churko, Five Finger Death Punch | FROM *American Capitalist* (Prospect Park, 2011)

'This is more than just a song,' guitarist Zoltan Bathory declared to *Metal Hammer* of his band's first US chart-topper. 'It was an outreach – and it's always going to be relevant. There are so many people who are bullied, mistreated; suffering emotionally and mentally. Some of them want out.' The point was amplified by an unflinching video, and Five Finger Death Punch put their money where their mouth is by partnering with the National Suicide Prevention Lifeline. 'If you talk one person off the ledge...' Bathory noted, 'it's been worth it.'

LOCUST
Machine Head

BY Robb Flynn, Phil Demmel | PRODUCED BY Robb Flynn | FROM *Unto the Locust* (Roadrunner, 2011)

'The whole "Locust" concept was mine,' guitarist Phil Demmel wrote on Twitter. 'Nothing Biblical about people coming into your life and harvesting everything from you before upping and flying away after they drain you of all they can.' Beneath the lyrical rage, the music lurches from a Cure-style intro to an ever-shifting riff fest. 'We rarely have a bar go by without something changing,' Robb Flynn noted to exclaim.ca. 'We still want to write songs in the classic pop sense of what a song is. But, in the middle of it all, we take the listener on a journey.'

WHITE TRASH MILLIONAIRE
Black Stone Cherry

BY Chris Robertson, Ben Wells, Jon Lawhon, John Fred Young, Zac Maloy | PRODUCED BY Howard Benson | FROM *Between the Devil and the Deep Blue Sea* (Roadrunner, 2011)

'I had a 1981 Trans Am,' frontman Chris Robertson explained to *Classic Rock*. 'Half the car was primered and the rest was in regular paint. That car was the inspiration for the song... It's all about being happy with what you got.' The cut almost didn't make it onto *Between the Devil and the Deep Blue Sea*. 'We had it too fast,' drummer John Fred Young admitted to rockaaa.com. 'It sounded almost corny but we couldn't figure out why, as we knew it had a hook and a good melody. But Howard [Benson, producer] just told us to slow it down. It worked really well.'

DEATHBOUND
Mastodon

BY Troy Sanders, Brent Hinds, Brann Dailor, Bill Kelliher | PRODUCED BY Mike Elizondo | FROM *The Hunter* (Reprise, 2011)

Crack the Skye pushed the proggy limits, but Mastodon returned to Earth (more or less) on *The Hunter*. Most of its songs weighed in at under five minutes, and the singalong 'Curl of the Burl' and gleeful 'Blasteroid' suggested a band that wasn't quite as earnest as we imagined. But tucked away at the end of a deluxe edition was the ferocious 'Deathbound'. Like its fellow bonus cut 'The Ruiner', the song had been penned for *Crack the Skye*, but was left off because, Brann Dailor explained, it was 'just too heavy and too fast and crazy'.

THE VAMPIRE FROM NAZARETH
Septicflesh

BY Christos Antoniou, Sotiris Anunnaki V, Seth Siro Anton, Fotis Benardo | PRODUCED BY Peter Tägtgren, Septicflesh | FROM *The Great Mass* (Season of Mist, 2011)

Greece is known for 'sand, Zorba dancing and vacations', Septicflesh frontman Seth Siro Anton told invisibleoranges.com. Yet his band and Rotting Christ have secured the country a niche in death metal, and *The Great Mass* – which 'The Vampire from Nazareth' opens – is an extraordinary landmark. Septicflesh are distinguished by symphonic elements, provided here by the Philharmonic Orchestra and Choir of Prague. 'Everything being played has a purpose,' Anton insisted. 'It's not merely inserted for an impression of false grandeur.'

NARCISSISTIC CANNIBAL
Korn featuring Skrillex and Kill the Noise

BY Jonathan Davis, James 'Munky' Shaffer, Reginald 'Fieldy' Arvizu, Skrillex, Kill the Noise, Luke Walker | PRODUCED BY Skrillex, Jim Monti, Kill the Noise | FROM *The Path of Totality* (Roadrunner, 2011)

'This album has taken over from *Untouchables* as my favourite Korn record,' Jonathan Davis declared to *Classic Rock* of the dubstep-soaked *The Path of Totality*. 'We've made some records that worked and others that didn't, but Korn's job is to shake things up.' The band brilliantly swerved getting swamped by the electronic shenanigans of Skrillex and Kill the Noise. That's most evident on the swaying, stadium-sized 'Narcissistic Cannibal' – a song about people who, Davis said, 'basically eat themselves alive because of their narcissism.'

SWERVE CITY
Deftones

BY Chino Moreno, Stephen Carpenter, Abe Cunningham, Frank Delgado, Sergio Vega | PRODUCED BY Nick Raskulinecz | FROM *Koi No Yokan* (Reprise, 2012)

'Stephen [Carpenter] and I were playing together a lot on this record,' Chino Moreno told *Kerrang!*, 'and it's my favourite thing when we hit our stride.... He and I have a history of not seeing eye to eye – so, when we're vibing together, we come up with my favourite stuff... Sometimes the music will be really heavy, but the vocals take the song in a different direction so it isn't just a boneheaded rock song.' Twenty years into their career, Deftones were still able to surprise: 'Swerve City' is so gleefully savage you'd swear they were kids.

NON-STATE ACTOR
Soundgarden

BY Chris Cornell, Kim Thayil, Ben Shepherd | PRODUCED BY Adam Kasper, Soundgarden | FROM *King Animal* (Universal Republic, 2012)

'Non-State Actor' originated with a riff by Ben Shepherd. 'We jammed it out,' the bassist sighed, 'overstructured it, overdid everything, ripped it down again...' 'We came up with other modes of the riff,' Chris Cornell explained to *Rolling Stone*. 'And every time we came up with a new mode, we weren't sure which one was better. Then we were trying to fit them all into one arrangement, which is never smart.' The effort paid off in one of the standout moments – 'punk rock world pop,' suggested Kim Thayil – from Soundgarden's comeback.

BLOOD
In This Moment

BY Maria Brink, Chris Howorth, Kane Churko, Kevin Churko PRODUCED BY Kevin Churko | FROM *Blood* (Century Media, 2012)

'I'm kind of a psycho,' Maria Brink confessed to loudwire.com (somewhat unnecessarily if you've seen her on video or in concert). 'I like things to thread together and have themes.' For In This Moment's best-selling album, that theme was 'the blood of the Phoenix, as in all death represents something new'. This resurrection was complemented by the band upping its visual game. 'When I first saw a picture of Kiss, and I heard them, I was so into that,' guitarist Chris Howorth explained to crypticrock.com. 'The make-up and the mystique.'

RISE UP
Testament

BY Chuck Billy, Eric Peterson, Del James | PRODUCED BY Andy Sneap, Testament | FROM *Dark Roots of Earth* (Nuclear Blast, 2012)

Testament fans have long argued that thrash's Big Four (Metallica, Slayer, Megadeth, Anthrax) should be a Big Five. The case was strengthened by *Dark Roots of Earth*, which earned Testament their highest chart placing (number twelve in the US) and added bangers like 'True American Hate' to their list of classics. Opener 'Rise Up' confirmed the fire burned brightly, with characteristically phenomenal drumming by Gene Hoglan, a Pantera-style groove, and a hooky chorus that bore the fingerprints of Guns N' Roses coconspirator Del James.

LOVE BITES (SO DO I)
Halestorm

BY Lzzy Hale, Dave Bassett | PRODUCED BY Howard Benson | FROM *The Strange Case of...* (Atlantic, 2012)

'Love Bites,' Lzzy Hale announced to noisecreep.com, 'is my little stab against the media's portrayal of love. Your heart cannot be measured or judged by the quizzes in magazines and scenes in movies.' The cut put Halestorm on the metal map and earned them a Grammy. 'It was meant to be an empowering song for people when love goes down the tubes,' Hale explained. 'This is a way of saying, yes, everything can end, but it's rejuvenating to stand up and go, "This sucks right now, but it's not going to take me down with it."'

R.A.T.S.
Cancer Bats

🇨🇦
BY Liam Cormier, Scott Middleton, Mike Peters, Jaye R. Schwarzer | PRODUCED BY Eric Ratz, Kenny Luong | FROM *Dead Set on Living* (Distort Entertainment, 2012)

'We didn't stray too far from what we started out doing, which was making banging party songs that we wanted to rage to,' singer Liam Cormier told soundspheremag.com of Cancer Bats' fourth album. 'I more just wanted to try and outdo everything we've ever done and write the best CB record ever.' And that's what they achieved. *Dead Set on Living* crashed the British top fifty, gave them their only chart placing in their Canadian homeland, and opened with a rollicking rage against hypocrisy that became their fans' favourite song.

THESE COLOURS DON'T RUN
Architects

🇬🇧
BY Tom Searle | PRODUCED BY Ben Humphreys, Architects FROM *Daybreaker* (Century Media, 2012)

The sun-kissed shores of California did not make Architects guitarist and writer Tom Searle happy. 'You go to Huntington Beach and you see the oil rigs on the horizon,' he grumbled to vice.com. 'You get this sense that it was once such a beautiful place but it's been destroyed.' That rage fed into an extraordinary song, interpreted as being anti-American. 'Their corporations and businesses are fried,' Searle seethed, 'and they've gone and destroyed other places in the world. And England is complicit in almost everything America does.'

KASHMIR
Led Zeppelin

🇬🇧
BY Jimmy Page, Robert Plant, John Bonham | PRODUCED BY Jimmy Page | FROM *Celebration Day* (Atlantic, 2012)

'They played "Kashmir" and dry ice comes rolling off the stage and the lights come descending down into this big, purple, metal spider,' Marilyn Manson declared of Zeppelin's triumphant 2007 reunion. 'It sounded perfect and I just declared immediately that this is almost as amazing as Evan [Rachel Wood]'s vagina. The guy right next to me goes, "That must be some vagina."' You need the *Celebration Day* DVD for the full kaleidoscopic effect, but the audio alone turns this warhorse into the classic that Zep-heads have always claimed it is.

LIES GREED MISERY
Linkin Park

BY Chester Bennington, Rob Bourdon, Brad Delson, Dave Farrell, Joe Hahn, Mike Shinoda | PRODUCED BY Rick Rubin, Mike Shinoda | FROM *Living Things* (Warner Bros., 2012)

'We've incorporated a lot of guitar work with big choruses and the heavier electronic stuff,' Chester Bennington explained to *Kerrang!* of *Living Things*, 'to give it that really big wall-of-sound feeling without getting too metal.' The album pushed Linkin Park's poppier elements, but short sharp shocks like 'Victimized' and 'Lies Greed Misery' kept their noise credentials intact. On the latter, Skrillex-style throbs combine with static blasts, hammering beats, Mike Shinoda's rapping and Bennington's screaming to create a gem that's deliciously deranged.

INTOXICATED
Lacuna Coil

BY Cristina Scabbia, Andrea Ferro, Cristiano Migliore, Marco Biazzi, Marco Coti Zelati, Cristiano Mozzati, Don Gilmore | PRODUCED BY Don Gilmore | FROM *Dark Adrenaline* (Century Media, 2012)

'I see a lot of other bands in our own genre – but I'm not going to name names – that are pretty much following what we did a few years ago,' Cristina Scabbia sniffed to radiometal.com. 'They're going into more melodic, mainstream sonorities, and we're doing the opposite... We went into something that is heavier. This album is the heaviest we've ever done.' The hit 'Trip the Darkness' and a cover of R.E.M.'s 'Losing My Religion' aside, that was true, with Lacuna Coil's trademark Eastern-tinged metal hitting a twisted peak on 'Intoxicated'.

LEAVE IT ALONE
Tremonti

BY Mark Tremonti | PRODUCED BY Michael 'Elvis' Baskette | FROM *All I Was* (Fret12, 2012)

'I'm not as heavy as this album is,' Mark Tremonti declared to *Classic Rock*. The weightiness of *All I Was* didn't come as a huge surprise: Tremonti's other bands Alter Bridge and even Creed have metallic moments, and the guitarist makes no secret of his old-school headbanger tastes. But if you want a slice of one of modern rock's greatest axemen, free of AB and C's more lighter-waving elements, check out *All I Was* and its muscular opener, on which Tremonti (aided by bassist Eric Friedman and drummer Garrett Whitlock) proves his might as a frontman.

IN THE END
Black Veil Brides

BY Andy Biersack, Jake Pitts, Jinxx, Ashley Purdy, John Feldmann, Martin Johnson | PRODUCED BY John Feldmann, Brandon Paddock | FROM *Wretched and Divine: The Story of the Wild Ones* (Lava, 2013)

A quasi-religious concept album wasn't what we expected from a bunch of cheery Mötley disciples, nor could we have predicted that its climax would be a musing on the nature of heaven. Yet that's what they delivered. 'Heaven is a legacy that you leave for the people around you,' observed frontman Andy Biersack. 'This song is about when you die, or you're gone, or when something's over, who is left to remember the moments that you had? Who will tell the story of your life... and what have you done that would make you someone of substance?'

IN UTERO: A PLACE OF HATRED AND THREAT
Svart Crown

BY JB Le Bail | PRODUCED BY Francis Caste | FROM *Profane* (Listenable, 2013)

'People say that we are "the evil Gojira",' main man JB Le Bail told echoesanddust.com. 'Their music is really different from ours, but we'd lie if we say that they're not an example to follow… We try to increase our level, maybe following their footsteps, but playing our kind of stuff; more aggressive, more evil.' The standout cut on Svart Crown's second album certainly ticked the aggressive and evil boxes, bringing the artwork's demonic gestation theme to spectacularly horrible life. However, Bail protested, 'We're not violent guys – not really.'

CHAOS IS KING
Onslaught

BY Nige Rockett, Andy Rosser-Davies
PRODUCED BY Onslaught | FROM *VI* (AFM, 2013)

'Just because you're not youthful any more doesn't mean you can't be angry,' guitarist Nige Rockett observed to metalassault.com. 'There is a lot of crap going on in this world… So there's always a lot of fuel for the fire.' Onslaught's ire was most explicit on *VI*'s epic 'Children of the Sand', but 'Chaos Is King' proved the British thrashers were as vital as ever. 'Definitely the most aggressive track,' Rockett confirmed to metalforcesmagazine.com. 'It was a real bitch to nail super-tight in the studio, but… we have to push ourselves to the limits.'

IN DUE TIME
Killswitch Engage

BY Justin Foley, Joel Stroetzel, Adam Dutkiewicz, Jesse Leach, Mike D'Antonio
PRODUCED BY Adam Dutkiewicz | FROM *Disarm the Descent* (Roadrunner, 2013)

'It's very heavy,' singer Jesse Leach told loudwire.com of the album that marked his return to Killswitch Engage, 'but still maintains the signature Killswitch hooky, melodic stuff… I pulled out some new styles vocally: yelling and screaming and growling and layers – and it sounds massive.' Massive indeed was 'In Due Time' – a gorgeous anthem that became their only US top ten single. 'We wanted to have a high-energy record,' guitarist Joel Stroetzel enthused to premierguitar.com, 'and express how excited we were to be playing again.'

TORDENBRAK
Kvelertak

BY Erlend Hjelvik, Maciek Ofstad, Vidar Landa, Bjarte Lund Rolland, Marvin Nygaard, Kjetil Gjermundrød PRODUCED BY Kurt Ballou | FROM *Meir* (Indie Recordings, 2013)

'We're not afraid to be catchy,' frontman Erlend Hjelvik noted to thequietus.com. 'We actually don't mind people liking our band.' There is plenty to like about the Norwegians' second album, which is spectacularly heavy, gloriously catchy and – even if you've no idea what they're singing – uniquely uplifting. Of the closing, nine-minute 'Tordenbrak', they warned, 'There is a storm coming. All you can do is pray.' But the song's old-school twin guitars and soaring sound make it a storm that anyone reading this book should run straight into.

ONE OF US IS THE KILLER
The Dillinger Escape Plan

BY Benjamin Weinman, Greg Puciato | PRODUCED BY Steve Evetts, Benjamin Weinman | FROM *One of Us Is the Killer* (Sumerian, 2013)

One of TDEP's most accessible songs was, ironically, rooted in the group's volatility. The title cut of their fifth album, Benjamin Weinman told ghostcultmag.com, 'is about the difficulties of maintaining relationships, especially for people in an active band like us. That's always a major challenge… Constant instability can be a threat, especially in the relationship between Greg [Puciato, singer] and I. We're so dependent on each other… but we're also such different people. Maintaining such a relationship is a constant battle.'

GOD IS DEAD?
Black Sabbath

BY Geezer Butler, Ozzy Osbourne, Tony Iommi | PRODUCED BY Rick Rubin | FROM *13* (Vertigo, 2013)

'When I first went to school, we read *The Iliad* and *The Odyssey*,' Geezer Butler recalled to *Classic Rock*. 'I can't remember anything of what they were about, but the Bible stuck with me.' That influence fed into the Grammy-winning highlight of Sabbath's comeback album. 'I love that song,' Rob Halford told shortlist.com. 'For them to release a single that was nearly nine minutes long just shows you that they still value everything that Black Sabbath represents. They were always against the grain; always against the system of the music world.'

ADDICTED TO PAIN
Alter Bridge

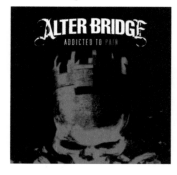

BY Mark Tremonti, Myles Kennedy | PRODUCED BY Michael 'Elvis' Baskette | FROM *Fortress* (Roadrunner, 2013)

The standout track on Alter Bridge's fourth album, Myles Kennedy explained to digitaljournal.com, 'came about early in the songwriting process… Lyrically, the song is about someone who is addicted to the drama of a toxic and unhealthy scenario, and the frustration involved with watching somebody in that situation.' It provided a vivid testament to Mark Tremonti's metal leanings and quickly became one of Alter Bridge's highest charting and most durable anthems. 'It's an exciting record,' Tremonti told *Billboard* of *Fortress*. 'It's got a lot of energy.'

SHADOW MOSES
Bring Me the Horizon

BY Oli Sykes, Lee Malia, Jordan Fish | PRODUCED BY Terry Date | FROM *Sempiternal* (RCA, 2013)

'The title is from a computer game called *Metal Gear Solid*,' bassist Matt Kean confessed to SugarScape. 'The opening bit with the people doing the spooky singing, that's a melody from the game.' The song was the first of four hits from *Sempiternal*. 'We actually never intended for it to be a single,' singer Oli Sykes noted to Metal Fucking Rocks. '[We] thought it'd be a good song to play and maybe put out for free, to bridge the gap between our last record and this new one... But management said, "This song's too good. You can't put that out for free!"'

DREAM HOUSE
Deafheaven

BY George Clarke, Kerry McCoy | PRODUCED BY Jack Shirley, Deafheaven | FROM *Sunbather* (Deathwish, 2013)

No one knew they needed a cross between Burzum and My Bloody Valentine, but along came Deafheaven to deliver it anyway. Their first defining song, frontman George Clarke explained to pitchfork.com, '[is] about the obsession with wealth... On "Dream House", that conversation is really a conversation I had with this girl I was totally in love with. I was really hammered one night and was texting her, like, "How are you?" She's like, "I'm dying." And I was like, "Is it blissful?" She said, "Like a dream"... It sounded nice at the time.'

FUTURE
Paramore

BY Hayley Williams, Taylor York | PRODUCED BY Justin Meldal-Johnsen | FROM *Paramore* (Fueled by Ramen, 2013)

After a split in the ranks, Paramore bounced back with their poppiest album (until 2017's *After Laughter*). Yet they closed it with a remarkable, post-metal-style blowout. 'Such a happy accident,' Hayley Williams told artistdirect.com. 'That's something I was playing around with on my guitar right after Josh and Zac Farro had left the band... It was this old thing I kept picking on guitar over and over again... The other half is the guys jamming at [Hollywood studio] Sunset Sound in the live room. It's a really special song. It's super-emotional for me.'

BLOOD HOST
Scar the Martyr

BY Joey Jordison, Henry Derek | PRODUCED BY Rhys Fulber, Joey Jordison | FROM *Scar the Martyr* (Roadrunner, 2013)

'If you like Slipknot you could like it,' Joey Jordison observed to Kerrang! Radio of the band he formed towards the end of his time with the 'knot. 'If you like Nine Inch Nails you could like it. If you like Neurosis you might like it too.' With Jordison on drums and bass, Blood Promise's Henry Derek on vocals, Strapping Young Lad's Jed Simon and Darkest Hour's Kris Norris on guitar, and Nine Inch Nails' Chris Vrenna on keyboards, Scar the Martyr's sole album was punishing – and 'Blood Host' perfectly summed up its hooky heaviosity.

DOC HOLLIDAY
Volbeat

BY Michael Poulsen | PRODUCED BY Rob Caggiano, Volbeat | FROM *Outlaw Gentlemen & Shady Ladies* (Vertigo Berlin, 2013)

A Western-themed album that owes as much to rockabilly as it does to Metallica... from Denmark? It was the most unlikely recipe for success since Lars Ulrich swapped a tennis racquet for drumsticks, but *Outlaw Gentlemen & Shady Ladies* topped European charts and crashed the US top ten. 'If you're into gunslinger and cowboy stories, everybody knows Doc Holliday,' main man Michael Poulsen declared to artistdirect.com. 'At least they should, if you ask me... It comes from watching movies, reading books, and being very nerdy about it.'

REVELATION OF MANKIND
Dir En Grey

BY Kaoru, Die, Toshiya, Kyo, Shinya | PRODUCED BY Dir En Grey | FROM *Arche* (Firewall Div, 2014)

This Osaka quintet have flirted with progressive, extreme and nü metal. And just as their name cherry-picks different languages to signify nothing concrete, so their music is defiantly fluid. Album number nine closes with a hammering cocktail of A Perfect Circle, Within Temptation, acoustic delicacy and death metal viciousness. 'When I was growing up, I listened to American bands,' guitarist and leader Kaoru observed to metalsucks.net. 'I had no idea what they were saying. But I still remember the excitement that I experienced.'

O FATHER O SATAN O SUN!
Behemoth

BY Nergal | PRODUCED BY Behemoth, Wojtek, Sławek Wiesławski | FROM *The Satanist* (Nuclear Blast, 2014)

Behemoth crashed the US top forty with their tenth album, following leader Nergal's recovery from leukaemia. 'Sickness is a sign,' he reflected to the *Guardian*. 'Now I know that there may not be a tomorrow... I'm giving you my very best.' That was embodied by *The Satanist*'s stirring, orchestra-embellished climax, 'O Father O Satan O Sun!' 'I've always been very fond of independence and autonomy and free-thinking and freedom and intelligence,' Nergal explained. 'Satan has always been a very strong symbol of all those values.'

TRYING TO CRACK THE HARD DOLLAR
Eyehategod

BY Mike Williams, Brian Patton, Jimmy Bower, Gary Mader, Joey LaCaze | PRODUCED BY Eyehategod | FROM *Eyehategod* (Housecore, 2014)

Drugs, death and Down added up to a thirteen-year gap between Eyehategod's fourth and fifth albums. Singer Mike Williams was jailed for narcotics (Phil Anselmo paid his bail), drummer Joey LaCaze succumbed to respiratory failure (*Eyehategod* is his swan song) and Jimmy Bower doubled as the drummer in Down. But when they reconvened, it was with their finest hour, full of stirring, Sabbath-esque sludge. As Williams suggested to invisibleoranges.com, 'If John Lee Hooker listened to Black Flag, he would sound like Eyehategod.'

PARADISE (WHAT ABOUT US?)
Within Temptation featuring Tarja

BY Sharon den Adel, Robert Westerholt, Martijn Spierenburg | **PRODUCED BY** Daniel Gibson, Robert Westerholt | **FROM** *Hydra* (WT Recordings, 2014)

People always saw us like we had some kind of competition going on, which we never did,' insisted Within Temptation singer Sharon den Adel to heavy.nyc of fellow symphonic metal mistress Tarja Turunen. 'The lyrics are about paradise, so it's showing all the people there's no competition.' What could have been a syrupy love-in turned out to be one of the hardest hitters on Within Temptation's sixth album – no mean achievement considering *Hydra* also included a duet with former Killswitch Engage singer Howard Jones.

NOW WE DIE
Machine Head

BY Robb Flynn, Phil Demmel | **PRODUCED BY** Robb Flynn, Juan Urteaga | **FROM** *Bloodstone & Diamonds* (Nuclear Blast, 2014)

Two decades on from their game-changing debut (*see 1994*), Machine Head remained untouchable. Fittingly, *Bloodstone & Diamonds* earned the highest US chart placing of their career, just short of the top twenty. The album set out its skull-crushing stall with 'Now We Die', which added strings and keyboards to evoke folk-tinged armageddon. 'This was one heck of a song to try and put together,' recalled Robb Flynn. 'I was like, "This song's killer!" And Dave [McClain, drummer] and Phil [Demmel, guitarist] were like, "This song sucks!"'

OUT OF THE BLACK
Royal Blood

BY Mike Kerr, Ben Thatcher | **PRODUCED BY** Royal Blood, Tom Dalgety | **FROM** *Royal Blood* (Black Mammoth, 2014)

Royal Blood weren't the first duo to emerge in the wake of The White Stripes: California's Middle Class Rut and Brooklyn's Sleigh Bells made plenty of awesome noise, and The Dresden Dolls covered 'War Pigs'. But something about Brighton bassist Mike Kerr and drummer Ben Thatcher caught fire – possibly their White Stripesy ability to sound like Led Zeppelin with half the personnel. 'The noise I was making was just big enough that we didn't add any more members,' Kerr told notreble.com. 'We decided to just keep it simple.'

CAPTIVATE YOU
Marmozets

🇬🇧

BY Becca Macintyre, Sam Macintyre, Jack Bottomley, Will Bottomley, Josh Macintyre | PRODUCED BY Larry Hibbitt | FROM *The Weird and Wonderful Marmozets* (Roadrunner, 2014)

'We were getting heavier and heavier,' guitarist Sam Macintyre recalled to montrealrocks.ca of his band's formative days, 'but then we chose to do more melodic stuff.' Amid inevitable comparisons to Paramore, Marmozets – two sets of siblings, fronted by singer Becca Macintyre – conjured an angular, punky energy, akin to friends and touring partners Enter Shikari. 'They're such a cool, individual band,' producer (and Hundred Reasons guitarist) Larry Hibbitt told BandApp. 'I didn't want them to sound like another metal band.'

TREND KILLER
The Haunted

🇸🇪

BY Marco Aro, Jonas Björler, Ola Englund, Patrik Jensen, Adrian Erlandsson | PRODUCED BY Tue Madsen | FROM *Exit Wounds* (Century Media, 2014)

'I *love* The Haunted!' declared Kerry King – high praise from a notoriously hard-to-please icon. The Slayer man favoured the band with singer Peter Dolving, but there's nothing wrong with his replacement, Marco Aro. 'He made it more hardcore,' King told knac.com. (Dolving replaced Aro in 2003, and the pair swapped yet again in 2013.) The Swedish stompers' thunderous eighth outing peaks on 'Trend Killer'. With Testament's Chuck Billy guesting, it's a scathing, 'Heretic Anthem' (*see* 2001)-esque putdown of bandwagon-jumpers.

GIMME CHOCOLATE!!
Babymetal

🇯🇵

BY Kobametal, Takeshi Ueda, Miki 'Mk-metal' Watanabe | PRODUCED BY Kobametal | FROM *Babymetal* (BMD Fox, 2014)

'Babymetal have a unique sound,' DragonForce's Herman Li observed to *Classic Rock*. 'Among heavy metal fans there is a hatred towards pop music... but I think people also like it because of that. People *love* it because of that.' People certainly love Babymetal, who leapt from Japan to festival stages and arenas worldwide. 'Rock music hasn't changed much,' producer Kei 'Kobametal' Kobayashi noted to the *Guardian*. 'When a group from the other side of the world suddenly appears, playing something so weird, it captures your attention.'

A SKELETAL DOMAIN
Cannibal Corpse

🇺🇸

BY Pat O'Brien, Paul Mazurkiewicz | PRODUCED BY Mark Lewis | FROM *A Skeletal Domain* (Metal Blade, 2014)

Cannibal Corpse's lucky thirteenth album was their highest-charting, almost hitting the US top thirty. You could attribute that to the *Walking Dead*-style video for 'Kill or Become', or to Cannibal Corpse fans probably not being overly concerned with trends. But you could also attribute it to the album being fantastic, with its title cut a particular highlight. 'We're not reinventing the wheel here,' drummer Paul Mazurkiewicz conceded to metalassault.com. 'We're just trying to hone our skills, refine our songwriting, and this is what you get.'

THE MOTHERLOAD
Mastodon

BY Bill Kelliher, Brann Dailor, Brent Hinds, Troy Sanders | PRODUCED BY Nick Raskulinecz | FROM *Once More 'Round the Sun* (Reprise, 2014)

'We have a dance video!' marvelled Brann Dailor. Controversy over the 'Motherload' clip's twerking posteriors brought Mastodon a new audience, but the song's swirling riff, crashing drums and heartwarming chorus were what made it truly irresistible. 'The four of us have a giant appreciation of and respect for a wide variety of music, from Beethoven to Bjork,' Troy Sanders observed to azcentral.com. 'To a very small degree, I believe that shows in the music, but ultimately it comes across as a bizarre, seventies space-rock band.'

SHOCK ME
Baroness

BY Pete Adams, John Dyer Baizley, Nick Jost, Sebastian Thomson | PRODUCED BY Dave Fridmann, Baroness | FROM *Purple* (Abraxan Hymns, 2015)

If you were a stoner who thought Mastodon had sold out, you shifted your allegiance to Baroness, who ploughed an old-school furrow on cult classics like 'March to the Sea'. Then they discovered the art of writing choruses and made 'Shock Me' – as splendidly swirling and singalong as Mastodon's 'The Motherload' (*see* left). 'It was important for us,' singer John Dyer Baizley told *Rolling Stone*, 'to write our new songs with the type of enthusiasm and expressiveness that could act as a counterpoint to [the *Purple*] album's dark themes.'

I AM THE VIRUS
Killing Joke

BY Jaz Coleman, Geordie Walker, Youth, Big Paul Ferguson | PRODUCED BY Tom Dalgety, Killing Joke | FROM *Pylon* (Spinefarm, 2015)

'An intense, angry, uncompromising shout into the abyss,' bassist Martin 'Youth' Glover declared of 'I Am the Virus', the pummelling standout on Killing Joke's fifteenth album. 'The virus is a metaphor for resistance against the corporate world,' frontman Jaz Coleman explained to heavymusicartwork.com. 'We're living in a time where people are more like zombies, really. And it's a combination of what they're eating, the air they're breathing, and what they're drinking, as much as media manipulation.'

SPEED OF LIGHT
Iron Maiden

BY Adrian Smith, Bruce Dickinson | PRODUCED BY Kevin Shirley, Steve Harris | FROM *The Book of Souls* (Parlophone, 2015)

'One of the greatest rock bands in history...' Lady Gaga instructed crfashionbook.com. 'Some people really don't know the importance of metal and the scope of it.' *The Book of Souls* was awash with epics that lived up to that billing, but least cerebral and most fun was its first single. 'Adrian wrote the riff,' Bruce Dickinson told *Spin*. 'I thought, "That sounds like something off *Burn*! Let's do a homage to Purple with an Ian Gillan-type scream in the beginning." The rest of the riffs sound like something that could have been on *Piece of Mind* [*see* 1983].'

HAPPY SONG
Bring Me the Horizon

🇬🇧

BY Oli Sykes, Lee Malia, Jordan Fish, Matt Kean, Matt Nicholls | PRODUCED BY Jordan Fish, Oli Sykes | FROM *That's the Spirit* (RCA, 2015)

'It's about making light out of a shitty situation,' Oli Sykes explained of the cheerily foreboding 'Happy Song'. 'We all live with depression to some extent... We all have so many problems, and the world has so many problems too. And we really need to probably address 'em, and be honest about 'em. But instead we choose to ignore, and replace it with something trivial or superficial. We're all guilty of that – myself included. And the way I see it is, if we don't laugh, we'll cry. So let's poke some fun at the fact that we're all fucked.'

THE DEATH OF ROCK 'N' ROLL
Venom

🇬🇧

BY Cronos, La Rage, Dante | PRODUCED BY Cronos | FROM *From the Very Depths* (Spinefarm, 2015)

'The Death of Rock 'n' Roll,' Cronos told therockpit.net, 'tells about how this thing we call rock 'n' roll progresses in such a way that it becomes unrecognizable... The so-called metal bands of today all play rock 'n' roll and it's so different to what Bill Haley and Elvis and Chuck Berry and all the guys did back in the day – but it's all just rock 'n' roll... and the fans stay with it forever... It's in your soul; it's in your bones.' He channelled that conviction into a song that proves Venom are as vibrant in the twenty-first century as they were influential in the twentieth.

REPENTLESS
Slayer

🇺🇸

BY Tom Araya, Kerry King | PRODUCED BY Terry Date | FROM *Repentless* (Nuclear Blast, 2015)

'It's about doing it and not giving a shit,' Tom Araya said. 'This band doesn't ask forgiveness for anything.' To Kerry King, 'This is my Hannemanthem... I wrote it from my perspective about how Jeff looked at the world.' The late Jeff Hanneman, noted Paul Bostaph, 'wasn't into being a "rock star". He didn't want the attention, he just wanted to get out there and play... He was great at what he did and basically loved to kick ass.' And for the guitarist's replacement Gary Holt, the song was simply 'killer... a great high-energy Slayer opening track'.

CRUSHED
Parkway Drive

BY Winston McCall, Jeff Ling, Luke Kilpatrick, Ben Gordon | **PRODUCED BY** George Hadjichristou | **FROM** *Ire* (Resist Records, 2015)

'None of us would get creative fulfillment out of writing another Parkway metalcore album,' frontman Winston McCall told *Metal Hammer*. 'There had to be a different way of doing it. It took a hell of a long time to get our heads around what that actually meant.' 'Crushed' suggested they listened to a Behemoth cut or two. 'Lyrically this song deals with the concept of power and control,' McCall explained. 'We have let the balance of power slip so far that a godlike will is able to be imposed upon the masses, with little to no way of breaking the cycle.'

CESSPITS
Napalm Death

BY Barney Greenway, Shane Embury | **PRODUCED BY** Russ Russell | **FROM** *Apex Predator – Easy Meat* (Century Media, 2015)

A cesspit, Barney Greenway explained thoughtfully, 'was used as a sewage overflow. A pit, basically. And what I wanted to suggest with that was just talk about people that live in holes, figuratively and literally. When you think about it, is that what it's come to in 2014? That people have to live that way? The mind just boggles... It almost suits some people for other people in the world to live in those holes, because it creates a separation... Their comparatively luxurious existence isn't threatened as long as those people over there are stuck in their holes.'

CHIENS DE LA CASSE
Mass Hysteria

BY Yann Heurtaux, Frédéric Duquesne, Mustapha 'Mouss' Kelaï, Raphaël Mercier, Vincent Mercier | **PRODUCED BY** Frédéric Duquesne | **FROM** *Matière Noire* (Verycords, 2015)

Anchored by the punky vocals of Mustapha 'Mouss' Kelaï, Mass Hysteria's eighth album explodes with spectacular, metallic riffing. 'Chiens de la casse' is the agenda-setting opener, but check out the anthemic likes of 'Vae Soli!' too. 'There are a lot of kids at our shows...' guitarist and main writer Yann Heurtaux observed to guitariste.com, 'and our album that matters most to them is *Matière Noire*.' Echoes of Mass Hysteria's industrial origins remain but, as bassist Vincent Mercier noted to sons-of-metal.com, the album is 'very metal, very sharp'.

NEVER TURN BACK
We Are Harlot

BY Danny Worsnop, Jeff George, Bruno Agra | **PRODUCED BY** Kato Khandwala, Danny Worsnop, Jeff George, Bruno Agra | **FROM** *We Are Harlot* (Roadrunner, 2015)

'We're going to be the biggest rock 'n' roll band in the world!' Danny Worsnop bragged to *Rock Sound*. 'You'll understand when you hear the record. Even I can't believe how good the album is.' In truth, the album was more fun than classic, and Harlot's 'supergroup' billing was stretching it: Worsnop fronted Asking Alexandria, but guitarist Jeff George, bassist Brian Weaver and drummer Bruno Agra were household names only in their own homes. However, 'Never Turn Back' is a stone-cold, old-school-style, swaggering classic.

SUPERHERO
Faith No More

BY Mike Patton, Bill Gould, Mike Bordin | PRODUCED BY Bill Gould FROM *Sol Invictus* (Reclamation!, 2015)

Faith No More's second comeback song followed the less radio-friendly 'Motherfucker'. It began, Bill Gould told marvel.com, 'from the sound of the song, where it has these pounding drums and it has this throbbing kind of pulse… We make movie scenes for movies that don't exist. "Superhero" was one of those where it was definitely a superhero comic… That was just the vibe of the song and, when Mike [Patton] came to me writing words about it, we were already calling it "Superhero". So it's kind of like in the DNA; it's a comic strip.'

CYGNUS
Cult of Luna & Julie Christmas

BY Julie Christmas, T. Hedlund, A. Johansson, K. Karlsson, F. Kihlberg, J. Persson | PRODUCED BY K. Karlsson, M. Líndberg, A. Schneider FROM *Mariner* (Indie Recordings, 2016)

'We had no idea what could come out of our collaboration,' said Cult of Luna guitarist and singer Johannes Persson. 'But when we heard her vocals on our song for the first time, we felt like we had something very interesting.' The union of the Swedish metallers with Brooklyn singer Julie Christmas created a career highlight for both: the spacey yet crushing *Mariner*. 'Cygnus', Persson told *Rolling Stone*, 'was inspired by the "Star Gate" sequence in *2001: A Space Odyssey*. It's how we imagine it would be to cross that final limit of the universe.'

ONE HAND KILLING
Twelve Foot Ninja

BY Nick 'Kin' Barker, Steve 'Stevic' Mackay, Rohan Hayes | PRODUCED BY Steve 'Stevic' Mackay | FROM *Outlier* (Volkanik, 2016)

'I really wrote what felt good,' rhythm guitarist Rohan Hayes told echoesanddust.com. 'Some of my favourite heavy riffs are from bands like Vildhjarta, Meshuggah and Deftones.' Hayes and his band contributed their own riff to the heavy hall of fame with the funk-tinged 'One Hand Killing', the big, bold opener on their second album. 'It's okay to like Pantera and The Doobie Brothers,' lead guitarist Steve 'Stevic' Mackay wrote on Facebook. 'It's okay to like Meshuggah and Adele… There are no rules with this sh!t! That is "metal" to me!'

WHITE LINE FEVER
Deströyer 666

BY K.K. Warslut, R.C. | PRODUCED BY Laurent Teubl, Mersus | FROM *Wildfire* (Season of Mist, 2016)

Deströyer 666 main man K.K. Warslut (Keith Bemrose to his mum) grew up in a small town, surrounded by 'long-haired hard rock fans who wore Black Sabbath, Motörhead and Harley Davidson t-shirts'. The influence of Lemmy's lot endured: note the umlaut in the band's name, a title looted from a 'head single, and the punky pummelling of the song itself. 'I play metal and surround myself with metalheads,' Warslut assured lordsofmetal.nl. 'Everything else falls into place. Albeit with lots of hard work and a healthy diet of sex, drugs and heavy metal.'

ROTTING IN VAIN
Korn

BY Jonathan Davis, James 'Munky' Shaffer, Reginald 'Fieldy' Arvizu, Brian 'Head' Welch, Ray Luzier | PRODUCED BY Nick Raskulinecz | FROM *The Serenity of Suffering* (Roadrunner, 2016)

'Rotting in Vain', Jonathan Davis explained, 'was written about being in that black place... be it relationships, or feeling when you're stuck and you're just being abused or you don't like where you're at, and you just sit there and rot. It takes you years and years to figure out how to claw your way out... I'm just sitting there, fucking dying and letting it happen for years and years and not helping myself to get out.' After pop Korn and dubstep Korn, this was Reassuringly Dark and Heavy Korn, complete with a Sepultura-style tribal breakdown.

SPIT OUT THE BONE
Metallica

BY James Hetfield, Lars Ulrich | PRODUCED BY Greg Fidelman, James Hetfield, Lars Ulrich | FROM *Hardwired... to Self-destruct* (Blackened, 2016)

Remember thrash? It seemed Metallica didn't. Then they snuck this onto the end of *Hardwired...* and we lost our minds (and did it again when they added it to their setlist nearly a year later). The song itself, James Hetfield told fan magazine *So What*, is about 'the wonder and fear' of ever more invasive technology: 'Without future-tripping too much, just the possibilities of *Terminator*, stuff like that... We're wearing smart watches, things are getting closer and closer to just being *in* us... So "Spit Out the Bone" is that your bones aren't needed. They break!'

MY CHAMPION
Alter Bridge

BY Mark Tremonti, Myles Kennedy | PRODUCED BY Michael 'Elvis' Baskette | FROM *The Last Hero* (Napalm, 2016)

The lyric of *The Last Hero*'s heartwarming highlight, said Myles Kennedy, 'was actually inspired by thinking back to my situation as a kid. I was this really small, underdeveloped kid who had to work extremely hard to keep up with all of my peers... I would hear a lot of words of encouragement from parents, coaches, or teachers though... They manifested themselves in this song.' Complementing the words was the chiming guitar of Mark Tremonti. 'I really liked that riff,' he told musicradar.com. 'It had kind of a seventies vibe that I dug.'

THE HOUSE OF SHAME
Lacuna Coil

BY Andrea Ferro, Cristina Scabbia, Marco 'Maki' Coti Zelati, Ryan Blake Folden | PRODUCED BY Marco 'Maki' Coti Zelati | FROM *Delerium* (Century Media, 2016)

A concept album about 'an old sanatorium up in the hills of Northern Italy… whose corridors are filled with the ghosts of a thousand tortured minds and souls'? So far, so *Silent Hill*. But it made for Lacuna Coil's heaviest album (despite their customary cover version being, this time around, a reconstructed version of Madonna's 'Live to Tell'). 'The House of Shame', singer Andrea Ferro informed *Metal Hammer*, 'was the perfect song to introduce the place, which is the album. Musically it has lots of double-bass drums and female screaming.'

MÅNEBLÔT
Myrkur

BY Amalie Bruun | PRODUCED BY Randall Dunn | FROM *Mareridt* (Relapse, 2017)

'I was in one of the worst times of my life,' Amalie 'Myrkur' Bruun recalled of the genesis of the *Mareridt* album. 'I was afraid to sleep.' Plagued by bad dreams, she channelled her unease into the album, and 'Måneblôt' 'portrays a nightmare engaging a woman, girl, animal, violence, sun and fire worship and the pagan ritual, Blôt'. That nightmare is evoked by a stunning blend of black metal and folk. Yet, as she sighed to *Kerrang!*, 'There are long think pieces about how I'm ruining black metal, and I'm the worst thing to happen to anything.'

DOOMSDAY
Architects

BY Sam Carter, Dan Searle, Alex Dean, Josh Middleton | PRODUCED BY Dan Searle, Josh Middleton FROM *Holy Hell* (Epitaph, 2018)

'It's the last song that Tom [Searle, late guitarist] started,' Searle's brother and drummer Dan told *Kerrang!* 'He was too consumed in his battle with cancer to be thinking about songwriting. But I remember him sending me the riff.' The result was issued in 2017 as the precursor to the band's greatest album. 'It's a song about those first few stages of grief,' singer Sam Carter explained. 'You wake up every morning feeling defeated… You work through the day to find some positivity… only to go to bed and wake up again with that same feeling of doom.'

EXECUTIONER'S TAX (SWING OF THE AXE)
Power Trip

BY Riley Gale, Blake Ibanez, Chris Ulsh | PRODUCED BY Arthur Rizk | FROM *Nightmare Logic* (Southern Lord, 2017)

'Imagine if Cro-Mags, Leeway, Slayer and classic Sepultura were cooked into a Christmas pie,' Trivium's Matt Heafy enthused to *Kerrang!* 'That's Power Trip.' The Texas quintet made major waves with their third album, mainly thanks to the irresistible, chugging 'Executioner's Tax'. A political allegory, according to singer Riley Gale, the song concerns the powers that be, '[that] love to get us addicted, fat, sick – so they can feed us, medicate us and nearly quite literally kill many of us.' When it turned up on Fox News, Power Trip were not happy.

RUN
Foo Fighters

BY Dave Grohl, Taylor Hawkins, Nate Mendel, Chris Shiflett, Pat Smear, Rami Jaffee | PRODUCED BY Greg Kurstin, Foo Fighters | FROM *Concrete and Gold* (Roswell, 2017)

'I couldn't even walk when I wrote "Run",' Dave Grohl told *Billboard* of a song composed when he was nursing a broken leg. 'There's some catharsis there; that I get to scream my brains out. I'm a huge fan of old-school thrash metal, so I was really excited, twenty-two years into being the Foo Fighters, to have a song that's probably the heaviest thing we've ever recorded.' There's stuff on *In Your Honor* and *Wasting Light* that's heavier, but the alternately swaying and screaming 'Run' is still remarkable, hence its two Grammy nominations.

STREET POWER
Ho99o9

BY theOGM, Eaddy, Eric Rogers, Ian Longwell, Dave Sitek | PRODUCED BY Michael Feinberg | FROM *United States of Horror* (Toys Have Powers, 2017)

'We're like the X-Men,' rapper Eaddy suggested to revolvermag.com. 'We're mutants that don't belong in society.' Like an unholy mix of Ministry and Death Grips, 'Street Power' is potent punk among the deranged hip-hop of *United States of Horror*. Ho99o9 even toured with The Dillinger Escape Plan and Papa Roach. And their name (pronounced 'horror')? 'At the time,' Eaddy recalled of their origins, 'Odd Future and Tyler, the Creator came out and he was into this real kind of playful, demonic, scary state and everything was just six-six-six.'

CIVIL WAR
Body Count featuring Dave Mustaine

BY Ernie C, Ice-T, Vincent Price, Dave Mustaine | PRODUCED BY Will Putney | FROM *Bloodlust* (Century Media, 2017)

'If a motherfucker comes through my door, I'm not grabbing a butter knife,' Ice-T observed to *Classic Rock*. 'It's like I say in the lyric of "Civil War": if you come to shoot me, I'm shooting back... I'm not going to let you militia motherfuckers just run over some shit.' Twenty-five years after 'Cop Killer', Body Count kept pushing buttons, this time with a thrash legend on introductory voice and guitar. 'I met Dave Mustaine,' Ice told Music Choice. 'I'm like, "You're the business. You're Megadeth." And I was like, "This shit's bad-ass."'

INTO THE FIRE
Asking Alexandria

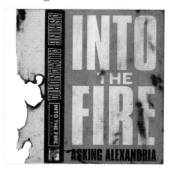

🇬🇧
BY Danny Worsnop, Ben Bruce, James Cassells, Matthew Good | PRODUCED BY Jonathan Davis, Matthew Good | FROM *Asking Alexandria* (Sumerian, 2017)

'"Into the Fire" is me doing the Asking [Alexandria] thing again and realizing that I've got these flaws,' returning frontman Danny Worsnop explained to rocksound.tv. 'I have these demons and I can either be depressed about them, and turn to drugs and turn to alcohol and turn to doing all these fucked-up things I used to do, or I could use them in a positive way and make them work for me and lean into the crazy.' The song was co-produced by Jonathan Davis, with whom Asking Alexandria covered Duran Duran's 'Hungry Like the Wolf'.

HOOK, LINE AND SINKER
Royal Blood

🇬🇧
BY Mike Kerr, Ben Thatcher | PRODUCED BY Tom Dalgety | FROM *How Did We Get So Dark?* (Black Mammoth, 2017)

The blistering highlight of Royal Blood's second album was premiered at the Reading Festival two years before its release. 'We were so desperate to play it,' Mike Kerr admitted to gigwise.com. The song confirmed the band were no flash in the pan and, as Kerr told Zane Lowe, 'just felt like a refinement of what makes Royal Blood work.' A Zeppelin vibe was obvious. 'They play with the spirit of the things that have preceded them,' Jimmy Page told nme.com, 'but you can hear they're going to take rock into a new realm... It's music of tremendous quality.'

FUCK YOU!!!
Autopsy

🇺🇸
BY Matt McCourt | PRODUCED BY Autopsy, Greg Wilkinson | FROM *Puncturing the Grotesque* (Peaceville, 2017)

Autopsy, founder and drummer Chris Reifert explained to metalsucks.net, 'wants to take you gently by the hand and lead you into a glowing sunset while rainbows smile at you and birds wink at you and then push you off a lovely little cliff where you will fall to your doom.' *Puncturing the Grotesque* closes with a cover of a cut by guitarist Danny Coralles' former band, Bloodbath. 'It came out awesome,' Reifert told metalcrypt.com, 'and it's also a cool tribute to Dane Petersen, who was the original Bloodbath vocalist and who has passed away.'

RITUAL
Soulfly

🇧🇷🇺🇸
BY Max Cavalera | PRODUCED BY Josh Wilbur | FROM *Ritual* (Nuclear Blast, 2018)

'The culture of tribes was always fascinating to me,' Max Cavalera told whatculture.com. 'I find it very mystic and very different... so, when we started incorporating that into *Roots* and *Soulfly*, it kind of became my trademark.' That trademark is spectacularly stamped on *Ritual*'s title track, which indeed harkens to *Roots*-era Sepultura and the first Soulfly album. (Neatly, *Ritual* was released twenty years after that debut.) 'Revisiting the tribal stuff felt like rewatching an old movie,' Cavalera observed. '"Oh my God, I forgot how great this movie was!"'

A FLOOD OF LIGHT
Rolo Tomassi

🇬🇧

BY Eva Spence, James Spence, Chris Cayford, Nathan Fairweather, Tom Pitts | PRODUCED BY Lewis Johns | FROM *Time Will Die and Love Will Bury It* (Holy Roar, 2018)

'It is pulling cues from people like John Carpenter and sounds on the *Blade Runner* soundtrack... that kind of big, sci-fi, spacey thing,' keyboardist James Spence informed echoesanddust.com of the stunning epic at the heart of an extraordinary album. To alreadyheard.com, he explained: 'That for me is the perfect embodiment of the whole record: finding the balance between the dark and the light... That would be a song that I would show to anybody that didn't know our band, and show them what we're capable of.'

MADE AN AMERICA
The Fever 333

🇺🇸

BY Aalon Butler, John Feldmann, Nick 'Ras' Furlong, Travis Barker | PRODUCED BY John Feldmann, Travis Barker | FROM *Made An America* (Roadrunner, 2018)

Rap-rock is so venerable that Fever 333 frontman Aalon Butler was only seven when Rage Against the Machine's first album came out. Having served fifteen years in the post-hardcore band Letlive, he formed The Fever 333 with guitarist Stephen Harrison and drummer Aric Improta. Despite a total lack of originality (you'll hear Limp Bizkit as well as Rage), the trio secured the patronage of Blink-182's Travis Barker, and repaid the hype with the irresistible title cut of their debut EP. 'We're trying,' Butler declared, 'to write the soundtrack to the revolution.'

RATS
Ghost

🇸🇪

BY A Ghoul Writer, Tom Dalgety | PRODUCED BY Tom Dalgety | FROM *Prequelle* (Loma Vista, 2018)

'It's about something spreading as wildfire and completely destroying things quicker than you know,' Tobias Forge pointed out to revolvermag.com. The theme was appropriate, and possibly not coincidental, given that Forge was (unsuccessfully) sued by former bandmates in 2017. Its inspiration was the then eight-year-old Forge's viewing of a metal show in 1989. 'Ozzy Osbourne opened with "I Don't Know" [see 1980] and it's such a fucking great opening track,' he recalled to loudwire.com. 'I wanted to have that feel with "Rats".'

SHADOW OF YOUR LOVE
Guns N' Roses

🇺🇸

BY Duff McKagan, Izzy Stradlin, Paul Tobias, Slash, Steven Adler, Axl Rose | PRODUCED BY Mike Clink | FROM *Appetite for Destruction: Locked N' Loaded* (Geffen, 2018)

'Shadow of Your Love' wasn't new even when GN'R cut it: Axl, Izzy and Paul Tobias wrote it for the band's forerunners, Hollywood Rose. Guns put a live version on the 'It's So Easy' single in 1987, then it languished in b-side and bootleg obscurity. But when *Appetite* got the deluxe reissue treatment, up popped a polished take from back in the day. 'To go in to remix and master that and release it after all this time, for me, it was, "Wow, this is a trip!"' Slash told revolvermag.com. 'You definitely get the spirit of the band from way back when.'

ALL OUT LIFE
Slipknot

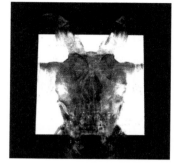

🇺🇸

BY Corey Taylor, Shawn Crahan, Jim Root | PRODUCED BY Greg Fidelman, Slipknot | FROM 'All Out Life' (Roadrunner, 2018)

A ferocious comeback after 2014's maudlin *The Gray Chapter*, the standalone single 'All Out Life' is, Corey Taylor told Zane Lowe of Beats 1, 'about this toxic idea that unless something came out ten minutes ago then it's not any good – and that bothers me. I love new music but, at the same time, don't turn your back on the music that's been. It's a rallying cry for everyone and saying, "You know what? Let's not talk about old, let's not talk about new; let's talk about what is. Let's talk about what's good and what's real and get behind that."'

STARLIGHT
Babymetal

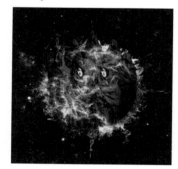

⬤

BY DKMETAL, Meg-Metal, TAKEMETAL | PRODUCED BY Kobametal | FROM *Metal Galaxy* (Babymetal Records, 2019)

Metal has seen no shortage of dramatic departures: Ozzy from Sabbath, Diamond Dave from Van Halen, Halford from Priest, Bruce Dickinson from Maiden, Joey from Slipknot, and nearly all of Guns N' Roses. Adding to that list, the exit of Yui 'Yuimetal' Mizuno sent Babymetal fans into a tailspin in 2018. But, barely stopping for breath, Suzuka 'Su-metal' Nakamoto and Moa 'Moametal' Kikuchi forged ahead with 'Starlight' – a tie-in with their *Apocrypha: The Legend of Babymetal* graphic novel and their most glorious single to date.

DRUGS
Falling in Reverse featuring Corey Taylor

BY Ronnie Radke, Cody Quistad, Charles Massabo | PRODUCED BY Charles Massabo | FROM 'Drugs' (Epitaph, 2019)

If Bring Me the Horizon's dabbling in Beiber-esque pop on *amo* gave you palpitations, say no to 'Drugs'. It pushes the same buttons, and throws in a verse that makes clear exactly how much band-leader Ronnie Radke was influenced by Eminem. But if you can get past all that, you'll find a storming cut that tips over into full-blown rage around two-and-a-half minutes in, with a Corey Taylor cameo that sounds unhinged even by Slipknot standards. The rest of Falling in Reverse's discography is excruciating pop-punk that can be safely ignored.

MANTRA
Bring Me the Horizon

BY Oli Sykes, Jordan Fish, Lee Malia, Matt Kean, Matt Nicholls | PRODUCED BY Oli Sykes, Jordan Fish | FROM *amo* (RCA, 2019)

'You never know how it's going to go when you take another sonic step,' Bring Me the Horizon observed when 'MANTRA' won *Kerrang!*'s best single of 2018 award, 'but the reaction from fans and newcomers alike reminds you why it's so important that we do.' As Ax7's M. Shadows noted to *Metal Hammer*, 'Bring Me The Horizon are able to add modern elements to their music where I feel everyone else who's tried has failed... People can talk all day about that band, but they will continue to be huge because of their songwriting and innovation.'

AFRAID OF WATER
Blood Command

BY Yngve Andersen | PRODUCED BY Yngve Andersen | FROM *Return of the Arsonist* (Fysisk Format, 2019)

Brilliantly bonkers, Blood Command spent their first few years unleashing gems like '(The World Covered In) Purple Shrouds' (from 2017's *Cult Drugs*) and supporting the likes of Biffy Clyro, Refused and Rolo Tomassi. In 2019, guitarist Yngve Andersen, singer Karina Ljone, bassist Simon Oliver Økland and drummer Sigurd Haakaas streamlined their sound to punk-pop, yet sacrificed none of their pyrotechnic charm, for 'Afraid of Water'. Not quirky enough for you? Try 'No Thank You, I'm More In To Fake Grindcore' instead.

HOW TO SURVIVE
Of Mice & Men

BY Aaron Pauley, Alan Ashby, Josh Wilbur, Phil Manansala, Valentino Arteaga | PRODUCED BY Josh Wilbur | FROM *EARTHANDSKY* (Rise, 2019)

'We decided to go heavier with this album...' singer and guitarist Aaron Pauley revealed to loudwire.com as Of Mice & Men toiled on their sixth effort. 'It's sounding huge and heavy, heavenly and absolutely demonic – all rolled into one.' Anyone who had heard their generic metalcore to date might have rolled their eyes, but then along came 2019's 'How to Survive' and 'Mushroom Cloud'. The latter is fun, the former is furious, and both are utterly crushing. While their contemporaries go pop, Of Mice & Men are heading in the opposite direction.

DEUTSCHLAND
Rammstein

BY Christoph 'Doom' Schneider, Doktor Christian Lorenz, Oliver Riedel, Paul Landers, Richard Z. Kruspe, Till Lindemann PRODUCED BY Olsen Involtini, Rammstein | FROM *'Rammstein'* (Universal, 2019)

'We come from the east and grew up as socialists,' Till Lindemann observed to *Rolling Stone* in 2011. 'We used to be either punks or goths... We used to fight with these right-wing idiots, and we would do that today.' Rammstein set the moral compass spinning with a provocative video for their comeback single, and remained tight-lipped on the thinking behind it. But the song itself was undeniable: a made-for-stadia, five-minute Greatest Hits. Fittingly, it became Rammstein's second number one in Germany, after 2009's equally controversial 'Pussy'.

SOURCES ▶

My thanks to all the writers, editors, webmasters and filmmakers whose work is quoted in this book. Particularly helpful resources are noted in **bold**

ONLINE

- 2warpstoneptune.com
- 4degreez.com
- 45cat.com
- **2112.net**
- adsofmetal.tumblr.com
- al.com
- alreadyheard.com
- altpress.com
- amiright.com
- andrewdarlington.blogspot.com
- arsenioorteza.blogspot.com
- artistdirect.com
- artistwd.com
- axs.com
- azcentral.com
- bassplayer.com
- bathory.nu
- bathoryhordes.com
- bbc.co.uk
- blabbermouth.net
- black-sabbath.com
- blastzoneonline.wordpress.com
- bluntmag.com.au
- bridgwatermercury.co.uk
- bullz-eye.com
- burnyourears.de
- cdandlp.com
- chroniclesofchaos.com
- classicrockrevisited.com
- cnet.com
- collectiveunconscious.org
- collideartandculture.com
- concertposter.org
- coveralia.com
- crfashionbook.com
- crueworld.com
- crypticrock.com
- **cygnus-x1.net**
- darkabyss.org
- darkside.ru
- defleppard.com
- deftonesworld.com
- demolishmag.files.wordpress.com
- derekriggs.com
- deviantart.com
- **discogs.com**
- djfood.org
- djnoble.demon.co.uk
- dontforgetthesongs365.wordpress.com
- downloadfestival.co.uk
- earofnewt.com

- echoesanddust.com
- enslain.net
- eonmusic.co.uk
- ew.com
- exclaim.ca
- facebook.com/KoRnKollection
- **faithnomoreblog.com**
- **faithnomorefollowers.com**
- fanart.tv
- feedtim.wordpress.com
- flashbak.com
- flickr.com/photos/digimeister
- flickr.com/photos/khiltscher
- foetus.org
- fontsinuse.com
- forbassplayersonly.com
- frankmaddocks.com
- fuckingrocks.blogspot.com
- fullinbloom.com
- **genius.com**
- ghostcultmag.com
- goldminemag.com
- guitarmessenger.com
- hardattackmag.com
- headbanger.ru
- heavymusicartwork.com
- heraldtribune.com
- herfitzpr.com
- hiponline.com
- homepages.gac.edu/~dkuster/zombie
- hornsuprocks.blogspot.com
- houseofrockinterviews.blogspot.com
- ink19.com
- invisibleoranges.com
- **ironmaidencommentary.com**
- izotope.com
- izzystradlin.wixsite.com
- janesaddiction.org
- jimfitzpatrick.com
- jimihendrixcollector.com
- jimsteinman.com
- joelgausten.com
- keyboardmag.com
- kkdowning.net
- knac.com
- laist.com
- lisaphillipsmediastudies.blogspot.com
- lollipopmagazine.com
- lordsofmetal.nl
- **loudersound.com**
- loudwire.com
- machinemusic.wordpress.com
- magazine.criticalmass.se
- makemyday.free.fr
- **mansonwiki.com**
- martyfriedman.com
- megadeth.rockmetal.art.pl

- members.ozemail.com.au/~cruekiss/
- menshealth.com
- metalassault.com
- metalcrypt.com
- metal-discovery.com
- metalexiles.com
- metalexpressradio.com
- metalfan.ro
- metalinsider.net
- metaljacketmagazine.com
- metalnoise.net
- metalrage.com
- metal-rules.com
- metalsludge.tv
- metalstorm.net
- metalsucks.net
- metal-temple.com
- metalunderground.com
- metalupdate.com
- misfitscentral.com
- mister-madman.tumblr.com
- mixonline.com
- m-magazine.co.uk
- moshpitsandmovies.wordpress.com
- msopr.com
- **musewiki.org**
- musicaficionado.com
- **music.avclub.com**
- music-bazaar.com
- musicomh.com
- musicfeeds.com.au
- **musicradar.com**
- newalbum.wordpress.com
- nin.wiki
- noisecreep.com
- **noisey.vice.com**
- notreble.com
- nuclearblast.de
- oxfordstudent.com
- pastemagazine.com
- **phoenixnewtimes.com**
- pitchfork.com
- planetmosh.com
- planetout.com
- premierguitar.com
- prongs.org
- providermodule.com
- queenarchives.com
- radiometal.com
- ramblinmanfair.com
- ranker.com
- rarerecordcollector.net
- rarerecords.com.au
- read.tidal.com
- recordmecca.com
- revgraeme.blogspot.com
- reynoldsretro.blogspot.com

- ritchieblackmoresrainbow.wordpress.com
- riverfronttimes.com
- roadrunnerrecords.com
- rockgighistory.wordpress.com
- rockrollnewspaperpresshistory.blogspot.com
- rocksbackpages.com
- rocksound.tv
- roughedge.com
- scorpscollector.wordpress.com
- scribd.com
- segabits.com
- shortlist.com
- sickthingsuk.co.uk
- skograt.tumblr.com
- sleazeroxx.com
- smnnews.com
- someofthetimesileftmyhouse.wordpress.com
- **songfacts.com**
- songmeanings.com
- soundonsound.com
- soundspheremag.com
- spfc.org
- spin.com
- **spotify.com**
- steppenwolf.com
- stereogum.com
- steven-knezevich.squarespace.com
- stickitonyourwall.com
- **superseventies.com**
- talkingmetal.com
- tapeop.com
- tempecarnivore.blogspot.com
- theaquarian.com
- thechilisource.com
- thegauntlet.com
- theguardian.com
- theguitargallery.com
- themusic.com.au
- theninhotline.net
- **thequietus.com**
- theringer.com
- therockpit.net
- thestreet.com
- **thetoptens.com**
- thevinyldistrict.com
- thrashhits.com
- tohereknowswhen.org
- tom-bryant.com
- toolshed.down.net
- trebuchet-magazine.com
- truemetal.org
- trust.connection.free.fr
- uberrock.co.uk
- udiscovermusic.com
- ultimateclassicrock.com
- ultimate-guitar.com
- unearthed.com

- uofmusic.com
- vhnd.com
- vintagevinyl.biz
- vinyl-never-dies.com
- visiblenoise.wordpress.com
- vivelerock.net
- voicesfromthedarkside.de
- washingtonpost.com
- web.stargate.net/soundgarden
- wildhearts-book.co.uk
- worthpoint.com
- yelyahwilliams.tumblr.com

BOOKS

- Aerosmith; Davis, Stephen: *Walk This Way* (Avon Books, 1997)
- Blows, Kirk: *Heavy Tales from the Hard Rock Highway* (Plexus, 2012)
- Brannigan, Paul: *This Is a Call – The Life and Times of Dave Grohl* (HarperCollins, 2011)
- Bream, Jon: *Whole Lotta Led Zeppelin* (Voyageur Press, 2008)
- Cerullo, John (editor): *Iron Maiden Guitar Tab Edition* (Cherry Lane, 1994)
- Dimery, Robert (editor): *1001 Songs You Must Hear Before You Die* (Cassell, 2010)
- Evans, Mark: *Dirty Deeds: My Life Inside/ Outside of AC/DC* (Bazillion Points, 2011)
- Fricke, David: *Def Leppard – Animal Instinct* (Zomba, 1987)
- Gooch, Curt; Suhs, Jeff: *Kiss Alive Forever* (Billboard Books, 2002)
- Ian, Scott: *I'm the Man* (Hachette UK, 2014)
- Jeffries, Neil (editor): *The Kerrang! Direktory of Heavy Metal* (Virgin, 1993)
- Leaf, David; Sharp, Ken: *Kiss: Behind the Mask* (Warner Books, 2003)
- Lee, T.; Mars, M.; Neil, V.; Sixx, N.; Strauss, N.: *The Dirt* (HarperCollins, 2001)
- Marsh, Dave: *The Heart of Rock & Soul: The 1001 Greatest Singles Ever Made* (Plume, 1989)
- Neil, Vince; Sager, Mike: *Tattoos & Tequila* (Orion, 2010)
- Popoff, Martin: *Rush: Album by Album* (Quarto, 2017)
- Prato, Greg: *German Metal Machine: Scorpions in the '70s* (CreateSpace, 2016)
- Red Hot Chili Peppers; Mullen, Brendan: *An Oral/Visual History* (HarperCollins, 2010)
- Rees, Dafydd; Crampton, Luke: *Q Encyclopedia of Rock Stars* (DK, 1996)
- Rosen, Craig: *The Billboard Book of Number One Albums* (Billboard, 1996)
- Roth, David Lee: *Crazy from the Heat* (Random House, 1997)
- Slash; Bozza, Anthony: *Slash: The Autobiography* (HarperCollins, 2007)
- Stroud, Graeme: *Status Quo* (Fonthill, 2017)
- **Sutherland, Mark (editor): *Kerrang! Proudly Presents: 666 Albums You Must Hear Before You Die* (Bauer, 2011)**
- Tannenbaum, Rob; Marks, Craig: *I Want My MTV: The Uncensored Story of the Music Video Revolution* (Plume, 2012)
- True, Everett: *Hey Ho, Let's Go: The Story of the Ramones* (Omnibus, 2002)
- Tyler, Steven; Dalton, David: *Does the Noise in My Head Bother You?* (Harper Collins, 2011)
- Wall, Mick; Halfin, Ross: *Classic Rock: High Voltage* (Future, 2007)
- Wenner, J. S. (editor): *Rolling Stone: The 100 Greatest Artists of All Time* (Rolling Stone, 2011)
- **Wiederhorn, Jon; Turman, Katherine: *Louder Than Hell: The definitive oral history of metal* (itbooks, 2013)**
- Yarm, Mark: *Everybody Loves Our Town: A History of Grunge* (Faber and Faber, 2011)

MAGAZINES

- *Billboard* (billboard.com)
- *Classic Rock* (**loudersound.com/ classic-rock**)
- *Decibel* (**decibelmagazine.com**)
- *Guitar World* (**guitarworld.com**)
- *Guitarist* (musicradar.com/guitarist)
- *Kerrang!* (**kerrang.com**)
- *Metal Hammer* (**loudersound.com/ metal-hammer**)
- *Mojo* (mojo4music.com)
- *Q* (qthemusic.com)
- *Revolver* (**revolvermag.com**)
- *Rolling Stone* (**rollingstone.com**)
- *Southern Cross* (Black Sabbath fanzine)
- *Total Guitar* (musicradar.com/totalguitar)
- *Uncut* (uncut.co.uk)

FEATURES

- Beaujour, T.; Begrand, A.; Beinstock, R.; Christe, I.; Considine, J.D.; Epstein, D.; Exposito, S.; Greene, A.; Grow, K.; Kelly, K.; Sheffield, R.; Shteamer, H.; Smith, S.; Spanos, B.; Weingarten, C.R.: *Rolling Stone: The 100 Greatest Metal Albums of All Time* (rollingstone.com/music/music-lists/the-100-greatest-metal-albums-of-all-time-113614)

VIDEOS

- Dunn, Sam; McFadyen, Scot: *Beyond the Lighted Stage* (2010)
- FaceCulture (YouTube)
- Guns N' Roses Central (YouTube)
- Music Choice (YouTube)
- Scam Truth Two (YouTube)
- Wishyouplease (YouTube)

▶ PICTURE CREDITS

Every effort has been made to credit the copyright holders of the images used in this book. We apologize for any unintentional omissions or errors and will insert the appropriate acknowledgement to any companies or individuals in subsequent editions of the work.

46TR: George Wilkes/Hulton Archive/Getty Images; **51BL**: Ebet Roberts/Getty Images; **53T**: Michael Putland/Getty Images; **53B**: Paul Natkin/Getty Images; **61TL**: AF archive/Alamy Stock Photo; **61B**: Paul Natkin/Getty Images; **65BL**: Paul Natkin/Getty Images; **65BR**: dpa picture alliance/Alamy Stock Photo; **67R**: © Raúl Vega; **75TL**: Aaron Rapoport/Corbis/Getty Images; **75BR**: Roger Chaisson; **87TR**: Ebet Roberts/Getty Images; **100B**: Mick Hutson/Redferns/Getty Images; **110TL**: Eric CATARINA/Gamma-Rapho via Getty Images; **123BR**: Mick Hutson/Redferns/Getty Images; **129TR**: Artwork by Emek Artman (Silkscreen, 1998); **133BR**: Jeff Kravitz/FilmMagic, Inc./Getty Images; **135BL**: Joe Traver/Liason Agency/Getty Images; **139TL**: Tim Mosenfelder/Getty Images; **139BL**: Pete Still/Redferns/Getty Images; **148TL**: Mick Hutson/Redferns/Getty Images; **149BR**: Lionel Flusin/Gamma-Rapho via Getty Images; **151BR**: Rob Verhorst/Getty Images; **163TR**: Dave Etheridge-Barnes/Getty Images; **163BL**: Mick Hutson/Redferns/Getty Images; **165TL**: Larry Carroll; **171BR**: Don Arnold/Getty Images; **175BL**: Araya Diaz/WireImage/Getty Images; **176BL**: Martin Philbey/Redferns/Getty Images; **177TL**: Photographer John Ross, Designer Frank Maddocks; **180BR**: Jakubaszek/Getty Images; **181BL**: Photographer Futura, Designer Frank Maddocks; **183BR**: Adrain Dennis/AFP via Getty Images; **185BL**: Ollie Millington/WireImage/Getty Images; **189BR**: Monica McKlinski/Getty Images; **191BR**: ITAR-TASS News Agency/Alamy Stock Photo; **195BR**: Alessandro Bosio/Pacific Press/LightRocket via Getty Images; **197BL**: © Gonzales Photo/Terje Dokken/Universal Images Group via Getty Images; **199BR**: David M. Brinley - Illustration/Design Tobias Forge – Art Director; **201BR**: PYMCA/Avalon/Universal Images Group via Getty Images; **202B**: Santiago Bluguermann/LatinContent via Getty Images.

Back cover: Clayton Call/Redferns/Getty Images